GALACTIC SUBURBIA

GALACTIC

THE OHIO STATE
COLUMBUS

SUBURBIA

RECOVERING WOMEN'S SCIENCE FICTION

LISA YASZEK

UNIVERSITY PRESS

Library of Congress Cataloging-in-Publication Data
Yaszek, Lisa, 1969–
Galactic suburbia : recovering women's science fiction / Lisa Yaszek.
    p. cm.
Includes bibliographical references and index.
ISBN-13: 978–0–8142–1075–8 (cloth : alk. paper)
ISBN-13: 978–0–8142–5164–5 (pbk. : alk. paper)
1. Science fiction, American—History and criticism. 2. American fiction—Women authors—History and criticism. 3. American fiction—20th century—History and criticism. 4. Feminism and literature—United States—History—20th century. 5. Women and literature—United States—History—20th century. 6. Feminist fiction, American—History and criticism. 7. Sex role in literature. I. Title.
PS374.S35Y36 2008
813.'08762099287—dc22
                    2007032288

This book is available in the following editions:
Cloth (ISBN 978–0–8142–1075–8)
Paper (ISBN 978–0–8142–5164–5)
CD ROM (ISBN 978–0–8142–9153–5)

Cover design by Dan O'Dair.
Text design by Jennifer Shoffey Forsythe.
Type set in ITC Veljovic.
Printed by Thomson-Shore, Inc.

9 8 7 6 5 4 3 2 1

For Doug

CONTENTS

ILLUSTRATIONS

A C K N O W L E D G M E N T S

mANY DIFFERENT people have helped make this book possible. Special thanks are due to Professor Emeritus Irving F. "Bud" Foote, who created the Bud Foote Science Fiction Collection at Georgia Tech and entrusted it to my care; the collection is where I first discovered the vibrant tradition of women's science fiction (SF) that is the subject of this book. Thanks also to my current colleagues in the School of Literature, Communication, and Culture at Georgia Tech, especially Ken Knoespel, Carol Senf, and Jay Telotte, who ensured that I had the time and resources to complete this book, as well as all the students in my SF classes who provided feedback on my ideas along the way. I am especially indebted to Katharine Calhoun and Martha Saghini of the Interlibrary Loan Program for patiently tracking down resources not available at Georgia Tech, and to my research assistants, Kellie Coffey and Jason Ellis, for their heroic efforts to sort and index those resources. I am often told that I am fortunate to work at an institute that supports SF studies, and I am delighted to confirm that this support permeates every aspect of life at Georgia Tech.

In the process of writing *Galactic Suburbia,* I was fortunate to work with equally supportive colleagues from the science fiction, science studies, and feminist studies communities. Justine Larbalestier, Javier Martinez, and Farah Mendlesohn provided invaluable feedback on my first articles about women's SF. Since then, I have continued to develop my ideas through my interaction with members of the Science Fiction Research Association and the International Association for the Fantastic in the Arts including Brian Attebery, Marleen Barr, Joan Gordon, Mack Hassler, Veronica Hollinger, Dianne Newell, Robin Reid, Alcena Rogan, and Sherryl Vint. My ideas about the relations of science and gender in SF were honed by discussions with members of the Society for Science, Literature, and the Arts including Ron Broglio, Carol Colatrella, Bob Markely, and Patrick Sharp. My thinking about these subjects is indebted to Rebecca Holden, Sue V. Rosser, and the anonymous readers at *Signs, Feminist History,* and *NWSA Journal* as well. And of course, special thanks to my fellow interdisciplinary traveler Doug Davis; writing this book would not have been nearly as much fun without you.

The institutional support I received along the way was also an integral part of my experience writing *Galactic Suburbia.* The School of Literature, Communication, and Culture at Georgia Tech granted me the semester sabbatical during which I began my research on women's SF, and I completed my first articles on this subject with funding from the National Endowment for the Humanities Summer Stipend Program. Thanks also to the Georgia Tech Tuesday Talk organizers and the Macon State College Women's Association for providing me with public forums for my work. Portions of chapter 3 appear in the *NWSA Journal* and *Extrapolation;* essays drawn from chapters 1 and 2 appear in *Foundation: The International Review of Science Fiction* and *Daughters of Earth: Feminist Science Fiction in the Twentieth Century,* edited by Justine Larbalestier (Wesleyan University Press, 2006); and articles inspired by chapter 4 are forthcoming in *Women in Science Fiction and Fantasy: An Encyclopedia,* edited by Robin Reid (Greenwood Press) and *Gender Myths and Beliefs,* edited by Sue V. Rosser (ABC Clio).

Finally, thanks to Sandy Crooms and the entire editing and production staff at The Ohio State University Press, especially Maggie Diehl and Karie Kirkpatrick for their sharp editorial eyes; Jennifer Shoffey Forsythe for the book design and typesetting; and Dan O'Dair for the cover. I hope that my readers enjoy this book as much as I've enjoyed working with all of you.

STRANGE READING

NEW SCIENCE fiction (SF) magazine called *The Avalonian* hit the newsstands in 1952. The debut issue featured an anchor story by Lilith Lorraine—an SF veteran who had been writing for more than two decades and who also published *The Avalonian*—and half a dozen more pieces by writers largely unknown to the genre's growing readership. Among the latter was a very short story by Helen Reid Chase entitled "Night of Fire." In less than four pages Chase rallies a galactic civilization, recapitulates cold war nuclear fears, ridicules religious zealots, razes planet Earth, and finally saves a select fraction of humanity for a destiny among the stars. "Night of Fire" is both utterly typical and truly remarkable for its time. An intergalactic alien council decides that humans, with their deadly combination of advanced atomic technologies and apocalyptic religious impulses, have set themselves on the path to total annihilation. Exhibiting a rather fine sense of irony, the council stages a fake rapture and spirits away those few earthlings "of very unusual intelligence" who have adhered to the principles of rational and benevolent behavior, leaving behind a scorched earth for the very same religious fanatics who prophesied apocalypse in the first place (33).

Because Chase valorizes empirical science over fundamentalist religion and reasoned intelligence over rote faith, her story is very much a recognizable part of the SF tradition. But in a historical moment when science and technology (not to mention stories about them) were considered primarily the province of male scientists, politicians, and artists, Chase's story departs from tradition by focusing on the fate of *women* in the high-tech world of tomorrow. "Night of Fire" is told from multiple perspectives, including that of Mrs. Brandon, a woman of "meager intellect" who shuns science, technology, and education in general while embracing strict religious piety and merciless domestic order (32). Not surprisingly, when she is left behind with all the other anti-intellectual zealots, Mrs. Brandon loses both her faith and her mind. As a parodic embodiment of the conventional feminine virtues celebrated by many postwar Americans, the character of Mrs. Brandon serves as a powerful warning about the inadequacy of traditional sex and gender roles in the modern era. If women refuse to embrace scientific and social change, Chase warns, at best they will be left behind and at worst driven insane by the demands of a world that is rapidly evolving past them.

But Chase also insists that women who look forward to the future need not suffer this fate. On the apocalyptic "night of fire" the aliens make good on their vow to save the best of humanity, quietly whisking away scientists, engineers, and housewives alike. Of course, the housewives they save are radically different from Mrs. Brandon. As one of the baffled husbands left behind on Earth remarks, "I know [my wife] did some strange reading. Well, maybe it was along science lines. I didn't notice much. As long as she took care of the house right, that's all I cared about. I don't know how she'd find out about anything big though. But I know she's gone" (33–34). Chase celebrates the possibility that women in the home—much like men in the laboratory and on the assembly line—might contribute to a new technocultural world order. Even more significantly, she celebrates the possibility that they might do so by engaging in precisely that kind of "strange reading" that Chase's readers themselves participated in as they turned the pages of her brief story.

In "Night of Fire" SF storytelling emerges as a powerful tool for women interested in reading—and writing—about their roles as citizens of a high-tech future. And writers such as Chase had good reason to place their faith in SF rather than other literary forms. Like the forsaken husbands in Chase's tale, mainstream publishers of the 1940s, '50s, and '60s usually assumed that women had little or no interest in scientific, social, or political issues. Feminist author Betty Friedan recollects that "by the time I started writing for women's magazines, in the fifties, it was simply taken for granted by editors . . . that women were not interested in politics, life outside the United States, national issues, art, science, ideas, adventure, education, or even their own communities, except where they could be sold through their emotions as wives and mothers" (50). At best, such editors assumed readers might be interested in service articles about how to have a baby in a bomb shelter; at worst, they expected women's eyes to drift away from such articles in search of more amusing tales about mischievous children and perfect party frocks. Either way, staff writers were expected to meet the supposed needs of readers by focusing on domestic issues at the expense of everything else.

But history is never that simple. Nearly 300 women began publishing in the SF community after World War II, and the stories they wrote both implicitly and explicitly challenged what Friedan called "the feminine mystique" by staking claims for women in the American future imaginary.[1] Leading SF author and editor Judith Merril recalls that she turned to the genre in the 1940s because it was "virtually the only vehicle of political dissent" available to socially conscious authors working in a historical moment marked by political paranoia and cultural conservatism ("What Do You Mean" 74). Whether or not SF was the only vehicle for such dissent, it was certainly a useful one. As a wildly popular mode of storytelling that ostensibly revolved around future worlds and alien peoples, SF provided authors with ideal allegorical narrative spaces in which to critically assess the here and now.

This book is about Helen Reid Chase, Judith Merril, and all the other postwar women writers who wrote SF set in a place called "galactic suburbia." Feminist SF author and critic Joanna Russ first introduced the concept of galactic suburbia in her groundbreaking 1971 essay, "The Image of Women in Science Fiction," to make sense of the large body of SF stories set in high-tech, far futures where gender relations still look suspiciously like those of "present-day, white,

1. Figures cited in this book regarding the number of women writers who began publishing in the SF community after World War II are derived from my personal count of those listed in Stephen T. Miller and William G. Contento, *The Locus Science Fiction, Fantasy, and Weird Magazine Index (1890–2001)*. My research assistants, Kellie Coffey and Jason Ellis, confirmed these numbers in two independent reviews of the *Index*. In all three cases we included only those authors who published short stories rather than novels because the paperback industry was still quite new at the time, and it is likely that authors who published novels also wrote short stories.

middle-class suburbia" (81). Although tales written by women including Chase and Merril generally "contain more active and lively female characters than do stories by men," Russ concludes that they are little more than space-age variants of "ladies' magazine fiction" in which a "sweet, gentle, intuitive little heroine solves an interstellar crisis by mending her slip or doing something equally domestic after her big, heroic husband has failed" (88).

Russ clearly recognizes that women's writing about galactic suburbia put a feminine face on the future. However, in direct contrast to the feminist fiction that authors such as herself were beginning to produce, women writing for the postwar SF community rarely seemed to take the next logical step and show how new sciences and technologies might produce new sex and gender relations as well. For pioneering critics such as Russ, distinguishing between different types of women's speculative fiction was key to the project of defining feminist SF as an emergent narrative tradition in its own right. But as artists and scholars turned their attention to this new narrative tradition, earlier women SF authors were relegated to the margins of literary and cultural history.[2]

Galactic Suburbia reverses this trend by demonstrating the significant contributions that women writers made to modern SF in the decades following World War II. This project begins by expanding upon the notion of galactic suburbia itself. As Russ rightly notes, stories set in galactic suburbia generally revolve around what appear to be surprisingly conservative sex and gender ideals. But this does not mean that all women writers automatically agreed on the meaning and value of these ideals. SF became central to the American imagination after World War II because it enabled people to explore their hopes and fears about the emergence of a technocultural world order. This was particularly important for women because postwar technoculture hinged on what were then new understandings and representations of sex and gender. Accordingly, women writers used stories about romance, marriage, and motherhood in galactic suburbia

2. For further discussion concerning Russ's ideas about the necessary distinction between different eras and modes of women's speculative fiction, see my essay, "A History of One's Own: Joanna Russ and the Creation of a Feminist Science Fiction Tradition," in Farah Mendlesohn's edited collection, *On Joanna Russ,* forthcoming from Wesleyan Press. For more general discussions concerning the aesthetic and political implications of the feminist SF canon as it has evolved over the past three decades, see Robin Roberts's "It's Still Science Fiction: Strategies of Feminist Science Fiction Criticism" and Helen Merrick's "Fantastic Dialogues: Critical Stories about Feminism and Science Fiction."

as focusing lenses through which to evaluate these concepts. In doing so they produced a unique body of speculative fiction that served as a potent critical voice about the relations of science, society, and gender as they were articulated first in the wake of World War II and as they continue to inform American culture today.

Women's Science Fiction in Theoretical Context

As a cultural history of postwar women's SF, *Galactic Suburbia* fulfills one of the oldest and arguably still most important dictates of feminist scholarship: to recover women's history in all its forms. I do this by reading postwar women's SF in relation to three areas of feminist inquiry: SF studies, science and literature studies, and cultural histories of women's work. I am particularly indebted to feminist SF critics who, over the past three decades, have surmounted skepticism on the part of scholars and SF professionals alike to demonstrate the vibrancy of a centuries-old women's speculative writing tradition. Scholars including Marleen Barr, Sarah Lefanu, Jane L. Donawerth, and Carol A. Kolmerton paved the way for better understandings of feminist utopian and science fiction by connecting it to historical periods of feminist political activity. More recently, Brian Attebery, Justine Larbalestier, Farah Mendlesohn, Helen Merrick, Dianne Newell, and Victoria Lamont have extended the feminist SF studies project to address the progressive nature of women's speculative fiction in other eras as well.[3] *Galactic Suburbia* continues this tradition

3. For pioneering feminist SF studies, see especially Marleen Barr's *Future Females: A Critical Anthology* and *Alien to Femininity: Speculative Fiction and Feminist Theory;* Sarah Lefanu's *Feminism and Science Fiction;* and Jane L. Donawerth and Carol Kolmerton's *Utopian and Science Fiction by Women: Worlds of Difference.* For more recent explorations of women's SF, see Brian Attebery's *Decoding Gender in Science Fiction;* Justine Larbalestier's *The Battle of the Sexes in Science Fiction;* Justine Larbalestier and Helen Merrick's "The Revolting Housewife: Women and Science Fiction in the 1950s"; Merrick's "Fantastic Dialogues: Critical Stories about Feminism and Science Fiction" and "The Readers Feminism Doesn't See: Feminist Fans, Critics and Science Fiction"; Farah Mendlesohn's "Gender, Power, and Conflict Resolution: 'Subcommittee' by Zenna Henderson"; and Dianne Newell and Victoria Lamont's "House Opera: Frontier Mythology and Subversion of Domestic Discourse in Mid-Twentieth-Century Women's Space Opera" and "Rugged Domesticity: Frontier Mythology in Post-Armageddon Science Fiction by Women." While Attebery and Larbalestier are primarily interested in the development of a feminist science-fictional sensibility over the course of the twentieth century, Merrick, Mendlesohn, Newell, and Lamont demonstrate how women writing SF in periods of feminist backlash strategically use conservative cultural beliefs about sex and gender to critique other social and political institutions.

of scholarship by demonstrating how what I call women's SF—that is, SF written by women about women—emerged in the postwar era as a product of both new cultural conditions for women authors and new narrative practices in the realm of SF itself.

To date, feminist SF scholars have been some of the most provocative theorists regarding the relations of gender and popular genre writing. Donawerth, Robin Roberts, and Patricia Melzer have been particularly innovative in this respect, as they have brought feminist theories concerning the relations of gender, science, and technology to bear on their studies of SF storytelling.[4] These authors show how women writers have used SF for nearly two hundred years to debunk the myths of objectivity and gender neutrality that often marginalize or exclude women from scientific research and technological development. *Galactic Suburbia* extends such projects by situating postwar women's SF writing in relation to the technoscientific, social, and moral orders that emerged after World War II. In this respect it demonstrates both the material forces informing women's SF and the natural compatibility between feminist SF studies and other kinds of critical inquiry, including science studies, literary studies, and cultural history.

When scholars explore the relations of science and literature, they often focus on those technosciences that are most central to the American imagination today. With *Galactic Suburbia* I extend such lines of inquiry to consider how authors represented sex and gender relations vis-à-vis the technosciences that first emerged in the 1940s, '50s, and '60s. As early as 1985, Donna Haraway called for feminists to attend to both women's participation in the "integrated circuit" of a technologically enabled transnational capitalism and the stories that authors tell about life in that circuit. In response, critics including N. Katherine Hayles and Susan Merrill Squier have demonstrated how information science and biomedicine give rise to new representations of human identity, and particularly gendered identity, in a range of scientific, literary, and popular narratives. Similar interests informed my own work in *The Self Wired: Technology and Subjectivity in Contemporary American Narrative,* which maps the emergence of what I call "cyborg writing" at the interface of new economic, technological, and literary practices. Meanwhile authors including Jenny Wolmark, Mary Flanagan, and Austin Booth have identified the nar-

4. See especially Donawerth's *Frankenstein's Daughters: Women Writing Science Fiction;* Roberts's *A New Species: Gender and Science in Science Fiction;* and Patricia Melzer's *Alien Constructions: Science Fiction and Feminist Thought.*

rative devices that women SF writers use to make sense of sex and gender in relation to cybertechnologies such as computers and video-games.[5]

By drawing attention to the scientific and technological develop-ments that most profoundly impacted women's lives and captured their imaginations at the beginning of the contemporary era—ranging from nuclear technologies and rocket ships to deep freezers and tele-visions—I show how women's science-fictional storytelling practices have evolved since World War II. In doing so I provide a rich historical and cultural context that enables us to more fully understand rep-resentations of technoscience, society, and gender today. I provide this context by connecting stories about women's work in galactic suburbia to cultural histories of women's work in America. Feminist scholars including Ruth Schwartz Cohen, Annegret Ogden, Sheila R. Rothman, and Susan Strasser have written extensively about the manner in which the most traditional form of women's labor—house-work—has evolved in relation to scientific, technological, and eco-nomic development. Meanwhile, Elaine Tyler May and the various authors included in anthologies edited by Joel Foreman, Lary May, and Joanne Meyerowitz call attention to debates over the nature of women's work in the cold war, a period when women were reconfig-ured specifically as subjects of an emergent technoculture.[6] But these scholars do not address how women themselves represented such

5. For works examining new representations of human identity vis-à-vis information science and biomedicine, see Haraway's "A Cyborg Manifesto: Science, Technology, and Socialist-Feminism in the Late Twentieth Century"; Hayles's *How We Became Posthu-man: Virtual Bodies in Cybernetics, Literature, and Informatics*; and Squier's *Liminal Lives: Imagining the Human at the Frontiers of Biomedicine*. For more specific evaluations of technoscience and its impact on cultural understandings of sex and gender, see Hayles's "The Life Cycle of Cyborgs: Writing the Posthuman" and Squier's *Babies in Bottles: Twen-tieth Century Visions of Reproductive Technologies*. For discussion of feminist SF authors and narrative representations of cyberculture, see Wolmark's *Cybersexualities* and Fla-nagan and Booth's *Reload: Rethinking Women + Cyberculture*.

6. For cultural histories of housework, see especially Ruth Schwartz Cowan's *More Work for Mother: The Ironies of Household Technology from the Open Hearth to the Micro-wave*; Annegret Ogden's *The Great American Housewife: From Helpmeet to Wage Earner, 1776–1986*; Sheila R. Rothman's *Woman's Proper Place: A History of Changing Ideals and Practices, 1870 to the Present*; and Susan Strasser's *Never Done: A History of American Housework*. For studies that specifically address women's work in the cold war, see Elaine Tyler May's *Homeward Bound: American Families in the Cold War* and Joanne Meyerowitz's *Not June Cleaver: Women and Gender in Postwar America, 1945–1960*. Finally, for studies that explore cold war politics (including sex and gender politics) in relation to aesthetic cultural production, see Joel Foreman's *The Other Fifties: Interrogat-ing Midcentury American Icons* and Lary May's *Recasting America: Culture and Politics in the Age of Cold War*.

change in their fiction writing. By wedding cultural studies insights and methodologies to their literary counterparts, I show how postwar women turned to SF as an important source of narratives for critically assessing the nature of feminine work and identity in a technology-intensive world.

The postwar era marks a transitional moment in contemporary thinking about gender and technology. The processes of domestic industrialization that began at the turn of the century and that were fully realized after World War II fostered images of women as scientifically and technologically savvy home management experts and consumers. Yet other technocultural developments associated with the cold war complicated these representations. On the one hand, the threat of nuclear annihilation reinforced conventional ideals about gender relations, binding women ever more closely to the private sphere of the home in the name of national security. On the other hand, early Soviet successes in the Space Race paved the way, however tentatively, for new ways of valuing women as technocultural workers in public spaces such as the laboratory and the launch pad. And throughout this era, women writers made their own innovative contributions to debates over emergent technocultural relations by boldly going where few women had gone before: into the SF community of the 1940s, '50s, and '60s.

Women's Science Fiction in Historical Context

If postwar women authors turned to SF to explore the relations of gender and technology after World War II, it is likely because the technoscientific developments of this period were themselves nothing short of science fictional. These developments included new wartime inventions such as atomic weapons, computers, and global communication technologies that promised to bring about widespread change in conventional social, political, and moral orders. But many Americans first experienced technocultural life in a manner that was both more humble and more profound: through the industrialization of the home. This was particularly true for American women who were, like their nineteenth- and early-twentieth-century counterparts, defined primarily by their labor in the private sphere. But whereas earlier generations of Americans understood the home as a sanctuary distinct from the public world of technology-intensive capitalism, postwar scientists, politicians, and authors treated the home as the fundamental unit of technoculture. By examining the changing relations of technology and domesticity, we can better understand how and why women became new kinds of citizens in a new kind of home.

The process of creating high-tech domestic citizens actually began at the turn of the century with four industrial innovations: modern plumbing, gas, electricity, and prefabricated household goods. Susan Strasser proposes that the first two were beneficial because they relieved women of the "staggering burden" that accompanied water transportation and fire building while "providing people the means for cleaner, healthier bodies, clothes, and houses" (103). Electricity and prefabricated goods also transformed housework, but in more complex ways. Wringers and washing machines saved many women from crippling bodily pain while the ability to purchase clothes reduced the visual problems that accompanied hand sewing in poor light. But these new technologies also produced new kinds of work. Washing machines tacitly encouraged housewives to do laundry more frequently, and new distribution centers for food and clothing required them to acquire new shopping skills and to engage in more travel as well (Ogden 156). Hence women's work changed in accordance with larger patterns of industrial production and consumption.

New patterns of industrialized domestic labor in the first half of the twentieth century gave rise to new representations of women as sophisticated home management experts. As Annegret Ogden explains, "New information was surfacing in matters of sanitation, medicine, nutrition, and many other fields affecting the well-being of the human race. Technology for production and concepts regarding production efficiency were becoming highly sophisticated by the early 1900s. Certain women in the new century saw how the new information, technology, and patterns of thinking could be applied in the home. The result was a new approach to housework and a new kind of housewife—the domestic scientist" (139). The concept of the domestic scientist was a wildly popular one, invoked everywhere from industrial studies of worker efficiency to women's service magazines. It also inspired a whole new field of scholarly inquiry: home economics.[7] Furthermore, in an era when suffragettes and other progressive women were demanding equality between the sexes, housewives who positioned themselves as domestic scientists implicitly (and sometimes explicitly) made the case that women deserved the same

7. For a discussion of domestic science in relation to the Progressive Era concept of "educated motherhood," see chapter 3 of Rothman's *Woman's Proper Place.*

social and political rights as men because they already had equivalent industrial skills and responsibilities.

Women's work as professional consumers also placed them at the interface of domesticity and technology. By the 1920s market surveys had established that housewives controlled almost the entire American retail dollar (Ogden 156). As the founding mother of home economics, Christine Frederick argued in her 1929 treatise *Selling Mrs. Consumer* that feminine demands for more and better goods were not mere vanity but signs of healthy self-expression that reflected women's growing confidence about their role in the marketplace. This role was crucial to the American economy because "the greater the demands made by women on industry, the more products industry would be able to turn out. . . . And the nation would be enveloped in prosperity" (Ogden 159). By putting housewives squarely at the center of the industrial world, Frederick and the businessmen she inspired demonstrated the increasingly close relations of the public and private spheres.

Of course, Progressive Era ideas about women as domestic scientists and consumers were primarily just that—ideas. In reality, women had uneven access to new labor-transforming technologies. For example, although prepared foods were available in most urban areas by the beginning of the twentieth century, three-fifths of the American population still lived in rural areas without access to modern grocery stores. Meanwhile, the urban poor still produced much of their own food to save money (Strasser 29–30). Efforts to fully modernize American homes were further delayed by the Great Depression and World War II, as industrialization projects were curtailed and individual households experienced dramatic declines in the liquid assets available for purchasing what suddenly seemed to be superfluous domestic technologies.

After 1945, new patterns of production and distribution combined with a booming postwar economy to foster the resumption of nationwide industrialization projects. By 1960, four-fifths of all American farms were wired for light, as opposed to the mere one-third that had electricity in 1940. Similar trends occurred in the dissemination of modern plumbing and gas lines: by 1960, 93 percent of American homes had piped water (up from 70 percent in 1940), and 65 percent had central heating (up from 42 percent in 1940) (Steidle and Bratton 222). It was not until the middle of the twentieth century, then, that Americans of all races and classes truly stood poised to take their place in the modern world.

As American families acquired homes with new technological amenities, they filled them with equally new appliances. By 1960, 10.5 percent of all modern homes had food waste disposals, 58.3 percent had automatic coffeemakers, and 56 percent had electric mixers. And although it might seem modest to us now, by this same year more than 15 percent of all American families had acquired the one device that truly makes every kind of work easier on warm and wet days: the air conditioner (Steidle and Bratton 222–23). If, in essence, Americans became technocultural citizens in the decades immediately following World War II, they did so largely in the privacy of their newly technologized homes.

The postwar diffusion of technological amenities and appliances had a particularly profound impact on American housewives as pioneers in the brave new world of postindustrial capitalism. Prior to this time, middle- and upper-class housewives often had both machines and servants to assist with household chores, while women with fewer economic resources relied on their own labor to maintain order in the home. After World War II, however, working-class women pursued new opportunities for work in America's rapidly expanding service sector. The gradual disappearance of servants combined with the increased availability of household appliances to create a unique situation. As Ruth Schwartz Cowan succinctly puts it, for the first time ever in the history of housework, both "the housewife of 'the professional classes' and the housewife of 'the working classes' were assisted *only by machines*" (199; my emphasis). Much like their male counterparts on the assembly line and in the computer lab, American women of the 1940s, '50s, and '60s were surrounded by the products of technoculture. Indeed, because many of these women spent so much time alone in the home with their machines, it may well be that they experienced a certain kind of technologically enhanced subjectivity even more intensely than those men who labored with both machines and other humans.

Given that the opening decades of the contemporary era marked the fulfillment of so many industrial ideals as they applied to the home, it is hardly surprising that this period also saw the revival and refinement of Progressive Era beliefs concerning women's work as domestic science and consumption. Not surprisingly, home economics books including Lillian Gilbreth, Orpha Mae Thomas, and Eleanor Clymer's *Management in the Home: Happier Living through Saving Time and Energy* (1954) and Rose Steidl and Esther Crew Bratton's *Work in the Home* (1968) continued to treat housewives as efficiency experts.

At the same time, prominent sociologists such as Talcott Parsons argued that modern technology had all but eliminated physical labor in the home, enabling women to pursue a new aspect of domestic science: the controlled production of happy children (Wajcman 239). Thus, the language of industry in the home extended to the efficient organization of the family itself.

And yet as the scope of domestic science expanded to include both people and things, women as family managers were systematically displaced from the positions of authority they had claimed for themselves just half a century earlier. Like their turn-of-the-century counterparts, postwar women were expected to be well versed in the newest and most effective modes of domestic management. However, family managers were rarely granted positions of authority in the new field of childhood development. Instead, they were treated as amateurs who needed the guidance of psychological experts such as Sigmund Freud and Erik Erickson and medical authorities such as Benjamin Spock to rear their children properly. "Ironically," cultural historian Annegret Ogden writes, "the role of supermother, in which women of the fifties put so much stock for personal fulfillment and social recognition, was really the role of an obedient child following rules drawn up by someone else—an authority figure in a far-off university laboratory" (177). As postwar women were drawn into the new networks of professionalized expertise and technoscientific knowledge that emerged at mid-century, they were required to give up what had long been seen as their natural authority over children.

One arena in which housewives were still treated as natural authorities was that of consumption. But the duties of "Mrs. Consumer" changed in the 1940s, '50s, and '60s in accordance with the changing priorities of the entire nation. As in the Progressive Era, postwar women were told that shopping was vital to the well-being of the economy. But now it was a fundamental aspect of cold war patriotism as well. Elaine Tyler May writes that postwar women's consumption "provided evidence of the superiority of the American way of life. . . . Although they may have been unwitting soldiers, women who marched off to the nation's shopping centers to equip their homes joined the ranks of America's cold warriors" (*Homeward Bound* 168). Consumption, then, remained a key sign of women's self-expression. But this expression took on new ideological significance as the United States sought to define itself in opposition to that other postwar industrial giant, the Soviet Union.

As May suggests, the cold war profoundly influenced popular representations of women's work as a kind of domestic patriotism, especially since housewives, as family managers and consumers, were perceived to be the first lines of defense against communist encroachment onto American soil. But at the same time that the Red Scare sent women homeward bound, the scientific and technological demands of the Space Race called them back into the paid workforce. When the Soviets launched their first artificial satellite, *Sputnik I,* months ahead of its U.S. counterpart, this unexpected event engendered a flurry of concern on the part of American scientists and government officials regarding the United States's ability to fully utilize American brainpower. The problem, according to studies published by the National Manpower Council (NMC) in 1957 and 1958, stemmed from the scarcity of American women in technoscientific professions: in Russia, women comprised 69 percent of all medical students and 39 percent of all engineers, but in the United States, less than 20 percent of all science and math majors were women (Kaledin 54).[8] To resolve this dilemma, the NMC—along with every major women's and labor organization—recommended increasing womanpower through salary raises, the construction of new childcare facilities, more part-time jobs for women, and equal rights legislation.

Although few employers followed the NMC's recommendations, the U.S. government tried to provide new opportunities for scientifically and mathematically inclined women. In 1958, Congress passed the National Defense Education Act, which guaranteed fellowships for all students regardless of race, class, or gender in mathematics, science, foreign languages, and other defense-related areas of research (Rossiter 63). And in 1959 the nascent National Aeronautics and Space Administration (NASA) quietly initiated the Women in Space Early (WISE) program, recruiting thirteen of the nation's top female aviators for astronaut training. Although it was unceremoniously shut down in 1962, the very existence of the WISE program in an era otherwise defined by exceedingly conservative notions of sex and gender ideals indicates the extent to which the imperatives of an emergent technoculture were already transforming those ideals.[9]

8. Furthermore, as Eugenia Kaledin notes, "between 1950 and 1960 the number of [American] women in engineering declined from 11 percent to 9 percent. . . . And in industrial and scientific technology the number of women dropped from 18 percent to 12 percent" (203).

9. The past few years have seen an explosion of interest on the part of feminist his-

Figure 1. Changing images of women and technology after World War II. On the left, WISE astronaut Jerrie Cobb poses next to a Mercury spaceship in a conventionally feminine matter. On the right, she works a Gimbal Rig much as any male astronaut might do. (Images courtesy of NASA)

If nothing else, the WISE program gave Americans new images of women's work. In February 1960, *Look* magazine ran a cover article on Betty Skelton, a national aerobatic champion who trained with the Mercury 7 male astronauts (Nolen 92). In August of the same year, *Life* magazine published an equally extensive article on Jerrie Cobb, a commercial pilot who held distance, altitude, and speed records for several types of planes and who served as a spokesperson for the WISE program (Freni 53). Meanwhile, NASA officials carefully documented every aspect of the WISE program for both scientific and publicity purposes.

Whether they appeared in coffee-table magazines or government reports, pictures of the WISE women clearly reflected changing ideas

---

torians regarding the first astronaut training programs for women in the late 1950s and early 1960s. See especially Martha Ackmann's *The Mercury 13: The Untold Story of Thirteen American Women and the Dream of Space Flight;* Pamela Freni's *Space for Women: A History of Women with the Right Stuff;* Bettyann Holtzmann Kevles's *Almost Heaven: The Story of Women in Space;* and Stephanie Nolen's *Promised the Moon: The Untold History of Women in the Space Race.*

about gender and technology. For example, NASA photographers often depicted Cobb as an avatar of conventional American femininity, replete with modern sports clothes, carefully styled hair, and impeccable makeup. But they also photographed her much like any other (male) astronaut, spinning in centrifuges, floating in buoyancy tanks, and proudly looking off into the distant future as she climbed into her jet cockpit (see figure 1). Much like their domestic counterparts, early women astronauts such as Cobb were surrounded—and in many ways defined—by their machines. But suddenly it seemed that women might be at home anywhere from the familiar environs of their own living rooms to the mysterious hinterlands of the stars.

Women's Science Fiction in Galactic Suburbia: A Brief Overview

As I argue in the following chapters, both the industrialization of the home and the new technocultural situations engendered by the cold war fueled the development of women's SF in the 1940s, '50s, and '60s. A number of factors unite the authors and stories I associate with this mode of SF storytelling. While women's SF—like SF as a whole—is too diverse to subsume under a single, categorical definition, stories written in this tradition share a number of characteristics and concerns. For the most part, women's SF was produced by authors who began their writing careers after World War II but before the revival of feminism in the mid-1960s. These authors wrote under decidedly feminine names and claimed for themselves conventionally (sometimes even stereotypically) feminine roles as housewives, teachers, and nurses. Although they occasionally published in older, action-oriented SF periodicals such as *Amazing Stories* and *Astounding Science Fiction,* most of their work appeared in the new SF magazines that emerged after World War II with reputations for printing thoughtful, offbeat stories of relatively high literary quality, such as *The Magazine of Fantasy and Science Fiction* and *If.*

Most importantly, the new women writers who published in these new magazines engaged in unique storytelling practices. Women's SF was recognizable as SF because it depicted futures extrapolated from the scientific and technological arrangements of postwar America. Additionally, women writers used classic SF story forms such as the space opera and the nuclear holocaust narrative and classic SF tropes such as the heroic scientist and the alien other to convey these futures. But women's SF was distinct from other kinds of postwar speculative fiction in two key respects: it revolved around the impact of science and technology on women and their families, and it was told from the perspective of women who defined themselves primarily (although not exclusively) as lovers, wives, and mothers.[10]

Taken together, these characteristics have led me to develop an account of women's SF that features somewhat different players than other SF histories. Some of the most famous mid-century women SF authors, including Leigh Brackett, C. L. Moore, and Andre Norton, are largely absent from this book. Although they were all innovative writers who used their chosen genre to critique the conservative tendencies of their own eras and espouse more progressive (and sometimes even protofeminist) futures, they rarely dealt with domestic relations or featured average human women as protagonists in their stories.[11]

Other SF luminaries who appear in these pages are presented in a new light. For example, while Judith Merril is largely remembered for her editing and anthologizing activities, she features prominently in this book as one of the foundational figures in women's SF. Similarly, women writers who are best known now for their work in slipstream and fantasy fiction, such as Carol Emshwiller, Marion Zimmer Bradley, and Anne McCaffrey, are also presented as leading figures in the creation of SF stories that directly engaged the relations of science, technology, and gender after World War II. And finally, by focusing on SF stories set in galactic suburbia, I recover popular mid-century writers such as Alice Eleanor Jones, Mildred Clingerman, and Doris Pitkin Buck who stopped publishing original work by the late 1960s and were all but lost to modern SF history. Taken together, these authors brought a wide range of social interests and literary skills to bear on the development of women's SF.

In chapter 1, "Writers," I examine why women were drawn to the SF community in the postwar era and situate their storytelling prac-

10. Postwar editors and fans regularly noted the unique characteristics of women's SF and furiously debated its meaning and value. For further discussion, see chapter 1 of this book.

11. For discussions of the protofeminist tendencies in Moore, Brackett, and Norton, see Sarah Gamble's "'Shambleau . . . and Others': The Role of the Female in the Fiction of C. L. Moore"; Virginia L. Wolf's "Andre Norton: Feminist Pied Piper in SF"; and Robin Roberts's *A New Species: Gender and Science in Science Fiction*. For discussion of these authors in relation to other, more overtly politicized postwar women writers such as Judith Merril and Marion Zimmer Bradley, see Newell and Lamont's "House Opera: Frontier Mythology and Subversion of Domestic Discourse in Mid-Twentieth-Century Women's Space Opera" and "Rugged Domesticity: Frontier Mythology in Post-Armageddon Science Fiction by Women."

tices in relation to broader patterns of literary production. Because women writers coupled stories about brave new worlds, sleek technologies, and exotic alien others with tropes of romance, marriage, and motherhood, fans and critics alike often treated their SF as a kind of literary anomaly, springing fully formed from the heads of a few isolated women. However, as my case studies of Judith Merril, Alice Eleanor Jones, and Shirley Jackson demonstrate, this kind of SF is more properly understood as a dynamic mode of speculative storytelling with close ties to other literary forms that centered on domestic tropes and themes including feminist utopian writing, women's magazine fiction, and early postmodernist literature.

Chapter 2, "Homemakers," illustrates how women used SF to comment on modern domesticity. As domestic cold warriors, postwar women were expected to protect their individual families through carefully executed acts of caretaking and consumption. While this simple ideal was promulgated throughout American culture, women complicated the meaning and value of modern homemaking in their everyday lives by creating cooperative daycare centers and consumer activist groups to meet their own needs for critical engagement with the larger world beyond the suburban home. In a similar vein, SF authors including Garen Drussaï, Ann Warren Griffith, and Kit Reed used the figure of the female alien to advocate alternate models of caretaking and the setting of the media landscape story to imagine how women might use truly fantastic domestic technologies to either escape or reconfigure the home. By telling SF stories about women's work as homemakers, such authors powerfully challenged the logic of the feminine mystique while defining new authorial traditions within SF.

Chapter 3, "Activists," explores postwar women's SF in relation to political activism. The dominant discourses of cold war America glorified women as domestic patriots who could best serve their country through housekeeping and childrearing in the suburbs. Meanwhile, women involved with peace organizations and the civil rights movement revised this rhetoric to their own ends, positioning themselves as municipal housekeepers driven to political action by concern for their children's future. Women's SF both anticipated and extended such arguments. As my analyses of authors including Carol Emshwiller, Mary Armock, and Mildred Clingerman illustrate, women's stories about nuclear war and the encounter with the alien other mirrored the political tactics of their activist counterparts. As such, these authors insisted on the necessity of including women's voices and values in ongoing debates about American policymaking.

In chapter 4, "Scientists," I demonstrate how women authors responded to debates over women's work in the fields of science and technology. Although the decades following World War II are now remembered as the golden age of American science, women were generally relegated to the margins of technoscientific labor as librarians, technical writers, and research assistants. At the same time, government agencies warned that the United States would fall dangerously behind the Soviet Union if it did not more fully utilize women's intellectual and technical abilities. Women writing for the postwar SF community claimed scientific authority for themselves—and by extension, all women—in two distinct ways. Journalists such as June Lurie, Sylvia Jacobs, and Kathleen Downe invoked and updated a centuries-old tradition of women's science popularization in the science essays they wrote for major SF magazines. Elsewhere, Marion Zimmer Bradley, Judith Merril, Doris Pitkin Buck, Katherine MacLean, and Anne McCaffrey created stories that celebrated women's domestic lives as inspiration for scientific and technological discovery while underscoring the danger of forcing women to chose between family and career. Taken together, these writers extended U.S. officials' growing conviction that women were needed as scientists, engineers, and astronauts on the front lines of the cold war.

I conclude this study with "Progenitors," in which I briefly explore how the thematic issues and narrative techniques of postwar women's stories about galactic suburbia continue to inform SF storytelling practices today. Although galactic suburbia has all but disappeared from feminist SF, contemporary women writers still engage many of the same issues as their postwar counterparts, including the history and future of race relations, the role of women in the media landscape, and the impact of gendered perception on scientific research and technological development. Meanwhile, as men begin to rethink their own domestic roles and experience the kind of economic displacement and technological alienation traditionally associated with women, male authors increasingly incorporate the settings and character types associated with galactic suburbia into their own writing. Taken together, these trends demonstrate that postwar women's SF is a major foundation upon which SF authors continue to build today.

WRITERS

*I*MAGINE IT. One world where women combine navy protocols with the practices of the free love movement to prepare their crews for long-term space travel; another world where housewives contemplate killing their husbands to more effectively rebuild an America torn apart by nuclear war; and yet a third world where shopping lists—not science—reveal the true nature of the universe. For readers who opened their postwar SF magazines expecting tales about sleek technologies, heroic engineers, and exotic alien worlds, such stories must have come as quite a shock: when did sex trump technology as the key to social progress? When did shopping lists replace science as the means by which we discover the world? And perhaps most urgently: why tell SF stories—usually the province of male scientists, soldiers, and politicians—from the perspective of housewives, mothers, and other markedly feminine characters in the first place?

The stories described above are all classic examples of the women's SF that emerged after World War II and flourished for the next two decades, providing the foundation for what we now call feminist SF. Like their male counterparts, women writing SF in the 1940s, '50s, and '60s were deeply interested in the impact of new sciences and technologies on society. In this respect they are very much a part of

SF history. Furthermore, because these authors illustrated fundamental connections between interpersonal relations in the private sphere and broad social relations in the public arena, their stories are very much a part of feminist history as well. Throughout this book I propose that stories about life and love in what Joanna Russ once called "galactic suburbia" are deeply enmeshed in the culture and politics of their historical moment. And as artifacts of that moment, they provide us with important insight into women's representations of the relations between science, technology, and gender at the beginning of the contemporary era.

In this chapter I map the emergence of women's SF after World War II. I begin by briefly considering why women authors chose this particular genre at this juncture in history and how the American reading public responded to them. I then situate women's SF in its specific literary milieus. As my case studies of Judith Merril, Alice Eleanor Jones, and Shirley Jackson show, women writing SF in this period had strong ties to a host of literary traditions including feminist utopian fiction, women's commercial magazine fiction, and early postmodernism. By combining the tropes and techniques of these other traditions with the narrative emphases of SF, postwar women writers created an aesthetically innovative and socially engaged mode of speculative storytelling that staked claims for women's place in America's future.

The Rise of Modern Women's Science Fiction

In the decades stretching from the end of World War II in 1945 to the revival of radical politics in the mid-1960s, American SF fully entered what Edward James calls its "Golden Age," a period when the genre reached new levels of mainstream popularity.[1] Before this time SF was published primarily in oversized pulp magazines; after World War II, innovations in mass-media manufacture and distribution led to the development of cheap, easily distributed paperback books. These innovations also led to a temporary boom in SF magazine pro-

---

1. More specifically, James defines the Golden Age of SF as a period that stretches from 1938 to about 1960. According to James, many of the themes and techniques commonly associated with Golden Age SF were established by the end of the 1940s, but it was not until the publishing boom of the 1950s that authors were able to explore these themes and techniques in the greater detail and length typically associated with "mature" SF. For further discussion, see Edward James, *Science Fiction in the Twentieth Century*.

duction. At least thirty-five new SF magazines—many of which even had the sophisticated production values of "slick" mainstream magazines and literary digests—appeared during the first half of the 1950s alone, paving the way for an ever greater number of authors to try their hand at this increasingly popular literary form (James 85–86).

SF also reached new levels of stylistic and thematic maturity in this period. Throughout the 1940s *Astounding Science-Fiction* editor John W. Campbell insisted that authors exchange the wildly speculative and often uncritically celebratory tone of earlier SF for more soberly accurate depictions of science and technology. Even more significantly, he encouraged writers to think through the social implications of science and technology and to put a human face on the sometimes overwhelmingly abstract issues attending new modes of knowledge and new inventions (Westfahl 184). By the 1950s these dictates had become the standard by which most written SF was measured. New publications such as *The Magazine of Fantasy and Science Fiction* (which quickly developed a reputation for literary quality) and *Galaxy* (which encouraged authors to question the social and moral conventions of cold war America) provided homes for a whole new generation of authors dedicated to producing thoughtful and critically engaged forms of SF (James 86).

This new generation of SF authors included nearly 300 women writers.[2] Of course, women have always been a part of SF history. Scholars generally recognize Mary Shelley's 1818 novel *Frankenstein* as one of the first SF (and first feminist) novels. A little more than a century later, stories by Leslie F. Stone, Clare Winger Harris, and Lillian Taylor Hansen were regularly featured in the pages of the first pulp SF magazines. By the 1930s and '40s a whole host of women had made names for themselves as SF authors, including, most notably, Leigh Brackett, C. L. Moore, and Andre Norton. However, few if any members of the early SF community treated these women writers as a unified group with overlapping thematic concerns or narrative techniques.[3]

2. For an explanation of how I derived these numbers, see footnote 1 in the introduction to this book.

3. Recent SF scholars—especially those dedicated to the historical recovery of women's writing outside moments of overt feminist activity—are beginning to identify certain similarities in early women's SF. For further discussion of the feminist impulses in pulp-era SF written by women, see Jane Donawerth's "Science Fiction by Women in the Early Pulps, 1926–1930." For further discussion of debates over representations of sex and gender in the early SF community, see Justine Larbalestier's *The Battle of the Sexes in Science Fiction*.

But by the late 1940s and early 1950s, no one doubted women writers' interest in SF. New authors including Judith Merril, Margaret St. Clair, and Zenna Henderson all published SF under their own, decidedly feminine, names. They also wrote about the relations of science, society, and gender more systematically than did their foremothers. As we shall see in the following pages, women writing for the postwar SF community regularly told stories about housewives, schoolteachers, and other conventionally feminine characters who grappled with the promises and perils of life in a high-tech era. And they began to focus on new characters in new situations as well: women engineers who balanced the paid work of starship design with the unpaid labor of childrearing; female scientists who resourcefully transformed their kitchens into laboratories; and even enlightened male doctors who aid human progress by taking on the work of mothering itself. Taken together, the stories written by postwar women authors anticipate one of the central tenets of later feminist thinking: that the personal is always already political.

What drew so many women to SF at the beginning of the modern era? Although there are a number of good answers to this question, three specific factors seem to have been particularly relevant to the rise of modern women's SF. First, as SF author and historian Brian Aldiss proposes in *Billion Year Spree,* women turned to this popular genre after World War II because new editorial imperatives and publishing patterns invited authors to write about "less dour technologies [for] wider audiences" (263). Second, as Judith Merril noted in a 1971 retrospective on McCarthy-era literary practices, SF was "virtually the only vehicle of political dissent" available to authors writing in a moment marked by intense political paranoia and cultural conformity ("What Do You Mean" 74). And finally, as Shirley Jackson—arguably one of mid-century America's most popular authors in any genre— told friends and family alike, SF editors could be counted on to publish tales that other editors deemed too outlandish or experimental for mainstream audiences (Oppenheimer 150). Simply put, women turned to SF in the 1940s, '50s, and '60s because it provided them with growing audiences for fiction that was both socially engaged and aesthetically innovative. In that respect they were not much different from their male counterparts.

And yet the stories these women wrote often differed significantly from those written by men, and so it should come as no surprise that American readers responded to women's SF in complex and sometimes contradictory ways. Vocal contingents of fans, editors, and writers (including a very young Isaac Asimov) condemned women's SF as "heart-throb-and-diaper" storytelling produced by a "gaggle of housewives" out to spoil the fun of the genre for everyone (qtd. in Larbalestier 172–73). For such members of the SF community, tales of marriage and motherhood seemed utterly incompatible with stories about high-tech galactic adventures.[4]

Women also encountered more subtle forms of sexism in their quest to be recognized as part of the SF community. In a 1955 letter to *Amazing Stories* editor Howard Browne, fourteen-year-old Cathleen M. M. Harlan enthusiastically announced her love of SF and her plan to pursue a career in SF writing. But she was troubled by one thing: "I've noticed most of the writers in the s-f field are men. This bothers me for one very good reason: I'm a girl. Could you tell me why this is so? (Not why I'm a girl)" (Harlan 117). Browne's reply was brief but telling: "few women write s-f because few women are interested in science" (118). This conclusion is particularly surprising because until *Amazing Stories* changed its format in 1953, it regularly featured science columns by June Lurie and Faye Beslow. Hence, Browne's response seems to reflect a certain historical amnesia. It also reflects the extent to which even the seemingly most open-minded of postwar Americans were invested in patriarchal assumptions about the necessary relations of science, society, and gender: even when they had proof to the contrary, they unthinkingly assumed that women simply were not interested in either science or stories about it.

But other members of the SF community were more generous in their assessment of women's interest in and contributions to the genre. *Fantasy and Science Fiction* editor Anthony Boucher described women's SF (which he regularly included in his *Year's Best* series) as a groundbreaking phenomenon that provided readers with "sensitive depictions of the future from a woman's point of view" for the first time in the genre's history (125). Similarly, in an editorial on what he cheerfully called "The Female Invasion," *Fantastic Universe* editor

4. Significantly, similar critical attitudes informed early feminist readings of postwar women's SF. In the 1970s both Joanna Russ and Pamela Sargent condemned what they called "housewife heroine" SF for simply reiterating conventional ideas about science, society, and gender. And even today echoes of this attitude can be found in Lisa Tuttle's assessment of postwar women's SF, which she sympathetically but insistently describes as comprising "sentimental stories dealing with . . . acceptable feminine concerns" (1344). For further discussion of feminist attitudes to prefeminist science fiction, see Helen Merrick's "Fantastic Dialogues: Critical Stories about Feminism and Science Fiction" as well as my essays "Unhappy Housewife Heroines, Galactic Suburbia, and Nuclear War: A New History of Midcentury Women's Science Fiction" and "A History of One's Own: Joanna Russ and the Creation of a Feminist Science Fiction Tradition."

Leo Margulies wrote that "today women work side-by-side with their men on every conceivable job in the world," and that in the job of writing SF, women were distinguishing themselves by virtue of "their intensely imaginative minds [and] their sensitive understanding of human emotions" (161). As editors dedicated to maintaining their respective magazines' reputations for cutting-edge fiction, Boucher and Margulies valued the new generation of women authors precisely because they brought new perspectives and literary techniques to bear on the craft of SF writing as it was then practiced. Little wonder that another such editor—*Fantastic*'s Paul W. Fairman—proudly proclaimed to readers, "we feel women are here to stay and that they'll be very much a part of our world in the future" (125).

Like their editorial counterparts, open-minded fans were also appreciative of women's writing. When *Astounding* editor John W. Campbell published Judith Merril's "That Only a Mother" in 1948 he did more than premiere the story that would set the standards for much subsequent women's SF. He induced an appetite for such stories in readers as well. Fans rated Merril's story as the second-best published in that particular issue—just behind Eric Frank Russell's "Dreadful Sanctuary" and well ahead of Isaac Asimov's "No Connection." And they begged *Astounding* for more. As Roscoe E. Wright put it in one of many such letters to Campbell: "this is about the finest short story I have ever seen. . . . If I ask for more, do you suppose Judith Merril would send you some more? . . . What Science Fiction needs is one—or maybe more—good yarn by a woman in each issue to give the magazine a better balance and wider appeal" (158). And when editors complied with such requests, fans were quick to provide them with positive reinforcement. In an open letter to *Fantastic* readers, Mrs. Lucky Rardin directly thanks Fairman and his editorial staff "for letting a couple of females into the science-fiction world. You'd think that all the women were left on Earth, forgotten, when the first space ships started climbing into space" (125). In direct contrast to those readers who dismissed women's SF as romance fiction with no real relevance to SF's future imaginary, fans such as Rardin were absolutely delighted to see characters resembling themselves within that future imaginary—especially when other women created them.

The wider literary community also recognized the innovative nature of postwar women's SF. In 1950 the *New York Times* compared Merril's *Shadow in the Hearth*—a nuclear war story told from the perspective of an average wife and mother—to the cautionary works of H. G. Wells and George Orwell, and in 1954 Motorola TV Theater broadcast a dramatic version of Merril's story under the title "Atomic Attack" (Merril and Pohl-Weary 99–100). And although Merril may have been the most prominent of the new women SF authors, she was not the only one to receive critical attention. In the 1950s and '60s editor Martha Foley featured SF stories by Merril and Shirley Jackson in her *Best American Short Stories* anthologies. The import of this honor becomes more evident when we consider that Foley included stories by only one male SF author (Ray Bradbury) during her tenure as editor of this anthology series and that subsequent editors have included only a total of six other SF stories in it since her time.[5]

Clearly the authors who helped shape women's SF as a distinctive mode of storytelling were literary forces to be reckoned with in their own day. But where did the impetus come from to take on this task? As I demonstrate in the following pages, women writing for the postwar SF community were inspired by a surprising range of literary traditions, including feminist utopian writing, commercial magazine fiction, and postmodern literature.

Judith Merril and Women's Speculative Fiction

When women wrote SF in the 1940s, '50s, and '60s, they did so in relation to a century-old tradition of speculative fiction about science, technology, and the home. As feminist literary scholars Carol Farley Kessler, Jean Pfaelzer, and Jane L. Donawerth and Carol A. Kolmerton have shown, nineteenth- and early-twentieth-century women published scores of utopian stories in which domestic reform was a central concern. In tune with the tenor of their times, utopian authors including Mary E. Bradley Lane and Charlotte Perkins Gilman linked such reform to advanced sciences that could yield "collective or mechanical alternatives" to traditional patterns of housework and childcare (Pfaelzer 50). For instance, the women of Lane's *Mizora: A*

5. The postwar women's SF stories selected for reprinting in Foley's *Best American Short Stories* are Judith Merril's "Dead Center" (1954) and Shirley Jackson's "One Ordinary Day, with Peanuts" (1955). The Bradbury stories that Foley included were "The Big Black and White Game" (1946); "I See You Never" (1948); "The Other Foot" (1952); and "The Day It Rained Forever" (1958). The six other SF stories that have been included in *The Best American Short Story* anthologies since Foley's tenure are Harlan Ellison's "The Man Who Rowed Christopher Columbus Ashore" (1991); Ursula K. Le Guin's "Sur" and "The Professor's Houses" (both originally published in 1982); Kelly Link's "Stone Animals" (2004); Cory Doctorow's "Anda's Game" (2004); and Tim Pratt's "Hart and Boot" (2004).

Prophecy (1881) chemically synthesize food, while those of Gilman's *Herland* (1915) delegate childrearing to scientifically trained professionals. This liberates women to pursue their personal interests, develop their professional talents, and otherwise express themselves as full human beings.

The first generation of women to write SF continued this tradition of utopian speculation in the pulp magazines of the 1920s and 1930s. As Donawerth argues, authors including Clare Winger Harris, Lillian Taylor Hansen, and Leslie F. Stone all published stories that, much like their utopian predecessors, imagined "the transformation of domestic spaces and duties" via chemically synthesized foods, automated houses, and robotic housekeepers ("Science Fiction" 138).[6] Elsewhere Lilith Lorraine and Sophie Wenzel Ellis speculated that new reproductive technologies such as incubators and artificial wombs would enable women of the future to pursue both "further education and . . . public responsibilities" ("Science Fiction" 142).[7] For these early SF women writers, advanced sciences and technologies could do more than simply alleviate the burden of women's work in the private sphere. They could produce new kinds of feminine (and sometimes even feminist) agency in the public sphere as well.

For Donawerth, however, the progressive tendencies of women's pulp SF are limited by two factors. First, like their male counterparts, women writing SF in the early part of the twentieth century tended to romanticize science and technology. This often led them to "displace their critique of the unfairly gendered social organization into unrealistic hopes for a science that would make the problem disappear" (*Frankenstein's Daughters* 15). Second, women "were limited . . . by their assumptions about literary form. . . . The brief science fiction tradition that women writers inherited was entirely male in narration, and mostly first person. . . . [Stories were told] in men's voices, about men making scientific discoveries and undertaking scientific exploration" ("Science Fiction" 145). Although women SF authors occasionally used male narrators to demonstrate how men might come around to enlightened feminist perspectives on science and society, stories written from masculine points of view threatened to erase women's voices altogether and to turn into conventional romances where hysterical, victimized women were rescued from

---

6. See especially Harris's "A Runaway World"; Hansen's "What the Sodium Lines Revealed"; and Stone's "Women with Wings."

7. See especially Lorraine's "Into the 28th Century" and Ellis's "Creatures of the Light."

galactic perils by rational, heroic men.[8]

At least one writer from this period depicts the promises and challenges of early SF authorship in similar terms. Leslie F. Stone recalls being drawn to this "young medium" in the 1920s because it was "fresh and new," providing her with the opportunity to create some literary "firsts," including the first depiction of women as astronauts and the first black SF protagonist (100). A leading member of SF editor Hugo Gernsback's inner circle, Stone claims that Gernsback "liked the idea of a woman invading the field he had opened" and that she never had trouble selling stories to him or his successor, T. O'Conor Sloane (101). Like many later feminist SF authors, Stone valued SF because it provided her with the opportunity to explore new scientific developments and the new social orders that might attend such developments.

But Stone also remembers being constrained by the masculinist assumptions of the early SF community. At the beginning of her career a friend advised Stone to publish under an androgynous name because SF was a men's genre and "back then, Women's Lib was but a gleam in feminine eyes" (101). And although some members of the SF community were willing to accept an SF "authoress," others used Stone's gender as an excuse to attack her work. For instance, fans roundly condemned "The Conquest of Gola" because it depicts a world of technologically advanced, telepathic women who fend off conquest by the rapacious men of a neighboring planet. The relative ease with which they do so only serves to confirm their chauvinist attitudes toward the subservient men of their own world. As Stone notes, the story clearly put "females in the driver's seat, females that dared to regard their gentle consorts as playthings. Male chauvinism just couldn't take that!" (100) Stone finally stopped writing SF in the late 1930s when she found herself contending with a new generation of editors (including *Astounding*'s F. Orlin Tremaine and John Campbell as well as *Galaxy*'s Horace Gold) who insisted that women could not write good SF (101).[9] Hence, early attempts to create woman-oriented,

8. Donawerth cites half a dozen of these stories, such as Louise Rice and Tonjoroff-Roberts's "Astounding Enemy" in which women scientists and soldiers combat insect enemies, but the story itself is narrated by a man, and Leslie F. Stone's "Out of the Void" in which a young female scientist attempts to voyage to Mars but is captured by an evil (male) politician and then must be rescued by her (male) lover turned revolutionary ("Science Fiction" 144–46).

9. Apparently Campbell and Gold eventually modified their opinions about women in SF, since both went on to publish authors including Judith Merril, Katherine MacLean, and Ann Warren Griffith.

feminist-friendly SF were limited not just by the narrative conventions of the field but by a network of socially conservative authors, editors, and fans as well.[10]

Chauvinism notwithstanding, many women continued to write speculative fiction, and by the late 1940s and early 1950s a new generation of women writers had made their way into the pages of SF magazines. Much like their pulp-era predecessors, the authors of this new generation continued to explore the relations of science, technology, and domesticity despite mixed reactions from the SF community. They also contributed to this tradition in two significant ways: by setting their stories in near futures where characters were still struggling with the social changes wrought by new sciences and technologies (rather than in faraway lands or distant futures where social change was already a fait accompli) and by narrating stories from women's (rather than men's) perspectives.

The close relations of women's early- and mid-century SF are particularly clear in the work of Judith Merril, a foundational figure in SF history. Merril's lifelong commitment to SF began during World War II when she moved to New York to support herself and her daughter through writing. There she joined the Futurians, a group of writers and fans (including such rising stars as Isaac Asimov, Frederik Pohl, and Virginia Kidd) who are often credited with setting the thematic and stylistic standards for modern SF. Over the next two decades, Merril edited a variety of prominent SF collections, including *Shot in the Dark* (1951) and all twelve of the *Year's Best of SF* anthologies (1956–67).[11] At the same time she was packaging SF for outside audiences in her anthologies, Merril worked to strengthen the genre from within by establishing some of the first professional SF writing groups, including the Milford Writers' Workshop and the Hydra Club (Merril and Pohl-Weary 270, 273).

This period of editing and organizing also marked the pinnacle of Merril's literary production. In 1948 Merril published her first SF story, "That Only a Mother," and in 1950 she published her first novel,

10. Of course, women readers also had strong opinions about how SF should be written, and many of them agreed with their male counterparts that there was no room for romance or domesticity of any sort in SF. For further discussion of the gender question in the early SF community, see Justine Larbalestier's *The Battle of the Sexes in Science Fiction*.

11. For further discussion of Merril's work as an SF anthologist and editor, see Elizabeth Cummins's "Judith Merril: Scouting SF"; "Judith Merril: A Link with the New Wave—Then and Now"; and "American SF, 1940s–1950s: Where's the Book? The New York Nexus."

Shadow on the Hearth. Both works depict American women trying to survive World War III, and both won Merril a great deal of recognition as a writer.[12] Throughout the 1950s and early 1960s Merril continued to win recognition for her experiments with female narrative voices. For example, "Dead Center" (1954), told from the perspective of a female rocket designer, appears in Anthony Boucher's *Treasury of Great Science Fiction* (1959), G. B. Levitas's *The World of Psychology* (1963), and Martha Foley's prestigious *Best American Short Stories* series (1955). Thus, Merril's stories set the paradigmatic standards for women's SF, especially as it evolved in relation to already-established traditions of women's speculative fiction.

In her autobiography, *Better to Have Loved,* Merril recollects turning to SF rather than other kinds of writing as a young author because it took as its basic premise "the idea that things could be different" (44–45). For Merril, SF embodied the very essence of great literature: "Some people, and I am one, also believe that art is by nature revolutionary: that a vital function of the artist is to produce and publish 'virtual realities' of social change. Certainly the inverse is true: no radical change can ever occur until a believable and seductive new vision is made public" (42). Much like Leslie F. Stone before her, Merril was drawn to SF by the narrative possibilities it afforded to socially conscious authors. Indeed, for Merril the task of imagining scientific and social "firsts" was more than a matter of literary pride; it was also a necessary first step toward actually enacting the kind of sweeping change that seemed to be at the very heart of the SF vision.

The continuities between postwar women's SF and its utopian and pulp predecessors are, of course, most apparent in Merril's stories. For example, her novella "Project Nursemaid" (1955) specifically explores how new sciences and technologies might transform conventional thinking about gender roles as they relate to childrearing. "Project Nursemaid" takes place on a future Earth where the U.S. military artificially gestates embryos on its moon base because "only those conditioned from infancy to low-grav conditions would ever be able to make the Starhop . . . or even live in any comfort on the moon" (15). To ensure that the moon children grow up feeling loved and secure,

12. "That Only a Mother" is one of the most extensively anthologized SF stories of all times, and one of the few postwar women's stories that feminist SF scholars have discussed in any depth. For an exemplary reading of this story, see chapter 3 of Jane Donawerth's *Frankenstein's Daughters.* For my own discussion of this story vis-à-vis the specific context of postwar women's political and literary activity, see chapter 2 of this book.

the military decides to hire hundreds of adventurous people as foster parents who will work together in small teams on rotating schedules so that no child is ever alone and no parent is ever faced with too long a stay in space. Thus Merril insists that new sciences and technologies—especially new reproductive technologies—demand new kinds of social and familial organization.

Merril's story follows the adventures of Colonel Tom Edgerly, a military doctor who has been tapped to run the Project Nursemaid foster parent recruitment drive. Initially the drive yields poor results. Although scores of people apply for the job, Edgerly's superiors insist that they can accept only those who are "healthy [women] of less than thirty-five years, with no dependents or close attachments . . . [but] with some nursing experience, and with a stated desire to 'give what I can for society'" (22). Not surprisingly, Edgerly finds himself rejecting ideal candidates for absurd reasons. One is labeled "unhealthy" because she has lost a hand in the same accident that killed her entire family; another is dismissed as having "questionable moral values" because she is a former madam; and a third candidate is put on hold for the simple reason that he is a man and "we need women in the nursery" (54). As the despairing Edgerly soon realizes, for all its talk of scientific and social advancement, the U.S. military remains hopelessly mired down by impossibly idealistic and woefully outdated ideas about who might make a good parent—or, more specifically, who might make a good mother.

Fortunately for Edgerly (and the moon children) Earth women themselves are quick to recognize the gap between military thinking about motherhood and the lived reality of modern women. For instance, the madam points out that her experience creating safe homes for young women in the hostile territory of the sex industry has more than adequately prepared her for raising children in the hostile terrain of space. Meanwhile, an elderly applicant argues that her experience traveling as a retiree makes her an ideal candidate for this new mode of parenting. Eventually, the situation comes to a head when two young women who have donated embryos to Project Nursemaid band together and demand that they be considered for foster parentage even though military regulations stipulate that donor parents and foster parents must never meet one another.

Faced not just with individual applicants who can be dismissed as aberrations from some hypothetical norm but also with a growing group of "grown women, with good reason[s] for wanting to do a particular job," Edgerly and his superiors finally reconsider their priorities (94). As a consequence, Project Nursemaid enters a new and highly successful phase where candidates of all ages, professions, and physical abilities are welcomed as potential parents—including the newly revitalized Edgerly himself. Much like her utopian and pulp fiction counterparts, Merril explores how new sciences and technologies might free women from the biological task of reproduction and therefore leads readers to think about motherhood as a socially constructed rather than biologically inevitable phenomenon. At the same time, Merril goes beyond her predecessors because she does not displace her desire for gender reform onto what Donawerth calls the "unrealistic hopes" for advanced technologies that will magically solve all social inequities. Instead, she dramatizes both the individual and collective psychological changes that must occur before such reform can truly begin.

Merril likewise extends women's pulp SF–writing traditions by using the transformation of a chauvinist male narrator to explore how patriarchal society as a whole might come to terms with the new social and sexual arrangements attending women's increased participation in the public sphere. To a certain extent, "Project Nursemaid" is one such story, although Edgerly is, from the beginning, a relatively enlightened character complete with his own parental (and perhaps even maternal) instincts. Merril more directly explores the difficulty of overcoming male chauvinism in "The Lady Was a Tramp" (1957), a story considered so racy at the time that she had to publish it under the pseudonym Rose Sharon.[13]

"The Lady Was a Tramp" follows the story of Terry Carnahan, a graduate of the United Nations Naval Academy who has been assigned to serve as the "IBMan" (what we would now call a computer engineer) on the merchant space ship *Lady Jane*. Although most graduates envy Terry's well-paying commission, the young naval officer is bitterly disappointed that he has not been tracked into the more glamorous job of Navy Space Scout. Terry's bitterness is further exacerbated by his first glimpse of the "potbellied, dumpy, unbeautiful" *Lady Jane* and its motley crew, which includes a pirate captain, a drunken pilot, a mechanical engineer who never bathes, and a nudist biotechnician (198). A serious young man "stuffed to the gills with eight full years of Academy training, precision, and knowledge," Terry seems to be the avatar of mid-twentieth-century manhood—not to mention the literal

---

13. Merril was enmeshed in a bitter custody battle with her former husband Fred Pohl and concerned that authoring a "dirty" story would be held against her in court (Merril and Pohl-Weary 159).

embodiment of the fresh-faced SF boy hero (199). However, as Merril goes on to contrast Terry's uptight behavior with that of the merchant tramp's relaxed crew, it soon becomes clear that he is at best an adolescent amongst adults and at worst a priggish relic of the past with no real place in the future.

Eventually, the combined kindness and obvious expertise of the *Lady Jane's* crew lead Terry to abandon his prejudices and embrace the tramp ship's laissez-faire social organization. When he learns that Navy protocol gives him the right to officially condemn "the psychological conditions onboard a ship," the IBMan realizes with some surprise that he has come to believe "that grease and nudity were perhaps as fitting uniforms in their ways for engine maintenance and bio work as knife-edge trouser creases were for precision computing" (212). Terry's allegiance to the *Lady Jane* is further cemented when the crew gives him full control of the ship's computer systems upon his first takeoff. After a few minutes of overwhelming pride the IBMan undergoes a final psychological transformation: "he forgot to be proud, and he forgot to be Terry Carnahan. . . . [he] gave back [to the ship] what she needed: the readings and scannings and comps and corrections that went to the driver's seat, to the pilot's board, to [the mechanical engineer] with the strength of ten and a tramp in his heart" (215). In the end, Terry gladly abandons his ascetic dreams of Scout glory in favor of the messy but even more thrilling reality of the tramp ship, where individual quirks (including his own primness) are tolerated and even fostered to encourage individual excellence.

At the same time he struggles to come to terms with the alternate social order of the *Lady Jane,* Terry finds himself struggling even harder to deal with its alternate sexual order. When Terry first meets Medical Officer Anita Filmord (who is, at the time, engaged in some heavy group petting with the nudist biotechnician, Chandra Lal, and the drunk pilot, Manuel Ramon Decardez), he is shocked to realize that "the hippy blonde was nobody's daughter or friend, but a member of the crew and an officer in the Naval Reserve" (201). He is even more alarmed to learn that Anita uses her extensive training in medicine, psychology, and sexual therapy to mold the *Lady Jane's* crew into the kind of well-adjusted family essential to long-term space travel. Unable to deal with what he perceives as a bizarre mingling of public and private behavior, the young IBMan denies Anita's professional status and tries to cast her into one of two familiar gender roles. As he complains to another crewmember, "if I go to a whore, I don't want her around me all day. And if I have a girl, I damn sure don't want every guy she sees to get into . . . you know what I mean!" (211). Bound as he is by rigid sexual mores that are as hopelessly outdated as his notions of social order, Terry cannot grasp the reality of life and love on the new frontier of deep space.

More specifically, Terry must come to terms with the fact that while Anita uses sex in her work, she is neither a whore nor somebody's girl, but a highly skilled officer who does her job extremely well. As the ship's medic, Anita is responsible for evaluating Terry's performance during the first stage of the ship's launch. Emotionally and physically drained by five hours of complete absorption in the ship's intricate computer system, Terry loses control of himself and unleashes all his pent-up emotions at Anita, calling her a whore and shouting at her to "get away, bitch!" (215). Rather than immediately relieving him of duty as he expects, Anita leaves for a few minutes, allows the young man to cool down, and comes back and sits with him for six more hours while he completes a second shift.

Only at that point does Terry accept what the other crewmembers have been trying to tell him all along: that his hostility toward Anita derives from his own insecurities about what it means to be a man. Once he proves himself through the successful completion of his first launch—and recognizes that he could not have done it without Anita's help—the IBMan takes his first tentative step toward embracing the adult sexuality of shipboard life: "he laughed and stepped forward . . . and the tramp was his" (216). This closing line drives home the parallels between the *Lady Jane* and Anita: although both initially appear to be the battered relics of a bygone order, they are ultimately revealed to be heralds of the new, more egalitarian social and sexual relations that might come into being in one particular high-tech future. Merril again extends the kind of political speculation initiated by her pulp-era counterparts, insisting that the conversion of the chauvinist male narrator is crucial not just to true gender equality but to true sexual liberation as well.

Merril's greatest contributions to modern women's speculative fiction may well have been her innovative experiments with stories told in women's voices from feminine and feminist perspectives.[14]

---

14. Scholars including Pamela Sargent, Sarah Lefanu, and Jane Donawerth all agree that Merril's narrative experiments are in fact precursors to the more overtly feminist experiments of later SF authors including Joanna Russ and James Tiptree Jr. However, these scholars focus exclusively on one story: the often-anthologized "That Only a Mother." Here, I demonstrate how Merril continued these experiments throughout her literary career.

Donawerth notes that women who wrote utopias often used female narrators to articulate the progressive principles of their all-female societies, but that when the SF community began to establish its own generic conventions in the 1920s and early 1930s, narrative voice was granted primarily to male scientists and explorers. At best, women's stories were related by sympathetic male narrators ("Science Fiction" 145–46). In the work of postwar SF authors such as Merril, female characters remain resolutely heterosexual and romantically involved with their male counterparts. However, this does not prevent them from having it all: families, careers, and, of course, stories of their own, told in voices of their own.

So how were writers including Merril able to introduce these protofeminist innovations into the SF community at a historical moment usually considered to be a low point in feminist history? Two distinct phenomena paved the way for this possibility. The first has to do with changes in the narrative conventions of SF. Scholars generally agree that after World War II the romanticism of early SF evolved into a more critical assessment of the relations of science, technology, and society. Merril herself attributes this change to two particularly influential editors: John Campbell of *Astounding Science Fiction* and Anthony Boucher of *Fantasy and Science Fiction.* As a "sociological science fiction" editor, Campbell extended the literary project of Hugo Gernsback before him, encouraging authors not just to explore how new sciences and technologies might develop, but also "to explore the effects of the new technological world on *people*" ("What Do You Mean" 67).

Meanwhile, Boucher, who was already an established professional in the relatively respectable literary genre of mystery and detection, brought to SF "a revolutionary concept: the idea that science-fantasy . . . *could be well-written.*" More specifically, Boucher encouraged authors to think about how they represented science and society in relation to the larger "history and traditions" of literature as a whole ("What Do You Mean" 78, 80). In contrast to those first-generation editors who defined SF as a distinct mode of popular literature for scientists and engineers, second- and third-generation editors such as Campbell and Boucher explored the relations between SF and other fields of creative endeavor. Consequently, they paved the way for authors to bring other histories and traditions—including women's histories and traditions—into SF itself.

The second change that paved the way for woman-centered SF was in the general political orientation of American women themselves.

Feminist scholars Leila J. Rupp and Verta Taylor note that the mid-century American press typically dismissed feminism as an old-fashioned political movement whose time had come and gone with the passage of the Nineteenth Amendment in 1920. Nonetheless, women who came of age in the postwar era grew up immersed in the legacy of feminism, both implicitly as they reaped its benefits and explicitly as they learned about it from college professors and family members who had been involved in the suffrage movement (45, 70–71, 108–11). In essence, mid-century women who simply thought of themselves as Americans and who expected the same rights and privileges as American men were living the dream that first-wave feminists had worked so hard to secure for themselves and their daughters.

Certainly the new narrative conventions of postwar SF and the legacy of first-wave feminism both played central roles in Merril's career as an SF author. As she recalls, "I grew up in the radical 1930s. My mother had been a suffragette. It never occurred to me that the Bad Old Days of Double Standard could have anything to do with me. . . . The first intimation I had, actually, was when the editors of the mystery, western, and sports pulp magazine where I did my apprentice writing demanded masculine pen names [and characters]. But after all these were pulps, and oriented to a masculine readership. It was only irritating; and as soon as I turned to science fiction, the problem disappeared" (Merril and Pohl-Weary 156).

For Merril, a lifelong feminist and progressive political activist in her own right, SF seems to have been an ideal genre precisely because by World War II it had abandoned its chauvinist pulp magazine roots. And although some editors and fans protested vigorously against those "sensitive [stories] of the future from a woman's point of view," at least SF provided women writers with a public forum in which to tell those stories in the first place. If anything, the very vigor of such protest suggests that when women wrote SF from feminine and feminist perspectives, they did so in ways that profoundly challenged the SF status quo.

This is certainly true of Merril's novella "Daughters of Earth" (1952), which follows six generations of women as they participate in the first waves of intergalactic exploration and colonization. Merril's story begins by revising three key patriarchal origin myths:

Martha begat Joan, and Joan begat Ariadne. Ariadne lived and died at home on Pluto, but her daughter, Emma, took the long trip out to the distant planet of an alien sun.

Emma begat Leah, and Leah begat Carla, who was the first to make
her bridal voyage through sub-space, a long journey faster than the
speed of light itself. . . .

The story could have started anywhere. It began with unspoken
prayer, before there were words, when an unnamed man and woman
looked upward to a distant light, and wondered. . . . Then in another
age of madness, a scant two centuries ago, it began with . . . the com-
pulsive evangelism of Ley and Gernsback and Clarke. It is beginning
again now, here on Uller. But in this narrative, it starts with Martha.
(97)

First and most strikingly, Merril opens her novella with a list of
mothers and daughters that parallels the patriarchal genealogies of
the Torah and the Old Testament. The founding of earthly civilization
may have been a masculine affair, she suggests, but the colonization
of space will be a decidedly feminine one.

Merril goes on to imagine an alternate history of humanity's fascination with space: rather than simply rehearsing the story of famous
male astronomers and astrologers, she claims that this fascination
begins with the simple, everyday speculation of "an unnamed man
and woman." And so she makes women central to space exploration
not just in the future but in the distant past as well. Finally, Merril
revises SF history. After beginning her recitation of this history with
a conventional list of male luminaries, Merril concludes with two
female narrators: Martha and Emma (the narrator of this opening passage). By making a space for women writers in the future, Merril also
implicitly reminds readers that women such as herself are already
part of the speculative writing tradition and that they, too, should be
remembered for their efforts to inspire the human imagination.

After staking claims for women in the past, present, and future of
space exploration, Merril invokes the two primary representations of
women that Donawerth attributes to early SF: the exceptional female
scientist explorer who is essentially one of the boys and the housewife heroine who might think scientifically within the home but who
depends on her husband to act and lead in the public sphere ("Science
Fiction" 142, 147).[15] In "Daughters of Earth," each generation of

15. Donawerth and Robin Roberts also identify a third female archetype in pulp-era
SF: the beautiful but sometimes treacherous alien other. Although she does not address
this stereotype in "Daughters of Earth," Merril (like many other women SF writers
before her) tends to treat her aliens quite sympathetically. For further scholarly discussion of early SF treatments of the alien other, see Donawerth's *Frankenstein's Daughters*

women swings back and forth between these two extremes: Martha, Ariadne, and Leah all delight in the stability of settled civilization, while Joan, Emma, and Carla are bound together by a wanderlust that leads them to the edge of the solar system and beyond.

While her pulp-era counterparts generally relegated the stories of housewives and women scientists to male narrators, however, Merril allows both of her character types to speak for themselves. "Daughters of Earth" takes the form of a family history compiled and related primarily by Emma for Carla, as the latter prepares to lead humanity's first subspace voyage. Although Merril grants Emma a certain narrative authority, she balances her protagonist's account of events with journal excerpts, newspaper clippings, and oral stories from Martha, Joan, Ariadne, and Leah. Like other feminist authors ranging from Virginia Woolf in the 1920s and 1930s to Joanna Russ in the 1970s and 1980s, Merril refuses to subsume the experiences of women into a single voice but rather insists on the multiplicity of women's subjective experiences.

In doing so, Merril profoundly complicates pulp-era images of women. In many respects, her female scientist explorers are much like their masculine counterparts, brilliant individuals who long for "new problems to conquer, new knowledge to gain, new skills to acquire" (111). But these are not the only reasons that Merril's characters long for the stars. Joan leaves Earth for Pluto because "in the normal course of things, [she] would have taken her degree . . . and gone to work as a biophysicist until she found a husband. The prospect appalled her" (103). By way of contrast, the Pluto mission enables Joan to have it all—a husband *and* a lifelong career. Later, Emma volunteers for the first mission from Pluto to Uller in part to fulfill her lifelong dream of emulating Joan and in part to escape the benevolent tyranny of her stepfather, Joe Prell, who loves Emma but believes that she is "too direct, too determined, too intellectual, too *strong*" to be a real woman—by which he means a docile wife and mother (112). Therefore, Merril insists that her characters' dreams of space travel are at least partly fueled by their desire to escape the very real gender discrimination they face on their home planets.

In "Daughters of Earth" gendered experiences also impact women's careers as scientist explorers in more productive ways. When her husband dies in a dome collapse on Pluto, Joan channels her grief

---

and Roberts's *A New Species: Gender and Science in Science Fiction*. For Merril stories that depict the female alien other in sympathetic ways, see especially "Homecalling" (1956) and "Exile From Space" (1956).

into the creation of a viable terraforming process that ensures that no other family will lose loved ones to closed city construction accidents (108). Similarly, when an Uller native kills Emma's husband, Emma rejects the retaliatory attitude of her fellow colonists and devotes herself to proving that the Ullerns are sentient beings that simply misinterpreted her husband's actions. After several decades Emma's work pays off, and when her granddaughter Carla leaves for the subspace voyage to Nifleheim, she does so "in profitable comradeship with the Ullerns" (159). The conclusions Merril draws throughout this novella about the relations of science and gender anticipate those proposed by feminist science studies scholars nearly four decades later: that subjective personal experiences, including commitments to other people and what Evelyn Fox Keller calls a "feeling for the organism" under investigation, are key aspects of scientific labor.[16]

Perhaps Merril's most striking innovation, however, is to grant voice to those housewife heroines who stay planetbound while their daughters venture off to the stars. This demonstrates how profoundly women are affected by scientific and technological development even when they do not directly participate in it. During the preflight ceremonies for the Pluto expedition Martha tries to forget her fear for Joan and instead "look the way the commentator said all these mothers here today were feeling" (99). And yet Martha quickly realizes that all the other mothers feel just as she does: "all around her, she saw with gratitude and dismay, were the faint strained lines at lips and eyes, the same tense fingers grasping for a hand, or just for air" (99). Thus Merril distinguishes between the rhetoric of patriotic motherhood and the complex emotions actually experienced by women whose children might be sacrificed in the name of patriotism. Moreover, by literally surrounding Martha with hundreds of likeminded women, Merril underscores the point that her protagonist is not just a single hysterical woman but representative of a larger group whose hopes and fears are also part of the story of scientific progress.

Elsewhere Merril uses her housewife heroines to explore how scientific progress might even work against women's social liberation. Although Joan becomes Pluto's leading scientific expert after her husband's death, Ariadne refuses to follow in her mother's footsteps and

16. For further discussion of the relations of science and gender, see especially Evelyn Fox Keller's *A Feeling for the Organism: The Life and Work of Barbara McClintock;* Hilary Rose's *Love, Power, and Knowledge: Toward a Feminist Transformation of the Sciences;* and the various essays collected in Evelyn Fox Keller and Helen E. Longino's *Feminism and Science.*

instead takes refuge in the role of consort to a succession of wealthy men. She does so, however, not out of any simple desire for marriage and motherhood but so she can obliterate the memory of a pioneer childhood in which "she was effectively mother and housekeeper and wielder of authority" over her younger siblings (108). Furthermore, when her first marriage breaks up, it is precisely because "colonial pressures pushed [her] into pregnancy" (109). New sciences and technologies might allow women like Joan to have it all, but unless they are used to relieve others like Ariadne of their domestic and reproductive duties, they can hardly be considered wholly liberating.

Although Martha, Ariadne, and Leah do not always benefit from the scientific and social arrangements of their respective worlds, they are not simply victims of these arrangements either. Rather, they are complex human beings who fully participate in their respective cultures. Nowhere is this more evident than in Leah's story. Like Ariadne before her, Leah resents pioneer life, especially as her mother's research into Ullern psychology leads them to exchange the relative comforts of the colonists' primary city for the more primitive conditions of a scientific outpost. At the same time, Leah feels "something amounting almost to compassion for her mother," especially as she begins to suspect that her mother's enthusiasm for the Ullern natives stems at least in part from the very real difficultly she has finding suitable romantic partners in either of the two small human colonies (160). Not surprisingly, the teenaged Leah rebels against the isolation and austerity of her early life by carefully cultivating a wide network of friends both in the primary Ullern colony and back on Earth as well.

When Emma and her colleagues finally establish communication with the Ullern natives, Leah surprises everyone and becomes her mother's "best ambassador" to the other colonists and to Earth itself, combining her knowledge of her mother's work with her own well-developed social skills—including "the tactful manipulation of other people"—to facilitate the first stage of human-Ullern space exploration (162, 163). Leah rises to the occasion not out of love for her mother or the Ullerns, but because, quite simply, she wants to become a colony leader in her own right and to attract a mate of her own by taking "a really intelligent part in discussions with the men back home" (162). Leah may not be an avatar of enlightened feminism, but she is not just a decorative ornament or submissive helpmeet, either. Instead, by concluding with Leah's tale, Merril insists that her readers take traditionally feminine characters seriously as subjects in their own right. After all, like their scientist-explorer counterparts, they are "all different, [and] all daughters of Earth" (97).

As one of the most prolific female authors in the postwar SF community, Judith Merril's name was (and for many scholars, still is) synonymous with the new mode of women's SF storytelling that emerged at this time. As close analysis of her fiction reveals, women's SF was not just an aberration in the genre's history but the logical extension of a speculative tradition initiated by those women who wrote utopias in the nineteenth century and pulp SF in the early twentieth century. Like her literary predecessors, Merril imagines that new domestic and reproductive technologies might ease women's lives and positively transform gender relations in the future. She also carries on the tradition of using chauvinist male narrators who convert to more progressive mindsets to demonstrate how scientifically advanced societies might evolve more enlightened social and sexual relations.

At the same time, Merril extends the literary tradition of her utopian and pulp-era predecessors by privileging female narration and point of view in many of her stories. Indeed, she is one of the first writers to put recognizably human women at the center of her stories. This enables her to more fully develop two key character types common to pulp-era SF: the female scientist explorer and the housewife heroine. For Merril, the former was not just one of the boys but a woman whose gendered experiences conditioned her relationship to science and technology. She also refuses simple depictions of the latter as a docile helpmeet or adjunct to her scientist explorer husband, instead insisting on the housewife heroine's complex subjectivity. Even more significantly, Merril uses the figure of the housewife heroine to interrogate the patriarchal biases often inherent in advanced scientific and technological practices themselves. And as we shall see in the next section, she was by no means alone in using this seemingly conservative figure for radical ends.

Alice Eleanor Jones and the Offbeat Romance

Perhaps the most striking characteristic of mid-century women's SF is not just that it gives voice to female characters but that it specifically gives voice to those associated with the home and other traditional areas of feminine influence: wives, mothers, children, and, as we shall see later, governesses and teachers. But why these figures? What exactly do they have to do with science and technology? As I suggested in my discussion of Merril's "Daughters of Earth," housewives and other domestic figures do not always simply endorse conservative ideas about sex and gender but can instead expose the contradictions buried in romantic ideas about science and technology. In this section, I elaborate on this claim by showing how other women writers used that most representative domestic character, the housewife heroine, to critically and creatively engage those values trumpeted by the keepers of cold war culture.

As conservative equations between women's SF and "heart-throb-and-diaper" fiction suggest, housewife heroines were most commonly associated with women's magazine fiction. And it is true that many of the authors who helped shape modern women's SF wrote for slick, widely circulated periodicals including *McCall's, Good Housekeeping,* and *Ladies' Home Journal* as well.[17] For these authors, women's magazine fiction was a potentially rich literary form that they could use to write something other than "happily ever after" romance stories that ended at the alter on a heroine's wedding day. Tropes including "marriage," "motherhood," and even "the home" served as lenses through which they explored otherwise taboo sex and gender issues. Not surprisingly, such authors brought this sensibility to SF, where the generic emphasis on world building enabled them to explore how dominant cultural understandings of sex and gender were shaped by new scientific and social arrangements.

Most scholarly discussions of mid-century women's magazine fiction are heavily indebted to Betty Friedan's groundbreaking work on the subject. As Friedan contends in *The Feminine Mystique* (1963), after first-wave feminists secured universal suffrage in 1921, a new heroine emerged on the pages of women's magazines. This New Woman actively pursued an independent identity for herself through education, adventure, and paid work. She also pursued egalitarian sex and gender relations with the New Man who admired and courted her because "individuality was something to be admired . . . men were drawn to [the New Woman] as much for [her] spirit and character as for [her] looks" (38). After World War II, however, the New Woman gave way to the Housewife Heroine, who was biologically designed for "sexual passivity, male domination, and nurturing maternal love"

17. Authors who published in both women's magazines and SF periodicals include Shirley Jackson, Mildred Clingerman, and Alice Eleanor Jones. I discuss Jones and Jackson in this chapter and Clingerman in chapter 2.

(43). In essence, Friedan concludes, the housewife heroine was part and parcel of the conservative—even repressive—gender ideologies characteristic of mid-century America.

Nonetheless, a few feminist scholars have proposed more complex histories of mid-century women's magazine fiction. In her study of women's magazines from the early 1930s to the late 1950s, Joanne Meyerowitz finds that editors and writers "asserted both a long-held domestic ideal and a long-held ethos of achievement" for women ("Beyond the Feminine Mystique" 249). More specifically, while women's magazines always celebrated marriage and motherhood, they recognized that women had lives beyond the home as well.[18] Literary scholars Nancy Walker and Zita Zatkin-Dresner have argued that "Housewife Writers" including Jean Kerr, Jean MacDonald, and Shirley Jackson used humorous, semifictionalized accounts of their own domestic lives as "a strategy for coping" with conservative gender ideals (Walker 102). By poking fun at the feminine mystique, housewife writers participated in a distinctly American tradition of humor whereby authors put seemingly lofty ideals and values in a homely context to deflate them (Zatkin-Dresner 32). In doing so, these writers—who were immensely popular and whose magazine stories inspired books, Broadway plays, and television shows—fostered a sense of community among those readers who sometimes felt trapped in their homes and overwhelmed by the demands of modern housewifery. Taken together, such studies indicate that the ideological encoding of the feminine mystique in women's magazines was not as complete as Friedan suggests. Instead, celebrations of women's achievements outside the home and subtle protest against the trivialization of their experience within it anticipate many of the issues that would be more directly voiced by women during the revival of feminism in the 1960s.

Although there have been no studies of romantic housewife heroine fiction to date, more general examinations of romance fiction can help us better understand how it, too, both invoked and interrogated the feminine mystique.[19] Anne Cranny-Frances posits that although

18. Janice Hume makes a similar point about the range of female types in postwar women's magazine fiction in her essay "Changing Characteristics of Heroic Women in Midcentury Mainstream Media."

19. For two groundbreaking studies of how romance narratives fulfill various psychosocial needs for women readers, see Janice A. Radway, *Reading the Romance: Women, Patriarchy, and Popular Literature,* and Tania Modleski, *Loving with a Vengeance: Mass-Produced Fantasies for Women.* For discussion of how romance authors themselves understand the relations of romance writing and feminism, see Jayne Ann Krentz, ed.,

romance narratives always run the risk of devolving into "bourgeois fairy tales" where heterosexual love erases social and political conflict, thoughtful women writers have used them to explore feminist concerns including "the nature of female/male relations in a patriarchal society and the constitution of the gendered subject" (9, 178). If authors want to write this latter kind of romance, they must meet conventional generic narrative expectations while providing readers with a "new and stimulating perspective" (2–3). Thus they must exert mastery over the codes of the romance narrative without being seduced by those codes themselves.

As we shall see in the following case study of Alice Eleanor Jones, authors of housewife heroine romances were often interested in providing readers with precisely this kind of new and stimulating perspective. In 1955, the first year of her literary career, Jones published five SF stories and two slick romance narratives, leading SF editor Anthony Boucher to predict that she would have a long career in both fields (125). Boucher was half right: although Jones never published any other SF after her initial debut, she continued to write for women's magazines including *Redbook, The Ladies' Home Journal,* and *Seventeen* on a regular basis for another decade. Her success in the women's magazine industry led to work as a columnist for the trade magazine *The Writer* as well.

Significantly, a number of Jones's essays for *The Writer* directly explore how commercial authors might write contemplative women's fiction. Unlike Judith Merril, Jones never directly connected her writing to feminism or to any other political philosophy. Nonetheless, her columns suggest that she was well aware of the relations between specific modes of storytelling and dominant cultural beliefs about sex and gender. In "Ones That Got Away" Jones tells readers that they can have successful careers "writing against the odds" and addressing "subjects considered taboo" by magazine editors if they carefully consider the codes informing different kinds of popular fiction (17). She particularly encourages young authors to pay close attention to editorial comments because "slick editors know their jobs or they couldn't keep them" (46). For Jones, editors are ideal readers because they understand both generic narrative conventions and the social and market forces informing them. As authors learn about these conventions and forces from editors, they learn how to manipulate them as well.

Dangerous Men and Adventurous Women: Romance Writers on the Appeal of the Romance.

Jones specifically explains how authors might bend generic conventions to explore taboo sex and gender subjects in "How to Sell an Offbeat Story." She begins by noting that there are two types of commercial romance stories. Women's magazine editors tend to prefer "sweet, fluffy, boy-girl stories" that end at the altar (18). But many slick writers such as Jones herself are drawn to a more complex type of romance story: "Suppose you simply aren't interested in the events that end with a wedding, but rather in what comes afterward: the problems of adjustment; the children; the troubles, the quarrels, and the crises; the accidents, the illnesses, even the deaths. Suppose your mind leans more to the dark than to the bright. What if your stories are offbeat, because *you* are offbeat?" (18). Jones makes an important point often missed by scholars who treat women's magazine fiction as an undifferentiated mass of fairy tales about the feminine mystique.[20] While stories written in the "sweet, fluffy, boy-girl" vein tend to reiterate stereotypical sex and gender relations, offbeat tales are produced by authors who quite literally write, as Rachel Blau DuPlessis puts it, "beyond the ending" of the traditional romance and the patriarchal ideology that it entails.

Because they write in relatively uncharted narrative spaces, offbeat authors can explore how gendered identities that seem to be fixed by archetypical events (a first kiss, a wedding, the birth of a child) might actually change over time. This literary activity closely resembles the feminist project of analyzing how dominant beliefs about sex and gender change in relation to specific historical and material forces. As such, authors like Jones who chose to write about "the dark" rather than "the bright" aspects of mid-century womanhood took the first important step toward identifying those social and sexual inequities that fueled the women's movement of the following decades.[21]

Understanding the narrative conventions of romance stories also enabled mid-century authors to better anticipate how they might successfully address taboo subjects without alienating readers. For Jones,

20. Scholarly assumptions about the conservative nature of romance fiction—and by extension all mass culture—derive from two primary sources: Marxist critics of the 1940s and 1950s (most notably, Max Horkheimer, T. W. Adorno, and Herbert Marcuse) and feminist critics of the 1970s and early 1980s (such as Ann Douglas and Germaine Greer). For further discussion of this critical legacy on contemporary scholarship, see Modleski, *Loving with a Vengeance*.

21. Contemporary authors continue this tradition of offbeat storytelling through the creation of "dark romances," where love stories frame serious explorations of women's physical, psychological, and social issues. For further discussion, see Mary Jo Putney's "Welcome to the Dark Side."

the litmus test is getting the offbeat story past the sharp-eyed editor:

> After you have been around a while you will learn to get around the
> taboos in many subtle ways without . . . compromising yourself. You
> do it by giving your story a switch. . . . Do you want to write about a
> forty-three year old heroine? Do it. Despite what editors profess to
> believe, women do not stop reading at the age of thirty-five. . . . To get
> past the editor, make her a young-looking forty-three, and give her
> charm, wit, and style. Maybe the editor is forty-three himself and has
> a wife the same age, who he still finds charming. . . . The first editor [I
> tried this on] didn't fall for my [forty-three year old character], but the
> second, third, or fourth one did. ("How to Sell an Offbeat Story" 20)

The switch that Jones describes here is, in essence, the careful manipulation of generic conventions. By giving editors and readers what
they think they want—conventional depictions of seemingly idealized
women—authors create spaces for themselves to explore issues that
seem to be outside the limits of light fiction.

This is certainly true of Jones's own magazine fiction. Every one
of her slick stories revolves around domestic affairs, and her protagonists are almost always married women or teenaged girls on the brink
of engagement. And yet the passage to marriage and motherhood is
never easy in Jones's fiction. Newlywed couples are too overcome
with sexual anxiety to consummate their marriage; men find that
they must be both father and mother to their children after their
wives die in childbirth; and women learn that both they and their
husbands secretly resent the demands of modern parenthood.[22]

Jones's very first slick publication, "Jenny Kissed Me," sets the pattern characterizing most of her romantic magazine fiction. Initially,
the story seems to be a simple coming-of-age tale in which a tall,
gawky, intellectual teenager named Jenny discovers the beautiful
woman inside her with the help of Paul, a wise and gentle family
friend. When the young woman concludes their first and only date by
asking if Paul believes that anyone will ever marry her, he immediately and sincerely replies, "I have no doubt of it. . . . If they don't, I'll
come back in five years and marry you myself" (17). Hence, Jenny's
initiation into the feminine mystique appears to be guaranteed, and
her fate as a future housewife heroine sealed.

And yet the interior details of Jones's story complicate this simple

22. See, respectively, Jones's short stories "The Honeymoon," "Morning Watch," and
"One Shattering Weekend."

narrative trajectory. The real drama here is not so much between Jenny and Paul as between Jenny and her mother, Margaret, an "exquisite" woman who embodies the ideals of postwar femininity. Margaret is a shallow but happy woman, comfortable in her middle-class respectability, who longs for Jenny to lead a life much like her own. Accordingly, she attempts to remake Jenny in her own image by giving her a party frock much like the one she herself wore as a teenager. On Jenny, however, the dress is nothing more that a nightmarish "froth of pink tulle with a voluminous overskirt that made her look enormous" (17). If Margaret embodies the psychosocial forces brought to bear on girls as they become women, the pink dress represents a specific kind of culturally sanctioned femininity that only underscores Jenny's discontent with the world around her.

Meanwhile, Paul turns out to be not so much the representative of a romantic love that smoothes out all ideological disruptions as a catalyst that brings them out into the open. A sophisticated political analyst from Washington, Paul responds to Jenny for what she is, buying her books of poetry and helping her transform the frilly party dress into a sophisticated evening gown that matches her personality. He also takes Margaret to task for browbeating Jenny, forcing her to admit that she has been "very stupid" in trying to change her daughter (17). Thus, Jenny gets to keep her intellectual independence and become a young woman on her own terms. As such, Jones's story echoes the tradition of New Woman magazine fiction as described by Betty Friedan, extending that prewar feminist tradition well into the antifeminist climate of postwar America.

Conversely, Jones's later housewife heroine stories look forward to the concerns of second-wave feminism. "The Real Me" (1962) follows several days in the life of Patricia Cameron, the wife of a university professor at a women's college and the mother of four small children. Like the heroines of other women's magazine stories, Patricia meets the chaos of family life with good grace and humor, deftly juggling dishes, a broken refrigerator, den mother duties, a cemetery plot salesman, a child with measles (which he of course passes on to his siblings and the rest of the neighborhood children), and an unexpected dinner party for her husband's boss, all in the course of a single day she insists "wasn't so bad" at all (140). Once again, Jones seems to have written a thoroughly conventional story, this time celebrating women's natural domestic talents.

However, Jones switches out her story by introducing an offbeat character who quite literally challenges the feminine mystique: the brashly feminist Miss Kent, whom Patricia and some other faculty wives meet during a public lecture night at their husbands' college. Miss Kent exhorts her listeners to remember the history of women's emancipation and to carry it over into their own lives, at least in their leisure moments: "when you marry, keep your own individuality, you own intellectual interests. Don't be 'just a housewife,' be a complete person" (137). Initially, Patricia rejects Miss Kent's words as those of an uninformed spinster; during what she calls "the measles day" she asks rather bitterly "Leisure, Miss Kent? What leisure?" (138). Even here, Jones's story seems to rigidly follow a pattern identified by Friedan in her own discussion of housewife heroine fiction, pitting the saintly, devoted wife and mother against the misguided single career woman (Friedan 46–47).

The twist in the end, interestingly enough, is one that Friedan herself would have recognized. After thinking about it for several days, Patricia admits that Miss Kent was "right in everything [she] said" and that "the measles day was not a typical day in my life—if it were, I'd be needing psychiatric help" (140). Accordingly, Jones's protagonist decides to reorganize her domestic duties and resume the writing career she gave up when she first married. In the end, she concludes, "I am a better wife and mother for being a private person, too. I am 'Mom' and 'Honey,' but I am also me. So thank you, Miss Kent" (140). Just one year later, Friedan similarly concluded *The Feminine Mystique* with a call for modern American women to "combine marriage and motherhood and even the kind of lifelong personal purpose that was once called 'career'" (342). In essence, both authors invite readers to engage in a new kind of romance, one centered upon love and respect for themselves and the other women around them.

A similar offbeat, critically engaged sensibility informs much of Jones's SF writing as well. Although she published only five SF stories at the beginning of her literary career in 1955, each demonstrates Jones's careful understanding of the genre and its narrative conventions. For example, her two stories written from masculine perspectives, "Life, Incorporated" and "The Happy Clown," are biting condemnations of postwar consumer culture along the lines of Frederik Pohl and C. M. Kornbluth's *The Space Merchants* (1952) and Fritz Leiber's *The Green Millennium* (1953). "The Happy Clown" is a particularly prescient example of what SF scholars David Pringle and Peter Nicholls call "the media landscape story" (792) because it explores how television advertising might literally shape the world of its viewers.

In her other stories, Jones invokes the tradition of women's speculative fiction writing. For instance, "Recruiting Officer" is a sex role-reversal story much like Leslie F. Stone's "The Conquest of Gola," where women are depicted as both intellectually and physically superior to men (Weinbaum 471).[23] In "Recruiting Officer," an alien from an all-female world is sent to Earth to "recruit" unwitting young men as sexual playthings for her people. After a long and successful career, Jones's protagonist encounters a series of mishaps that force her to withdraw from Earth without the one boy she wants for herself. Although she is saddened by this loss, she takes comfort in the prestige she has already earned in her own world—and in the arms of another, equally charming young man because, "as is the custom, they had saved one of the best for me" (101). Like her pulp magazine predecessors, Jones imagines alternate worlds where women might enjoy men without being particularly dependent on them in any significant way.

But Jones did more than simply extend older traditions of women's speculative fiction into the present day of mid-century America. She was also, as Anthony Boucher noted, an important contributor to the new tradition of women's SF (125). The two Jones stories that most clearly belong to this new mode of SF, "Miss Quatro" and "Created He Them," demonstrate two very different ways that women writers could import the thematic concerns and literary techniques of offbeat magazine fiction into science-fictional landscapes.

"Miss Quatro" is a conceptual breakthrough story in which characters (and readers) are suddenly presented with a new body of knowledge that transforms their perception of reality (James 91). Given Jones's affinity for slick magazine storytelling that relies on a twist in perspective, it is hardly surprising that she would gravitate toward its generic equivalent in SF as well. "Miss Quatro" tells the tale of a shy, selfless woman whom other characters describe as "the perfect housekeeper and perfect nursemaid" (58). When she is not scrubbing her employers' house or meticulously polishing their silver, Miss Quatro devotes herself to the neighborhood children, cheerfully entertaining them with endless hours of stories. More than mere spinster lady or hired help, Miss Quatro transcends her station to become a living avatar of the feminine mystique.

The twist occurs when her employers and their neighbors begin to wonder if the saintly Miss Quatro could really be of this Earth. The answer, of course, is no: she is actually the enslaved scout of an alien race who feed on human children. But Miss Quatro has come to love

---

23. For further discussion of women's celebratory sex role-reversal stories, see Roberts, *A New Species*.

humanity, and so she declares that "I will not go back!" and destroys herself to foil her masters' plans. Thus, Jones implicitly critiques postwar gender ideals, suggesting that the only women who can really embody the feminine mystique are enslaved aliens. As such, "Miss Quatro" articulates a point of view that must have been very familiar to those unhappy wives and mothers whom Friedan documented so extensively in *The Feminine Mystique.*

Significantly, Jones is careful to prevent readers from assuming that Miss Quatro's death is just another example of the good little woman who sacrifices herself for her children, depicting it instead as a gesture of solidarity with the human women around her. With a few cynical exceptions, the human women who know her treat Miss Quatro affectionately, showering her with compliments and gently admonishing her to take more time for herself; at one point her employer, Edith Horton, quite literally takes work out of Miss Quatro's hands and begs her to rest. In the end, Miss Quatro makes clear that her death is a gift to these women. With her last breath Miss Quatro tells the children who surround her to "go home. . . . [Your mothers] will be kind to you as they have been kind to me. I was not a slave here. A slave has no pride, and I am proud now" (63). More than mere protest against the deathly confines of the feminine mystique, "Miss Quatro" holds out the hope that women might overcome domestic isolation and become something more than obedient housekeepers and submissive nursemaids.

Finally, "Created He Them" illustrates how Jones applies the techniques of offbeat storytelling to SF to perform both gender and social critique. Once again, the story revolves around a housewife heroine who seems too good to be true. Living in a near future where the United States has just barely managed to survive a massive nuclear war, the "plain but proud" Ann Crothers seems to have single-handedly preserved the mid-century ideal of feminine domesticity and fecundity. In contrast to the majority of her neighbors, who have been rendered sterile by atomic radiation and are rendered further helpless by chronic food and medical shortages, Ann has married, created a fairly comfortable home for her family, and borne seven healthy children (an eighth is on the way at the beginning of the story). And so Jones's protagonist seems to be a testament to the endurance of the feminine mystique in even the most catastrophic circumstances.

Again, however, Jones gives her story a twist that invites readers to ponder the taboo subject of how personal relations are constituted by public forces. Here, the culprits are not faceless aliens but the men of Earth themselves. The United States survives World War III precisely because the government enforces strictly regulated marriages between those few individuals who can still "breed true" (36). Additionally, parents must contend with the dreadful knowledge that if their offspring survive past the age of three, they will be taken away to mysterious government centers where, "if any child were ever unhappy, or were taken ill, or died, nobody knew it" (34–35). Therefore, Jones suggests that nuclear war does more than merely produce genetic mutation. It mutates the natural order of marriage and motherhood as well.

Here Jones appears to depart from the message inherent in her other stories. Elsewhere, protagonists like Jenny, Patricia, and Miss Quatro chafe against their psychosocial conditioning into the feminine mystique. In "Created He Them," the tragedy seems to be that women like Ann are permitted only a gross parody of it. However, that argument is something of an oversimplification. Throughout all her stories Jones challenges the notion that women are solely destined for hearth and home, suggesting instead that those things should be part of a much larger and richer life for women. As such, "Created He Them" extends the argument Jones offers elsewhere: that women are confined to specific, socially constructed roles by forces beyond their control in the name of both nature and necessity. In this story the dramatic circumstances of World War III create a situation where women are harnessed as breeding machines but denied even the dubious comfort of believing that they therefore fulfill their natural roles as homemakers and caretakers.

Moreover, by showing how mid-century America's most dearly held beliefs about sex and gender might be twisted almost beyond recognition by nuclear war, Jones creates a protofeminist critique of masculinist science and technology.[24] In this postapocalyptic world nuclear war does little or nothing to preserve the nuclear family. Rather, it pits parent against child and wife against husband in depressing and potentially disastrous ways. Consider Henry Crothers's behavior toward his family. Upon learning that Ann is pregnant with their eighth child, Henry moans, "Oh God, now you'll be sick all the time, and there's no living with you when you're sick" (35). However, he perks up when he remembers that another child equals "another

---

24. As I shall discuss extensively in chapter 3, the nuclear holocaust narrative as domestic tragedy became one of the primary ways mid-century women writers voiced dissent from what they saw as the masculinist and militaristic tendencies of cold war America.

bonus" from the government—one that he immediately decides he will invest in the stock market rather than in the renovations that the children's nursery so desperately needs (35). Because Jones has already established that this is a world where parents have very little control over their children's lives, Henry's attitude is reprehensible but understandable. The logic of a war-oriented culture reproduces itself at every level of society: just as the government treats its adult citizens as objects of genetic manipulation, individual citizens like Henry Crothers treat their own children as objects of economic exchange.

And Jones insists that even the most devoted women are subject to these terrible new forces as well. Ann loves her children, but that does not stop her from using them as barter. Noting in despair that "things [are] so hard now, and Henry [is] difficult about what he likes to eat," Jones's housewife heroine spends her day on the street with her childless neighbors, trading quality time with her children for black market goods including eggs, cigarettes, and sleeping pills (32). Although Ann claims to detest these "transactions," she does nothing to stop them and returns home each day only after her shopping bag is full (32). Much like fatherhood, motherhood in this story is not just natural instinct. It is also, and even more specifically, a collection of behaviors produced by the bad social arrangements of an embattled world.

Jones makes what is perhaps her strongest case against the cultural logic of the nuclear age in the final scenes of her offbeat story, where she suggests that total war between nations will inevitably lead to total war between the sexes. From the beginning of "Created He Them" it is clear that Ann is less than sanguine about her husband; she freely admits, "I hate him. I wish he would die" (31). At the end of the story Ann almost makes good on this wish when she responds to Henry's bullying behavior with the threat that "I'll hit you back, I'm bigger than you, I'll kill you!" (36) Jones's protagonist seems ready to shed the role of the housewife heroine once and for all as she refuses to submit to either her husband or the entire social order that demands her submissiveness.

Although Ann's defiance stops Henry in his tracks—and leaves the reader hoping that somehow individual will can triumph over social convention and that Ann really will follow through with her threat—it is not to be. Perversely excited by his wife's words, Henry begins to laugh—and promptly orders Ann to have sex with him. Deflated by her failure to change anything, Ann tells Henry she is simply too tired. When that fails, she glumly follows Henry up the stairs, comforting herself with the hope that she can mitigate the horror of her husband's embrace with the sleeping pills bartered earlier that day over the bodies of her unwitting children (37). In the end, Jones suggests that although some divine being may have originally "created he them" to go forth and multiply in joy and sorrow alike, in the brave new world of the atomic age the best a woman can hope for is to go forth and multiply in a drug-induced haze.

As the case of Alice Eleanor Jones suggests, stories about housewife heroines and other domestic figures were often anything but mundane reiterations of conservative mid-century gender ideologies. Instead, when authors put such characters in "offbeat" situations, they held the power to critically engage a range of emergent scientific and social relations, especially as those relations impacted women and their families. Much like Judith Merril, Jones produced fiction that bridged the concerns of feminists at the beginning and end of the twentieth century. While mainstream stories such as "Jenny Kissed Me" hold forth hope that the liberated New Woman of first-wave feminism might somehow survive the family "togetherness" of the postwar era, SF tales such as "Created He Them" explore the cost of such togetherness in brutal detail.

By placing domestic figures in fantastic science-fictional landscapes, authors including Merril and Jones created, as Cranny-Frances puts it, "a site for the allegorical description of social injustices displaced in time and/or place from the reader's own society, but still clearly recognizable as a critique of that society" (9). But this was not the only way that mid-century women writers used domesticity in their fiction. As Shirley Jackson's writing reveals, the seemingly mundane tropes of family and home could serve as powerful tools through which to explore the limits of rational knowledge and the social construction of reality. As such, postwar women's SF anticipated both feminist *and* postmodern literary practices.

Shirley Jackson and Domestic Fabulation

As Robert Scholes argues in his groundbreaking literary study, *The Fabulators,* interest in the social construction of reality permeates the writing of many early postmodern authors including Lawrence Durrell and Iris Murdoch in England and John Barth, Thomas Pynchon, and Kurt Vonnegut in the United States. Taken together, the antirealist stories produced by these authors comprise a coherent body of "fabulist fiction" that "tends away from the representation of reality but returns to actual human life by way of ethically controlled fantasy" (11). More specifically, fabulators invoke the conventions of genre fiction to orient readers to a certain representation of reality and then gradually direct them to a "more abstract and philosophical level" through the adventures of characters that move effortlessly (if sometimes unwillingly) between different worlds ruled by different systems of meaning (111). In doing so, fabulist authors illuminate the narrative forces that inform our shared understandings of reality.

In *Structural Fabulation* Scholes directly links postmodern fabulation to SF, proposing that fabulation "offers us a world clearly and radically discontinuous from the one we know, yet returns to confront that known world in a cognitive way" (29). This definition, Scholes notes, parallels Darko Suvin's oft-cited description of SF as storytelling set in an alternative historical framework that operates upon the reader through "the technique of defamiliarization or estrangement" (46). As practitioners of "cognitive arts" produced by humanist thinking, both fabulist and SF authors turn their critical gazes on intellectual order, especially as it is expressed through the "attitudes and values that shaped science itself" (31, 30). The stories produced by this critical engagement can either show how scientific modes of thinking expand our understanding of what constitutes the world around us, or they can demonstrate how such thinking might limit us by its insistence on the primacy of the rational and the material.

Although Scholes focuses primarily on men such as Walter Miller, Theodore Sturgeon, and Frank Herbert in his discussion of "borderline or extreme" authors who blur the boundary between postmodern fabulation and SF, women also produced this kind of literature throughout the postwar era.[25] Nowhere is this more apparent than in the work of Shirley Jackson. Darryl Hattenhauer notes that much of Jackson's fiction is fabulist in both form and content, as it revolves around seamless transitions between reality and fantasy and the different epistemologies that attach to different orders of being. In essence, her stories are modern morality tales where "the protagonist may not perceive or benefit from an epiphany, but sometimes

---

25. Scholes devotes a great deal of attention to one woman who blurs the boundaries between mainstream fabulation and SF in her writing: Ursula K. Le Guin. However, in doing so he implicitly reinforces the conventional belief that most women did not engage in politically or philosophically progressive writing until the revival of feminism in the 1960s.

the reader can" (6). Much like her contemporaries John Barth and Kurt Vonnegut, Jackson is an early postmodernist who uses generic themes and narrative techniques drawn from different aspects of modern literary history to interrogate the philosophical, moral, and intellectual arrangements of present-day America.

Jackson said as much herself soon after the publication of her first novel, *The Road Through the Wall* (1948):

> I have had for many years a consuming interest in magic and the supernatural. . . . I think this is because I find them a convenient shorthand statement of the possibilities of human adjustment to what seems at best to be an inhuman world. . . . [I am also interested in] the preservation of and insistence on a pattern superimposed precariously on the chaos of human development.
>
> I think it is the combination of these two that forms the background of everything I write—the sense which I feel, of a human and not very rational order struggling inadequately to keep in check forces of great destruction, which may be the devil and may be intellectual enlightenment. (qtd. in Oppenheimer 125)

In this passage Jackson identifies both the popular genres with which her fiction would come to be most closely associated—gothic and weird fiction—as well as their roles within her larger body of work. Rather than simply celebrating the irrational, Jackson deploys elements of the fantastic to explore one of the most peculiar (and irrational) beliefs of the modern era: absolute faith in moral and intellectual order.

And yet, Jackson's fabulation differs from that of her male counterparts in that it typically revolves around women's lives and concerns. In this respect her writing anticipates what SF scholar Marleen S. Barr calls feminist fabulation: "Feminist fabulation is feminist fiction that offers us a world clearly and radically discontinuous from the patriarchal one we know, yet returns to confront that known patriarchal world in some cognitive way. Feminist fabulation is a specifically feminist corollary to Scholes' 'structural fabulation.' Structural fabulation addresses man's place within the system of the universe; feminist fabulation addresses woman's place within the system of patriarchy" (*Lost in Space* 11). As Barr suggests, fabulation is a useful narrative tool for women writing from a distinctly political perspective because it enables them to do more than simply ask questions about the social construction of reality or the limits of the scientific knowledge used to describe that reality. It enables them to identify patriarchy as the specific historical and material force informing consensus reality and its representations. As such, feminist fabulation takes the first critical step toward transforming the world into a more productive and equitable place for all.

Because Jackson's stories are so often set in the home and peopled by women who understand themselves as wives, mothers, or daughters, they are most accurately thought of as a variant on feminist fabulation that I call "domestic fabulation." James Egan notes that in many stories "searches for the domestic and the familial lead Jackson's characters into the realm of the fantastic" (17). In other tales, S. T. Joshi contends, characters stumble into fantastic worlds in the course of mundane pursuits such as "riding a bus, employing a maid, taking children shopping, going on vacation, [and] putting up guests" (11). Elsewhere, John G. Parks, Darryl Hattenhauer, and Lynette Carpenter all suggest that Jackson draws on gothic tradition to depict homes as social microcosms for larger battles between patriarchal and feminist ways of knowing the world. From this perspective Jackson's houses are both places of constricting male authoritarianism and spaces that enable "female self-sufficiency" (Carpenter 32).[26] Taken together, these diverse arguments about Jackson's use of what Joshi calls "the domestic weird" indicate the diverse ways that domestic fabulation can be used to demonstrate how preferred ways of knowing the world may be limited and self-contradictory.

Domestic fabulation encompasses a surprising range of Jackson's stories. It is perhaps most evident in Jackson's domestic comedies—semiautobiographical sketches published in various women's magazines and collected in two books, *Life Among the Savages* (1953) and *Raising Demons* (1957)—which often revolve around meditations on the universal relations of order and disorder as they are filtered through the lens of domesticity. Even the most homely modes of order take on cosmic significance in these vignettes. For example, in *Life Among the Savages* Jackson begins a story about housewives' shopping lists with the claim that "I have always believed, against all opposition, that women think in logical sequence" (77). However, she goes on to demonstrate a very different and much larger point about human perception. As readers soon learn, Jackson's academic

26. While Parks and Hattenhauer focus primarily on Jackson's use of the gothic house as an allegorical space in which to expose patriarchy as limiting and deforming female subjectivity, Carpenter explores how Jackson depicts the home as a space of female creativity and resistance to masculine authority.

husband cannot decipher her shopping lists because they are based on Jackson's walking routes through the local village rather than abstract logic (77–78). Meanwhile, Jackson herself cannot communicate with other housewives because conversations turn into "double-listings" based on different households' needs rather than true meetings between individual minds (82). Therefore Jackson suggests that no two humans can ever truly share the same sense of logical sequence.

The ultimate problem for Jackson, however, is not the disparity between individual minds but the wild proliferation of order itself. By the end of the shopping list vignette Jackson the narrator completely loses control of her lists as they spawn ever more fabulous permutations: a list of china Jackson wants leads to a new list of ways she imagines upper-class families with nice china might behave, which leads to a new list of the domestic help she would require if she were rich, which leads to another list about family heirlooms that would make her feel rich, which leads to a new list about the price of household goods, and so on. Eventually, Jackson concludes, "you can start from any given point on a list and go off in all directions at once, the world being as full as it is, and even though a list is a greatly satisfying thing to have, it is extraordinarily difficult to keep it focused on the subject at hand" (79). And so the housewife's shopping list represents what Jackson elsewhere calls the ineffectual but necessary attempt to take control of an indifferent universe.

While Jackson's domestic comedies treat the problem of order in a relatively lighthearted way, her mainstream novels provide readers with more serious meditations on the social construction of reality. As in her comedies, these domestic fabulations most often take place in the private sphere of the home. For example, *The Sundial* (1958) follows a group of women as they seek control over the Halloran estate.[27] Although the women strategically enact violence to get what they want, their preferred methods of battle are narrative. The primary contest occurs between the current matriarch of the family, Orianna

27. Although *The Sundial* was perhaps the least warmly received of Jackson's novels during her lifetime, it is the one that receives the most extensive critical attention today. For discussion of the novel's proto-postmodern elements, see Hattenhauer's *Shirley Jackson's American Gothic*. For discussion of how Jackson uses gothic elements to critique the debilitating legacy of patriarchy in *The Sundial,* see Egan's "Sanctuary: Shirley Jackson's Domestic and Fantastic Parables." And finally, for an assessment of this novel as one of Jackson's most explicit commentaries on contemporary life, see Richard Pascal's "New World Miniatures: Shirley Jackson's *The Sundial* and Postwar American Society."

Halloran, and her sister-in-law Fanny. Orianna attempts to secure the estate through a series of legal and illegal maneuvers: marrying the family heir; providing him with a son; and then pushing the son down a staircase and killing him so that, as a grieving mother, she may claim the Halloran fortune for herself. Fanny fantastically but powerfully contests Orianna's claim to the estate by announcing that her dead father has prophesied an apocalyptic cleansing of the Earth. Only those who remain in the Halloran household—and who follow the deceased patriarch's rules as Fanny relates them—can hope for salvation. In response, Fanny redirects the attention of the Halloran household to a different and presumably higher order of reality. This enables her to trump Orianna's legalistic claims to the estate and secure it as her own domain.

These two contesting versions of reality inevitably cancel out other, more benign narratives of order. Tempted by the thought that she might rule not just a single estate but a whole new world, Orianna temporarily allies herself with Fanny and encourages all the members of the Halloran household to throw themselves into preparation for the end days. When it becomes clear that there is not enough room in the house to store all the supplies they have been stockpiling, Fanny orders the Halloran library cleared of its books and Orianna cheerfully burns them to ashes, noting that "they were none of them of any great value. . . . Not a first edition among them" (120). Jackson concludes that there is little room for the life of the rational mind in the face of materialism and moral fervor.

Of course, these new modes of order are open to contest and reinterpretation—and once again, especially by those with their own interests in the Halloran estate. When another local apocalyptic group, the True Believers, learn about Fanny's visions, they immediately descend on the Halloran home to ally themselves with Fanny and Orianna. However, they do so not out of sympathy for their fellow believers but because "we got to get a place to meet" (100). Meanwhile, Orianna's friend Augusta Wilson—a bold woman who freely admits "it's money we need"—attempts to make herself indispensable to the Halloran family by leading a number of séances to clarify Fanny's original visions (58). Fortunately for Augusta and her daughters, the séances predict that in contrast to the True Believers, the Wilsons will be allowed to stay at the Halloran house during the coming apocalypse. Although Fanny's visions might succeed in balancing the chaos implied by Orianna's illegal ascendancy to the head of the Halloran household, her model of order is by no means a definitive one. Instead, the ambiguity of religious prophecy makes it susceptible to manipulation by those with ulterior motives.

Even the secondary household members who have no chance of wresting control away from Orianna or Fanny take advantage of the clean break from history implied by apocalypse to exercise their own narrative powers in small but astonishing ways. As a kind of psychological defense against manipulation by their overbearing mothers, Orianna's daughter-in-law, Maryjane, and Augusta's daughter, Arabella, tell each other elaborate stories based on popular film scenarios, casting themselves as brave heroines who defy all odds to become mistresses of their own destinies. Meanwhile Essex the librarian copes with the loss of his beloved books by madly spinning sordid tales about the Halloran women as morally depraved creatures ruined by pirates and Indians who casually pick up serial killers for their amusement. Storytelling in this novel operates much like shopping lists do in Jackson's comic vignettes: although it provides a starting point from which to organize one's relations to the larger world, it also "goes off in all directions at once" (*Life Among the Savages* 79).

Like other fabulators including Kurt Vonnegut and Thomas Pynchon, Jackson ultimately refuses the kind of narrative closure that would enable readers to determine which set of stories—and which set of power relations—will prevail in the end. When Jackson's characters find Orianna dead at the bottom of a staircase on the eve of the apocalypse, it seems that the game is over and that rough justice has been served by Orianna's granddaughter, Fancy, who has threatened to avenge her father's death in just this way from the very beginning of the novel. However, when Fancy takes Orianna's tiara and proudly announces that it is "my crown now" (239), are we to assume that she has stopped her grandmother's madness, or that she will simply repeat it in some exacerbated form? Jackson's readers never find out because the novel ends a few pages later, with Fancy and all the other members of the Halloran estate boarded up inside their house, waiting for the apocalypse to begin. Jackson's characters (and readers) are left hovering on the edge of an endlessly deferred revelation.

Given the similarities between structural fabulation and SF, it is not surprising that some of Jackson's most critical examinations of epistemological order appeared in SF magazines. Her first SF story, "Bulletin" (1954), takes the form of a history exam from the year 2123 that asks students to assess the veracity of claims ranging from "the aboriginal Americans lived above-ground and drank water" to "the hero Jackie Robinson is chiefly known for his voyage to obtain the golden fleece" (47, 48). Meanwhile, "The Missing Girl" (1957) relates the tale of a teenager who disappears from her summer camp. Frustrated by campers who do not remember her, counselors who claim to have rejected her application, and a family who does not remember sending a child to camp, the local police soon abandon the case. By this point, however, the story has taken on a life of its own, and when the local townspeople find a young woman's body they claim it is the missing girl and quickly bury her in their own cemetery, despite various signs indicating that it is not the same girl at all. Although these two stories are quite different in form, both reflect Jackson's interest in the social construction of reality: while the former insists on the mutability of historical knowledge, the latter underscores the equally real human desire to impose narrative order on a chaotic, indifferent, and possibly even hostile world.

Jackson's two most often anthologized SF stories, "One Ordinary Day, with Peanuts" (1955) and "The Omen" (1958), specifically reflect her interest in domestic fabulation.[28] The first of these stories uses an old married couple to demonstrate the arbitrariness of moral order. "One Ordinary Day" follows a day in the life of Mr. John Philip Johnson, a seemingly "responsible and truthful and respectable man" who wanders through New York City doing small good deeds for people: babysitting a child while his mother supervises moving men, arranging a promising romance between two lonely young people, giving a homeless man lunch money, and feeding peanuts to stray dogs and hungry seagulls (299). In this respect Jackson's story begins on a relatively benign note, as Mr. Johnson attempts to create order and happiness in the obviously disordered and unhappy lives of everyone he meets.

In contrast, Mrs. Johnson spends her day engaged in small acts of chaos and nastiness. As she tells her husband upon his return home: "[I] went into a department store this morning and accused the woman next to me of shoplifting, and had the store detective pick her up.

---

28. "One Ordinary Day, with Peanuts" is one of Jackson's most anthologized stories, along with "The Lottery" and "The Demon Lover." It has appeared in at least twelve anthologies including Anthony Boucher's *The Best from* Fantasy and Science Fiction: *Fifth Series*, Judith Merril's *SF: The Best of the Best,* Terry Carr and Martin H. Greenberg's *A Treasury of Modern Fantasy,* and Lawrence Jackson Hyman and Sarah Hyman Stewart's *Just an Ordinary Day.* "The Omen," like many of Jackson's stories, has been republished in one genre-specific anthology and one author-specific collection: Boucher's *The Best from* Fantasy and Science Fiction: *Eighth Series* and Hyman and Stewart's *Just an Ordinary Day.* For further information, see Charles N. Brown and William G. Contendo's *The Locus Index to Science Fiction and Index to Science Fiction Anthologies and Collections.*

Sent three dogs to the pound—*you* know, the usual thing" (304). This final aside seems to confirm what Jackson has hinted at throughout her story: that the Johnsons are not mere mortals but living embodiments of much larger cosmic forces. More specifically, they appear to embody the naturally opposed forces of good and evil in a perfectly balanced relationship that is as comfortable and predictable as that of an old married couple.

But Jackson invokes her readers' faith in the certainty of moral order only to shatter it at the end of her story:

> "Fine," said Mr. Johnson [after learning about his wife's adventures].
> "But you do look tired. Want to change over tomorrow?"
> "I *would* like to," she said. "I could do with a change."
> "Right," said Mr. Johnson, "What's for dinner?" (304)

Thus, Jackson asks readers to consider the unsettling possibility that good and evil might not be eternally balanced forces but arbitrarily constructed concepts. Moreover, she underscores the very banality of such concepts by equating the fantastic choice to do good or evil with the mundane choice of what to eat for dinner.

Jackson returns to her interest in shopping lists and the construction of reality in "The Omen." After announcing her plan to buy presents for her family and herself one morning, Granny Williams constructs a list that seems purposely designed to obscure rather than aid her memory. At first, Granny's abbreviations make a certain kind of sense: when her daughter asks for a specific kind of perfume, she writes down its name, "Carnation," and when her son-in-law requests some El Signo cigars, she writes down their name in translation as "the sign." But as Granny becomes confused about what other family members want, her abbreviations become increasingly arbitrary: her granddaughter's clamoring for stuffed animals is reduced to "blue cat"; her grandson's request for a walkie-talkie gets translated as "telephone"; and the dime-store jewelry she covets for herself becomes simply a "ring" (119–20). From the very outset of this domestic fabulation, Jackson reiterates the sentiment she has proposed elsewhere in her domestic comedies: that the relations of signifier to signified are tenuous at best.

This point is made all the more clear by the movement of the shopping list through the city. When Granny loses her list on the bus ride into town, both the list and the narrative focus of Jackson's story shift to Edith Webster, a timid young woman torn between a tyrannical mother who does not want her to leave home and a loving but increasingly frustrated boyfriend who wants her to marry him. Paralyzed by indecision, Edith prays for "somebody, something, somehow [to] show me the way, make up my mind for me, give me an omen" (122). After discovering Granny's list on the bus and finding herself deposited in a strange part of town bereft of any "familiar sign," Edith whimsically decides that the list is an omen that will guide her to her mother's home (124). Instead, it guides her toward a new home of her own. When Edith meets a man headed to his own wedding, replete with a carnation in his label, she is suddenly convinced that the flower is "the sign" that she should also get married. Accordingly, when she finds a restaurant with a blue cat on the front window and a telephone in the back, she promptly calls her boyfriend to accept his marriage proposal and secure for herself the final item on Granny's list: a ring. The ease with which Edith uses the list to secure her heart's desire underscores the ease with which signifiers may be detached from one set of referents and reattached to another.

Although readers might expect Edith's gain to be Granny's loss, Jackson refuses this kind of simple cosmic balancing. Instead, Granny's shopping trip turns out to be just as successful without a list as it might have been with one. No one gets the presents they asked for, but they seem equally pleased with what they do receive: as Granny's grandson "immediately" announces upon receiving a toy gun rather than the requested walkie-talkie, "this is what *I* wanted" (130). Without the concrete presence of Granny's list, her family cheerfully rewrites the memory of their earlier desires to match the reality of the evening as it unfolds. Even when Granny's son-in-law eyes his garishly colored tie rather "dubiously," the problem seems more directly tied to Granny's atrocious sense of aesthetics rather than to the randomness of the gift (130). As in "One Ordinary Day, with Peanuts," Jackson gives her story one final twist. After asking readers to consider the possibility that order might sometimes derive from a highly arbitrary matching of signifiers to signifieds, she asks them to consider an even more fantastic possibility: that order might sometimes be achieved without reference to any referents whatsoever.

Jackson's interest in the social construction of reality leads her to explore the limits of those epistemologies most prized by scientists and SF writers alike. Associated as they are with magic and superstition, omens appear to be diametrically opposed to rational, deductive modes of inquiry. And it does seem that the first part of Jackson's story prepares readers for the failure of magical thinking. For example, when Edith calls out for a sign to guide her, the narrator sternly warns that this is, "of course, a most dangerous way of thinking" (122). After Edith finds Granny's list, the narrator predicts that Edith is about to learn her first lesson regarding omens: "that their requirements are usually much more difficult than they seem to be" (124). And yet the second half of the story belies the narrator's warnings because Edith attains her heart's desire without any major problems.

So why does Jackson's narrator insist that omen reading is so dangerous? Perhaps because such reading reveals how rational ways of knowing the world might be transformed by individual desire. Almost immediately after the narrator's warning against magical thinking, Jackson introduces a subplot that revolves around a contest held by Murrain Brothers' Groceries on the opening day of their newest store. To win $100 worth of free groceries, contestants must decode a series of clues that will lead them to "Miss Murrain," a young woman wearing a hat "the color of the bags in which Murrain Brothers pack their special coffee" (125). Thus the contest requires participants to make sense of the world around them by decoding clues, matching them to external phenomena, and verifying the relations between the two congruent modes of inquiry.

The contest begins well enough with all participants politely following the rules of the game, but desire for the grand prize soon leads them to abandon all pretenses of logic and civility. When a group of contestants spot Edith wearing a hat that matches the red of the Murrain Brothers' coffee bags, they immediately assume she is Miss Murrain. Without bothering to ask her the designated follow-up questions, the contestants descend upon Edith as a mob and drag her to the grocery store despite her protests that they have the wrong woman. When they learn that someone else has already found the real Miss Murrain, they quickly turn against Edith. "You mean to say," one particularly belligerent woman screams, "*you mean to say* you told me you were that girl and you *aren't?*" (127) Like Edith, the contest participants engage in a mode of sign reading that is guided by personal desire. However, because they confuse interpretation with observation, they are left without a template for productive action when interpretation fails. As the physical threat to Edith indicates, in some cases omen reading truly is "a most dangerous way of thinking."

Ultimately, "The Omen" serves as a narrative instantiation of what Jackson observed more prosaically elsewhere: that superstition and science are not so much opposed epistemologies as they are variations of the same "pattern superimposed precariously on the chaos of human development" (qtd. in Oppenheimer 125). If Edith's subjective sign reading turns out to be more productive than the contest participants' pseudo-objective deduction, it is because she acknowledges her own participation in the construction of reality. At the beginning of the story Edith admits that she wants to elope with her fiancé but that "the courage required to defy her mother was more than she could muster" (122). Of course, this is precisely why she needs an omen: to give her courage. Furthermore, when Edith receives her sign in the form of Granny's shopping list, she treats it rather playfully, "smiling at herself, although not with so much amusement as she might have felt if this omen had not arrived exactly on schedule" (124). In the end, Jackson suggests that the construction of reality can be a joyous and liberating event when it is the product of a playful seriousness that is, as she puts it in the final lines of her story, an "amazing . . . charming . . . [and] positively *sentimental*" business (130).

Conclusion: Revisiting Galactic Suburbia

In this chapter I have examined the rise of women's SF in relation to broader patterns of literary production in the first half of the twentieth century. Since its heyday in the "long domestic decade" stretching from the end of World War II in 1945 to the revival of feminism in the 1960s, the relative merits of women's SF have been at times heatedly debated within the SF community. For some, this SF was nothing more than a disastrous attempt to tell stories about the social and sexual relations of today in what would surely be the otherwise new scientific and technological worlds of tomorrow. For others, it was a logical step in the evolution of SF as a socially engaged and aesthetically innovative literature. Either way, arguments both for and against postwar women's SF rarely addressed the relations of this new SF to other kinds of women's writing, implying, at best, that it sprung more or less fully formed from the minds of a few women who crossed over from the mid-century women's slick magazine market to produce a new kind of speculative fiction.

As my case studies of Judith Merril, Alice Eleanor Jones, and Shirley Jackson suggest, postwar women's SF is properly understood as a dynamic form of storytelling that emerged at the intersection of diverse popular and experimental literary forms. Although Judith

Merril is most often remembered for her editing and anthologizing activities, she was also one of the first contemporary authors to write women's SF, and the stories she produced in this vein at the beginning of her career in the late 1940s and 1950s set the standards for this type of fiction. This new kind of SF did not emerge in a vacuum but engaged a century-long tradition of women's speculative fiction. Like many feminist utopian and SF writers before her, Merril imagined that new sciences and technologies would create the conditions for more egalitarian sex and gender relations. However, she nuanced the work of her predecessors by exploring how men and women alike might confront—and, ultimately, overcome—the social and psychological difficulties attending the development of new scientific and social relations.

While Merril turned to the past for inspiration, authors like Alice Eleanor Jones looked to the present. In many ways, Jones seems to be the avatar of postwar women's SF authorship as it is typically conceived: although she wrote five well-received SF stories at the beginning of her literary career in the 1950s, she devoted most of her efforts for the next decade and a half to the more popular (and lucrative) market of women's magazine fiction. This does not mean, however, that either her women's magazine or SF stories simply celebrated those "happy housewife heroines" that Betty Friedan condemned in *The Feminine Mystique*. Instead, Jones used a variation on the ideal women's magazine story—the offbeat romance—to explore what she called "the dark side" of courtship, marriage, and motherhood. In doing so, she showed how sex and gender roles were produced by unspoken but widely accepted social arrangements. When Jones put the offbeat romance to work in science-fictional landscapes, this story type became a focusing lens through which to explore how new scientific and technological arrangements might also contribute to the devastating legacy of the feminine mystique and the reduction of women to decidedly unhappy housewife heroines.

Popular women's writing traditions may have provided both the political and poetic inspiration for a good deal of domestic SF, but they were by no means the only ones informing this kind of fiction. Authors such as Shirley Jackson also used the proto-postmodern literary form of structural fabulation to explore the mutability of moral and intellectual order and the social construction of reality. Although this wildly popular author published just five stories in SF magazines over the course of her long career, she is increasingly considered to be, like her male counterparts Walter Miller, Theodore Sturgeon, and

Kurt Vonnegut, an important example of those "borderline" authors whose work blurs the boundaries between structural fabulation and SF. She is also an important member of that group of SF authors including Merril and Jones who used the conventionally feminine tropes of marriage, domesticity, and the home as microcosms through which to explore larger social and intellectual concerns; accordingly, her stories are best understood as "domestic fabulations." And Jackson's domestic fabulations are particularly interesting because they demonstrate the convergence between protofeminist and proto-postmodern concerns, including a deep suspicion of master narratives and overly rational ways of knowing the world, especially as they are expressed in dominant scientific (and science-fictional) discourses.

Taken together, these case studies of three very different postwar women writers demonstrate that the rise of women's SF was less of an anomaly than it might at first seem. And yet, although this kind of mapping activity provides us with some insight into the basic thematic concerns and narrative techniques of women's SF, it also raises at least two other pressing questions: Why would women writers choose to conduct their political and aesthetic experiments in the realm of SF, an increasingly popular but still relatively marginal literary form in the postwar era? And why make seemingly conventional—if not explicitly conservative—domestic tropes central to these experiments, especially in an era of feminist backlash when such tropes were most often used to glorify the gendered status quo? As we shall see in the following chapters, these choices actually made a great deal of sense because they enabled women writers to engage in debates over some of the most pressing political and cultural issues of the day—including debates over the nature of women's work in the home itself.

HOMEMAKERS

WHEN POSTWAR women SF authors were not advocating feminist ideals, criticizing new technocultural arrangements, or exploring the limits of Enlightenment thought, they turned their attention to the promises and perils of housework. In "Woman's Work Is Never Done!" (1951) Judith Merril relates the tale of Leslie Caster, a teenage girl from a far future Earth where homemaking is a highly technical licensed art. As Merril describes it, even the simple act of purchasing bread is an action-packed adventure for her young heroine, one that involves navigating through throngs of servocars to Supply Town, programming the proper supply computer with the correct parameters for her father's favorite bread, and then, when she learns about a new plastic wrap that will keep her bread fresher than ever, cracking the codes that will enable her to secure this amazing new product for her own family. Emboldened by her success with this new technology, a triumphant Leslie returns home and rejoices to her mother, "the first time I ever went alone, and everything came out perfect. . . . Fourteen more and I can get a prelim license!" (51). And so Merril gestures toward a future world where homemaking is every bit as creative and fulfilling an experience as building rocket ships or exploring new galaxies.

But as Merril's readers soon learn, Leslie has a long way to go to earn her license. First she must meet the exacting standards of an established homemaker—her mother. Described as a "well-built, graceful woman of middle age" who is just a "trifle too much of a perfectionist," Mrs. Caster has already made three of her daughters brilliant successes in the family business and is determined to do the same with Leslie (51). But from the very start she is stymied by her daughter's unorthodox ways. When Mrs. Caster learns that Leslie drives manually rather than using her servocar's automatic pilot she threatens to withhold her homemaking license because "*no* lady navigoes herself!" (97). And when she finally sees the end product of her daughter's labor her worst fears are confirmed: "You had this bread smooth-sliced instead of rough-cut! *What* do you think your father's going to say, the way he likes home-made-style? Leslie Caster . . . you'll just never be a decent housekeeper. I can feel it in my bones. Never!" (98) Successful homemaking in Mrs. Caster's world is not about satisfying the individual woman's desire for technical prowess or creative expression; it is about conforming to socially accepted gender ideals and meeting the needs of others, even at the expense of the homemaker's own interests and enthusiasms. If woman's work is never done, it is because the work of adapting oneself to the cultural ideal of homemaking in an ongoing process that demands constant vigilance on the part of the homemaker herself.

Although Merril deploys a lighthearted tone throughout this vignette, it is a serious piece of fun. After World War II, homemaking became not just one aspect of women's identity but its totality. Cold war historian Elaine Tyler May explains that for Americans facing the uncertainties of the nuclear age, the home "seemed to offer a secure private nest removed from the outside world" (*Homeward Bound* 3). Accordingly, women's work as caretakers and consumers was celebrated throughout politics, psychology, and popular culture as key to preserving the American family and the American way of life. At the same time, these ideals were heatedly contested by public actors ranging from social critics and religious counselors to suburban mothers and, as Merril's piece suggests, even SF authors because they seemed to contradict older American values including the pursuit of happiness through self-determination and the right to participate in the public life of the nation.

By speculating about the promises and perils of women's work in the future, SF authors helped create a new tradition of literary homemaking in their own day. Catherine Wiley and Fiona R. Barnes explain that since World War II women writers working in diverse genres across the globe have approached the concept of home in remarkably similar ways, insisting that "home is not always a comfortable place to be. . . . [But it] is always a form of coalition: between the individual and the family or the community, between belonging and exile, between home as a utopian longing and home as a memory, between home as a safe haven and home as imprisonment or site of violence, and finally, between home as a place and home as a metaphor" (xv). While contemporary authors maintain faith in home as a potentially utopian space where women might connect with one another and express themselves freely, they recognize—as in Merril's vignette—that it is also a complex and sometimes contradictory place shaped by the demands of the larger public world. As such, the trope of the home serves as a powerful focusing lens through which to explore the relations of individual women to the broader cultural and historical forces that inform their lives.

When women writers rethink the home, they also rethink women's identity and agency as homemakers. In some cases this involves imagining new modes of domesticity and new kinds of families; in others it involves reclaiming and revaluing the physical act of housework itself. Either way, as Wiley and Barnes put it, "home is not therefore an endpoint, but a constant movement toward or reconfiguration of the self" (xvi). And as women authors reconfigure themselves in relation to the home, they engender new forms of creative community as well. Rather than simply inserting themselves into "the margins of literary traditions that have historically been male-dominated preserves," women who write about the home—especially as a space of creative female culture—have "redefined male-dominated literary spheres to create their own traditions and territories" (xxi). As they map the diverse social and political dimensions of homemaking, such authors make new literary homes that provide readers with new ideas about what constitutes good aesthetic practice as a whole.

Like other participants in this literary tradition, women writing SF after World War II made new homes within their chosen genre by telling stories from distinctly feminine points of view. They also used the thematic and stylistic toolkits of SF to critically assess the new understandings and representations of homemaking that emerged in this period. For example, authors including Carol Emshwiller and April Smith appropriated the figure of the alien other—a figure that male SF authors had long equated with femininity—to illustrate the limits of modern gender ideals and denaturalize the feminine mystique. But such authors also used the encounter with the alien other to explore how women might reclaim the act of caretaking itself. This is particularly apparent in Rosel George Brown's and Zenna Henderson's teacher stories, where intensely feminine spaces such as the car pool and the classroom enable women to connect with one another across species and thus create new kinds of family and home.

SF authors also explored the promises and perils of women's work as consumers. This is particularly apparent in the media landscape stories of Ann Warren Griffith, Garen Drussaï, Margaret St. Clair, and Kit Reed. By combining the surreal imagery of modern advertising with the future-forward sensibility of SF, these authors created shocking—and often shockingly funny—worlds where women appropriate household technologies to literally reshape their families and homes. Although such stories did not necessarily challenge postwar gender ideals, they did not simply treat women as victims of them, either. Rather, they illustrated how housewife consumers might act as scientific and social agents in their own rights.

Homemaking and Caretaking in Postwar Culture

Although homemaking might strike contemporary readers as one of the oldest and most traditional of women's activities, the new domestic technologies of the early twentieth century—including indoor plumbing, electricity, and prefabricated goods—led Americans to treat domestic labor as a symbol of economic and social progress.[1] After World War II, homemaking became a sign of political progress as well. "In the rhetoric of Cold War competition," feminist historian Susan M. Hartmann writes, "American leaders stressed women's traditional roles as wives, mothers, and consumers to demonstrate the superiority of the nation's institutions and values" (86). For example, as Adlai Stevenson told Smith College graduates during their 1955 commencement ceremony, homemaking was not just menial work to be feared by educated women. Instead, it presented them with the perfect opportunity to "defeat totalitarian, authoritarian ideas" by cultivating

1. For a focused discussion of housework in relation to late-nineteenth- and early-twentieth-century discourses of modernity, see Francesca Sawaya's *Modern Women, Modern Work*. For more general explorations of new domestic technologies and the transformation of women's work in this same period, see Susan Strasser's *Never Done: A History of American Housework*, Ruth Schwartz Cowan's *More Work for Mother: The Ironies of Household Technology from the Open Hearth to the Microwave*, and my own discussion of this subject in the introduction to this book.

in their families "a vision of the meaning of life and freedom" (qtd. in Hartmann 86). Thus, postwar women were invited to serve their country as domestic cold warriors dedicated to maintaining the security of America's most fundamental social unit: the nuclear family.[2]

In their capacity as patriotic caretakers, women were encouraged to devote themselves to the physical and emotional integrity of the nuclear family. As May notes, affective labor was part and parcel of "the first wholehearted effort to create a home that would fulfill virtually all its members' personal needs through an energized and expressive personal life" (*Homeward Bound* 11). For example, while Victorian women were expected to tolerate sex for reproduction only, cold war wives "were recognized as sexual enthusiasts whose insistence on conjugal satisfaction . . . would enhance family togetherness, which would keep both men and women happy at home and would, in turn, foster wholesome childrearing" (103). Much like those male scientists, soldiers, and politicians who strove to contain the threat of Soviet power within clearly defined spheres of influence, homemakers strove to contain the threat of social and moral corruption within the clearly defined space of the home itself.

Homemaking was not just patriotic; it was also, as the rhetoric of the feminine mystique assured a generation of Americans, the natural thing for women to do. In her groundbreaking book on the subject, feminist author Betty Friedan explains that

> [t]he feminine mystique says that the highest value and the only commitment for women is the fulfillment of their own femininity. . . . It says this femininity is so mysterious and intuitive and close to the creation and origin of life that man-made science may never be able to explain it. . . . The mistake, says the mystique, the root of women's troubles in the past is that women envied men, women tried to be like men, instead of accepting their own nature, which can find fulfillment only in sexual passivity, male domination, and nurturing maternal love. . . . The new mystique makes housewife-mothers, who never had the chance to be anything else, the model for all women; it pre-

---

2. While postwar domestic ideals were primarily targeted at white, middle-class women, other Americans embraced them as well. Elaine Tyler May explains that postwar prosperity enabled some working-class men to earn enough money so that their wives might, for the first time in many cases, stay home with their children. This was particularly important for African American women, who historically spent their lives tending to other (white) people's children. Little wonder, then, that the editors of *Ebony* magazine cheerfully participated in the new cult of domesticity with articles such as the provocatively entitled "Goodbye Mammy, Hello Mom" ("Ambivalent Dreams" 152).

supposes that history has reached a final and glorious end in the here and now, as far as women are concerned. (43)

This notion of feminine biology as destiny articulated neatly with political narratives of American superiority: democracy enabled individual women to choose how they would conduct their lives, and American capitalism provided them with the opportunity to follow their instincts and stay at home while their husbands went to work in the larger world.

The feminine mystique also appealed to many Americans because scientific experts said it was so, and in an era that was undergoing rapid scientific and social change, young people actively sought out expert advice about how to live in the modern world. The rhetoric of the feminine mystique derived from Freudian notions of anatomy as destiny, and those notions were disseminated in hundreds of works by sociologists and psychoanalysts throughout the postwar era.[3] In *Modern Woman: The Lost Sex* (1947), psychiatrist Marynia Farnham and sociologist Ferdinand Lundberg argued that "[f]eminism, despite the external validity of its political program and most (not all) of its social program, was at core a deep illness. . . . The dominant direction of feminine training and development today . . . discourages just those traits necessary to the attainment of sexual pleasure: receptivity and passiveness, a willingness to accept dependency without fear or resentment, with a deep inwardness and readiness for the final goal of sexual life—impregnation" (qtd. in Friedan 119–20). Farnham and Lundberg further proposed that therapists should treat women who did not naturally embrace these traits much like any other client who expressed estrangement from social and cultural norms. Rather than encouraging patients to explore their alienation from the feminine mystique, therapists were to help women identify strategies by which they could simply adjust themselves to it. Although these views were considered extremely conservative even in the 1950s, *Modern Woman* quickly became a best seller and was liberally quoted throughout academic and professional psychiatric culture.

The feminine mystique was widely celebrated in popular culture

3. Betty Friedan notes that by the 1940s and 1950s, most sociologists and psychoanalysts recognized that Freud had identified many issues key to understanding personality development, but that his interpretations of psychic events were very much culture-bound. Somewhat ironically then, even as experts began to carefully reassess all other aspects of Freudian theory, they continued to apply the notion of biology as destiny quite literally to women. For further discussion, see especially chapters 5 and 8 of *The Feminine Mystique*.

as well. Historian J. Ronald Oakley points out that Hollywood executives tried to lure audiences to the box office with new starlets who embodied the principles of the mystique: "in contrast to the forties, when women had often been portrayed as strong, individualistic, career-oriented or patriotic women doing their best for the war effort, the movies of the fifties paraded before audiences a variety of stereotyped women in stereotyped sex roles . . . [such as] the girl next door, the sexy mammary bombshell, and the temptress" (296). Similar—if less sexy—stereotypes permeated television as well. While family sitcoms such as *Father Knows Best* and *Leave It to Beaver* depicted women almost exclusively as wives and mothers, other TV shows including *Our Miss Brooks* and *Private Secretary* suggested that when women had to work, they would naturally gravitate to feminized, nurturing labor such as teaching or secretarial work (Oakley 296–98). Taken together, these visual representations of women both elaborated upon and reinforced the conservative gender ideals promoted by American politicians and psychologists.[4]

Even postwar homes were designed in accordance with these ideals. Architectural historian Clifford E. Clark Jr. explains that the ranch house—with its informal, one-story structure, large expanses of glass windows and walls, and generous open patios—was ideally suited for the young couple who wanted a "relaxed, comfortable, and casual" living space that would promote family happiness and togetherness (174). They also reinforced new ideas about women as domestic warriors. As domestic architecture expert Annmarie Adams notes, ranch homes were designed so that all major living zones opened onto centralized kitchens. This enabled women to "keep visual control" over children and husbands while showing off good housekeeping practices to visitors (168). Much like their modernist counterpart Le Corbusier, postwar architects approached the home as a machine for living in. In this case, however, they also treated it as a tool by which women ensured that their families lived in accordance with the American way of life.[5]

4. Over the past three decades feminist scholars have published a number of excellent studies on gender stereotyping in postwar visual media. For key discussions of gender and film, see Molly Haskell's *From Reverence to Rape: The Treatment of Women in the Movies;* Marjorie Rosen's *Popcorn Venus;* and Jeanine Basinger's *A Woman's View: How Hollywood Spoke to Women, 1930–1960.* For groundbreaking explorations of gender and television, see Ella Taylor's *Prime-Time Families: Television Culture in Postwar America* as well as Lynn Spigel's *Make Room for TV: Television and the Family Ideal in Postwar America* and *Welcome to the Dreamhouse: Popular Media and Postwar Suburbs.*

5. For an excellent discussion of how postwar gender ideals informed the design and construction of the new suburban shopping malls that proliferated throughout the 1950s and 1960s, see Lizbeth Cohen's "From Town Center to Shopping Center: The

But dominant notions of homemaking and the feminine mystique were both celebrated and contested throughout postwar American culture. For example, popular melodramatic films such as *Mildred Pierce* and *The Three Faces of Eve* explored the tension between new domestic ideals and older American values including individual achievement in the public sphere. Elsewhere, Protestant pastoral counselors sought to balance traditional theological ideals with new psychological theories of human development as a journey toward self-realization; in doing so, they developed new attitudes toward women's work. While the majority of these counselors still treated the home as a distinctly feminine space, they rejected the notion of anatomy as destiny and encouraged women who were not content with domestic labor to seek fulfillment in paid work and community service instead. Even that seemingly most traditional of all household accoutrements—the cookbook—acknowledged women's ambivalence regarding the principles of postwar domesticity. While recipe books produced by General Foods celebrated the modern homemaker's ability to maintain traditional family values with new technologies and prepackaged goods, others including *The Working Wives' Cookbook* and the *I Hate to Cook Cookbook* explicitly acknowledged that many women had other demands on their lives or did not find deep fulfillment in domesticity.[6]

Perhaps not surprisingly, the most critical and creative engagements with homemaking came from women themselves. For example, while the open plan of suburban ranch homes were designed to promote family togetherness, and fenced-in backyards were designed to encourage isolation from neighbors, homemakers "assumed active roles in the 'construction' of their own spaces, contesting many of the relationships presumed by the house . . . through the rearrangement of furniture and the appropriation of spaces intended for other uses" (Adams 171). More specifically, women refused their roles as surveillance officers by hanging curtains across open doorways and large windows and encouraging children to play in basements, side yards,

---

Reconfiguration of Community Marketplaces in Postwar America."

6. For further reading about postwar melodrama as expressing the contradictions imposed on modern women, see Justine Lloyd and Lesley Johnson's "The Three Faces of Eve: The Postwar Housewife, Melodrama, and Home" and Jackie Byers's *All That Hollywood Allows: Re-Reading Gender in the 1950s Melodrama*. For further discussion of protofeminism in postwar pastoral counseling, see Susan E. Myers-Shirk's "'To Be Fully Human': U.S. Protestant Psychotherapeutic Culture and the Subversion of the Domestic Ideal, 1945–1965." And finally, for further exploration of gender ideals in postwar cookbooks, see Jessamyn Neuhaus's "The Way to a Man's Heart: Gender Roles, Domestic Ideology, and Cookbooks in the 1950s."

and quiet streets. Meanwhile, children quite literally forged new connections between families by tunneling under backyard fences, and women created those connections metaphorically by meeting in public spaces such as swimming pools and social clubs. Rather than simply adjusting to domestic ideals, postwar women adapted those ideals to their own needs, especially as they articulated with other American values including the right to privacy and individual expression.

Elsewhere, women transformed caretaking into a collective activity that fostered participation in the public life of the nation. Suburban women challenged prevailing notions of motherhood as a biological duty that could be carried out only within the realm of the individual family by creating cooperative daycare centers where they shared childrearing and decision-making duties communally. Co-ops also enabled women to control their relations to professional child-care experts (who were, after all, these women's employees) and to engage with some of the most meaningful political issues of their day, including racial integration and anticommunism. As historian Robyn Muncie explains, "these small, local institutions supported democratic practices as well as social networks that directed members into other areas of community life, including local and state politics" (286). Rather than reinforcing the isolation of women and their families in the suburban home, cooperative daycare centers served as gateways for women to connect with one another and to engage the larger world around them.

Homemaking and Caretaking in Postwar Women's Female Alien Other Stories

Like their counterparts in the ranch home and the cooperative daycare center, women writing for the SF community challenged the feminine mystique by imagining how women might engage in alternate modes of homemaking and caretaking. Indeed, the fantastic tropes and narrative forms of SF provided them with ideal ways to do so. This is particularly apparent in stories about the female alien other. First popularized by male authors as a symbol of feminine power in the nineteenth century, the female alien became particularly central to SF storytelling in the 1940s and 1950s. Robin Roberts writes that

[t]he sudden reemergence of female aliens in the science fiction pulps

during this time may well have been a by-product of the post–World War II glorification of femininity. . . . In [stories such as Philip Jose Farmer's "The Lovers" and Paul W. Fairman's "Invasion from the Deep"], female aliens who are rulers and superior to men—politically, scientifically, or both—renounce their achievements and defer to human males, sometimes at the cost of their lives. Because of their maternal qualities, woman's self-abnegation is presented as admirable. These stories describe a patriarchal symbolic order in which the maternal is expected to destroy itself to preserve the patriarchy. (*A New Species* 42)

Much like those politicians and psychologists who encouraged women to exchange their careers for homemaking because it was both the patriotic and the natural thing to do, authors such as Farmer and Fairman reaffirmed conservative gender relations by telling stories about seemingly independent women who turn out to be most at home with themselves when serving others. By insisting time and time again that even the most alien and threatening of women could be converted to docile helpmeets—and that they would inevitably be happier for this conversion—men writing for the postwar SF community seemed to confirm the notion that feminine biology truly was destiny across Earth and the galaxy as a whole.

But as Brian Stableford notes, male authors including Arthur C. Clarke and Theodore Sturgeon also used "aliens as contrasting exemplars to expose and dramatize human folly" ("Aliens" 17). Not surprisingly, women writers used female aliens to expose and dramatize the folly of conventional sex and gender relations. In doing so, they anticipated a central practice of feminist SF: the use of the alien other to explore what Jenny Wolmark describes as the "slippage between sameness and difference [and] between centre and margins" that define "the limits of social and cultural identity" (*Aliens and Others* 28). More specifically, postwar women writers told stories about female aliens who physically travel between their home planets and Earth to represent the psychological journeys human women embark on as they explore what are often the opposing poles of self-determination and culturally sanctioned identity. In such stories, this latter form of identity is usually a variation of the feminine mystique. Thus, the figure of the female alien enabled authors to explore the complexities and contradictions of homemaking for modern women.

This is certainly true of Carol Emshwiller's "Adapted," which uses the figure of the female alien who is trapped on Earth to explore the devastating effects of the feminine mystique on women. First published in *The Magazine of Fantasy and Science Fiction* in 1961, "Adapted" is told from the perspective of an unnamed half-alien woman born on an Earth that closely resembles postwar America. Although her extraterrestrial father disappears before she is born and leaves behind no information about her alien ancestry, Emshwiller's protagonist is acutely aware of her unique nature from an early age:

> There was a time . . . when I liked being different. I used to like to look into a mirror and I even did not mind my long, thin nose and sharp chin. I would wonder about myself, staring into my own eyes, and every time I did it I would feel a kind of excitement. I could see how different I was, and I could see a look about me (it seemed to come more and more as I grew older) of something going to happen. I didn't know at all what it could be but sometimes I would think of it as flying. I could fly if I wanted to, I'd think, only what I meant was . . . well, not flying at all but something I could do that had to do with this floating feeling inside me. (32)

As a young girl who is alien to human society but who needs to make some kind of home for herself within it, Emshwiller's narrator experiences a tension "between belonging and exile, [and] between home as a utopian longing and home as a memory" much like the one that Wiley and Barnes associate with mainstream contemporary women's writing.

Terrified of drawing attention to herself in a world where even the mildest forms of social deviancy are viewed with great suspicion, Emshwiller's protagonist survives by passing first as an ordinary human girl and later as "just a housewife" (36). However, while the rhetoric of the feminine mystique assured mid-century women that adaptation to conventional gender ideals was both natural and healthy, Emshwiller insists that it is both artificial and dangerous. And indeed, her narrator undergoes extensive plastic surgery to be conventionally pretty, marries a man she does not love to be conventionally feminine, and represses her artistic and athletic skills to be conventionally domestic. The high cost of adaptation is driven home to both Emshwiller's protagonist and her readers during the alien woman's first and possibly last encounter with another of her kind: "I took a grip on my grocery bag and started towards him. . . . I kept thinking, in a minute he'll know me, in one minute more. *We*, I thought. I can say *We*. I'm his kind. But I walked up to him and past him and he didn't recognize me. . . . He looked right at me, my whole surface, and didn't recognize me at all" (38). Rather than making herself at home on Earth by adapting to human sex and gender roles, Emshwiller's narrator only succeeds at alienating herself from those people who might genuinely accept her as family.

Throughout "Adapted" Emshwiller connects her protagonist's search for identity with the literal act of homemaking. Soon after she is married and secure in her new identity as "just a housewife," the alien narrator decides to boldly paint her ceilings red. But when her husband gently mocks this decision she abandons her plan and paints the house neutral colors instead, noting "after a while I didn't mind them and the ache I had to have just one red ceiling went away" (33). In a similar vein, after giving birth to her daughter, Emshwiller's protagonist finds she must repress an incredible urge to replace all the flowers in her garden and house with cornstalks, an experience that causes her to resentfully ask herself, "who made up all these silly rules about beauty?" even as she complies with them (31). Emshwiller's alien narrator edits both herself and her home into a blandly acceptable version of the middle-class dream.

For Emshwiller, houses are more than just material places where women enact their identities; they are also psychic spaces where women learn to inhabit specific sex and gender roles. For example, as a child the narrator is proud of her unusual features, but when she is old enough to recognize that they inspire fear and anger in her mother, she quickly learns "to hunch my shoulders and hang my head" (32). Later, she takes great pleasure in swimming but gives it up when her husband complains that she does not devote enough time to her cooking. But the greatest tragedy is that as Emshwiller's protagonist adapts to the reduced circumstances of her life, she tries to make her equally talented—and equally alien—daughter do so as well: "I stopped swimming then and I wouldn't let you go, either. . . . You've always held your eyes away since then, and you took on my slouching walk, my hanging head, and I, I never told you to stand up straight" (36). As a result, the narrator alienates herself not just from her own people and her own home but from her own daughter as well.

In the final passages of "Adapted" Emshwiller does hold forth the possibility that home might also be a place where women create new selves and new communities. After she recovers from the shock of going unrecognized by her own race, the alien protagonist vows to ensure that life will be different for her daughter. Accordingly, she gives in to her repressed desire to decorate with cornstalks rather than flowers. More than idiosyncratic self-expression, the cornstalk decorations are, the narrator believes, a kind of homing beacon for others of her kind. As the narrator tells her daughter in conclusion, if and when the aliens do arrive, "I want you to go with [them] and I'll stay. I'll stay with your father and be what I've made myself into. But you, Darling, sit up. Don't slump so anymore" (39). Tenuous as this gesture might seem—after all, the narrator admits that she has repressed her alien instincts for so long that she might have mistaken the significance of cornstalks to her people—it does enable Emshwiller's protagonist, like her counterparts in suburban America, to subvert the logic of postwar domesticity and transform her house from a surveillance state into a place of self-expression.

In other stories, authors contrast the traveling female alien with the planet-bound human woman to explore the debilitating effects of conventional gender ideals on both individuals and the human race as whole. April Smith and Charles Dye's "Settle to One" (1953) relates the tale of Melandra, a kind, gentle, and brilliant alien who happens across Earth in her galactic wanderings. Delighted with the similarities between humanity and her own race, Melandra offers to give humans the knowledge they need to attain space travel and visit her own planet. After initial skepticism that a mere woman might really have this kind of technical knowledge, the human men realize that "she's advancing science at the rate of a decade a day. . . . By fusing the science of our two planets, we'll be able to explore whole galaxies" (74). In direct contrast to Emshwiller's unnamed female alien narrator, Smith and Dye's protagonist successfully establishes an independent intellectual identity in dialogue with that of her human male counterparts.

Unfortunately, Melandra cannot overturn human prejudices regarding sex and gender difference nearly so easily. In addition to possessing great generosity and intellect, Melandra is breathtakingly beautiful. Described as a tiny, graceful woman with cascading silver hair and sparkling green eyes that "could soften into tenderness or passion," Smith and Dye's protagonist seems to be a kind of extraterrestrial Marilyn Monroe—a reference further reinforced by artist H. R. Van Dongen's illustration of her in the story itself (see figure 2). Much like the movie star on whom she is clearly based, men are irresistibly attracted to Melandra. As one scientist puts it, "It's not [just] that she's so beautiful . . . it's the way she moves I think. And that soft voice blending in with her gestures. Something about the way she moved—it seemed to catch the rhythms of my blood and do strange

Figure 2. Original illustration for April Smith and Charles Dye's "Settle to One" (1953). Artist H. R. Van Dongen makes literal Smith and Dye's message that married togetherness in galactic suburbia is always haunted by the specter of the female alien other who offers both women and men new ways of relating to one another.

things to it. . . . I'm turning into a poet, but no words are like what I felt" (70).

Terrified that they will lose their men to the alien and her sisters (who, as it turns out, outnumber the men of their planet five to one), human women lash out with anger and fear—not at their wayward husbands but at Melandra herself. One woman even physically attacks the alien at a party, "clawing and biting at her like an animal suddenly gone mad" (76). Soon after this event Melandra vanishes, taking along most of her science and technology and leaving behind a single message: "Our peoples could not come together without spreading unhappiness among you. Your marriage-system would have been disrupted and destroyed, your women made full of hate and misery, your men tortured with confusion. And there is no happiness where there is not happiness in love" (81). By juxtaposing the alien's empathy and generosity of spirit with the insensitivity and pettiness of her human counterparts, Smith and Dye extend the insight offered by Emshwiller in "Adapted": that uncritical adherence to rigid ideas about proper sex and gender relations jeopardizes human progress as a whole.

This message is further reinforced by the central drama of Smith and Dye's story: Melandra's relationship with linguist Kathryn Owens. Kathryn is the first human to make contact with the alien and, as Melandra's host during her stay on Earth, the only woman who learns anything meaningful about her. What she learns profoundly complicates Kathryn's notion of women and their possible connections to one another. Coming from a world where women outnumber men does not make Melandra a dangerous manhunter, as it turns out, but an ideal woman friend. As the linguist reluctantly admits to herself, "she liked Melandra. She could not help it, even when she wanted not to like her. Used to the smallness, the cold and reserved relations of most women of her society to one another, she could not help contrasting the frankness of Melandra to their hypocrisy" (68). Kathryn's encounter with the female alien other prompts her to extrapolate beyond the social order of her own world to a utopian alternative where women are truly at home with one another precisely because they do not define themselves in terms of men.

Sadly, the linguist's tentative new understanding of what might be possible for women collapses when Melandra asks if she might have a baby with Kathryn's husband, Ron. In Melandra's world, women share men in amiable communal marriages, and so the alien assumes that once Kathryn gets to know her, she will understand that this request is meant to seal their own burgeoning friendship. Furthermore, she hopes that as a scientist Kathryn will understand the import of a hybrid baby for Melandra's race as a whole. The current imbalance between women and men in Melandra's world is the result of a planet-wide industrial accident that genetically damaged the alien woman's people and drastically reduced the number of live male births. Melandra hopes to introduce a new genetic strain that will rectify this situation, but Kathryn cannot make the imaginative leap that Melandra asks of her: "I used to be considered the most beautiful woman around here. Now I know how the drab ones feel. . . . I don't think you even think of comparisons. . . . [But] you've been through three generations of adjusting to a situation with very few men. The first generation must have suffered horribly, but by now you've worked out cultural patterns and compensations. Your mores have changed. . . . But what about us? If it gets easy enough to go between our planets, you're going to have an awful lot of Earthmen around. And we're going to have to go through what your people went through three generations ago" (79). As a scientist, Kathryn knows this is not quite true. Melandra's people have never developed the concept of monogamous love, and they are interested in human men as genetic resources rather than marital partners—as the alien woman explains to Kathryn, she wants Ron's baby because "he is excellent stock for our race" (73). The real problem is that Melandra's request requires Kathryn to relinquish her investment in what Betty Friedan called "married togetherness." No wonder that this outburst from the one human she trusts prompts Melandra to quit Kathryn's house and Earth as a whole.

The tragedy of this situation is further underscored by the fact that Melandra's sacrifice cannot reaffirm the married togetherness that humans in Smith and Dye's story hold so dear. When she first learns of the alien woman's departure, Kathryn rejoices that "her problem—the problem that would have belonged to the women of Earth—was solved" (82). However, the linguist quickly realizes that this solution only generates an even more complicated problem. Not only has she lost the friendship of the one woman she has ever met who knows "how to be happy" with herself and other women, but she has lost the companionship of her husband as well (82). Although Ron stays with Kathryn after Melandra's departure, his attention remains permanently elsewhere: "he had seen a dream, and he would never be the same again, never be completely hers again" (82). By "saving" her world from the bold new social and sexual orders embodied by Melandra, Kathryn dooms herself, like the narrator of Emshwiller's "Adapted," to a life of reduced expectations in her own home.

Not all stories about human women's encounter with the female alien end in tragedy. Instead, many postwar women SF authors imagined that such meetings might enable women to successfully reconfigure their identities and make new homes for themselves in the world. Stories that follow this narrative trajectory often feature two distinctive characteristics. First, they relocate women's work from the private sphere of the home to liminal spaces such as the car pool and the classroom. Much like the home, these liminal spaces are feminine ones where women exert emotional and intellectual authority. Unlike the home, however, they are public places where women from different walks of life pool their various talents to achieve the common goal of educating and otherwise caring for children.

Second, such stories often feature alien women who immigrate to Earth to make new homes. In dystopic fictions such as Emshwiller's and Smith and Dye's, the female alien trapped on Earth represents the human woman trapped by the feminine mystique, while the alien who travels freely between worlds stands in sharp contrast to her human counterpart who cannot escape patriarchal sex and gender relations. By way of contrast, the immigrant alien embodies the possibility of change and growth. Whether she comes to earth voluntarily or not, the alien immigrant understands both her rich cultural heritage and the fact that she cannot ever return to the home that fostered this heritage. Instead, she looks forward to making a new home on Earth by blending the best traditions of both worlds. As such, this figure serves as both mirror to and metaphor for the human woman who seeks new roles for herself in her own world.

For example, in "Car Pool" (1959) Rosel George Brown uses the encounter with the female alien other to champion the cause of motherhood as a public and communal activity (see figure 3). Brown's story relates the tale of Verne Barrat, a human woman who chairs the car pool to the local daycare center, and Mrs. His-tara, an alien woman from the gentle Hiserian race whose son Hi-nin has recently joined the car pool. Verne and Mrs. His-tara bond quickly, but chaos ensues when the children start roughhousing and a human girl named Gail bites off Hi-nin's hand. As a Hiserian, Hi-nin can regenerate lost limbs easily. Nonetheless, both children wind up in the hospital because they are allergic to the Hiserian aggressor hormones that are triggered in Hi-nin by his encounter with Gail. The human girl responds quickly to antibiotics, but the alien boy's poisoning is psychogenic and cannot be cured by medical intervention. As Mrs. His-tara tells Verne, "an adult Hiserian, perhaps, could fight his emotions and cure himself. [But] Hi-nin has no weapons—so your physicians have explained it to me, from our scientific books. How can I doubt it?" (92). Tragedy is averted, however, when Verne realizes that psychogenic problems need psychogenic cures and that Hi-nin, much like a human child, simply needs a gesture of affection to assure him that everything will be fine. And sure enough, when Gail apologizes and explains that she was only teasing, the alien boy perks up and begins to mend. As precious as this ending might seem, it demonstrates how the knowledge of interpersonal relations that women acquire in the home both complements and extends the scientific and medical knowledge accumulated by men in the laboratory and hospital.

Elsewhere in "Car Pool" Brown uses different humans' reactions to Mrs. His-tara as a focusing lens through which to explore the different models of motherhood available to postwar women. Most strikingly, Brown suggests that the real cause of Hi-nin's brush with death is not

Figure 3. Original illustration for Rosel George Brown's "Car Pool" (1959). Brown's tale is both a lighthearted depiction of cross-species parenting and a serious meditation on motherhood in the postwar era.

Gail but her mother, Regina Crowley. A seemingly uninhibited and bohemian artist who enjoys nothing more than teasing Verne about her sober commitment to community activism, Regina is actually the epitome of the cold war security mother: a profoundly conservative woman determined to protect her child from alien influences at any cost. In Brown's world, such attitudes are both craven and dangerous. Not only does Regina argue against letting Hi-nin into the car pool, but when Gail bites him she reacts with hostility and selfishness, throwing Hi-nin's hand out the window and dumping the boy on Verne's lawn while she rushes her own child to the hospital. Later, Regina unfairly blames the entire incident on Hi-nin, denouncing him as a "little animal" that "shouldn't have been in the car pool [and] shouldn't be with human children at all" (92). It is precisely Regina's hostile reaction to the alien child that enables Verne to pinpoint the source of Hi-nin's illness: he is so devastated by Regina's reaction to the hand-biting incident that he would rather die than face her again. Much like Emshwiller and Smith, Brown insists that rigid adherence to modern models of appropriate feminine behavior reduces women to less than they can or should be. And in this case it nearly results in the death of a child as well.

By way of contrast, Verne's encounter with Mrs. His-tara and her child lead her to embrace the alternative values of cooperative motherhood. As car pool chairwoman, Verne already participates in communal practices much like those established by women in real-world daycare centers. Moreover, as Brown makes clear to readers, Verne does not simply save the day by drawing on some magical, intuitive source of universal feminine knowledge. Rather, she carefully analyzes Hi-nin's problem in relation to both her own experience as a mother and the child development information she collects from Mrs. His-tara and Mrs. Baden, headmistress of the children's nursery school. When Regina peevishly tells her to mind her own business, Verne links hands with her new alien and human friends and tells Regina "it *is* our damned business" (93). In doing so, she transforms childcare from a private act grounded in anxiety and fear to a communal one based on the principles of mutual support and intellectual collaboration.

Finally, Brown suggests that cooperative motherhood is more than just morally and ethically correct; it is also downright sexy. In the first half of "Car Pool" Regina maintains a certain psychological hold over Verne by dismissing her political convictions as distinctly unfeminine. For example, when Verne accuses her of racism, Regina counters with the command to "*Stop* looking so intense. That's what keeps you from being the boudoir-slip type. You always look as though you're going to break up a saloon or campaign for better Public Child Protection. The boudoir slip requires a languorous expression" (87). But Regina misjudges the men of her world just as badly as she misjudges the Hiserians. When Verne saves Hi-nin and puts Regina in her place, her husband, Clay, responds by presenting her with her very own negligee—"a gorgeous blue fluffy affair of no apparent utility"—and then lustily chasing her around the house while the children sleep (94). By striving to reach her potential as a new kind of public mother, Verne gets to have it all—adorable children, close women friends, and a devoted husband.

While Brown uses the encounter with the alien immigrant to explore how women might secure new and more satisfying roles for themselves within preexisting social structures, Zenna Henderson imagines that such encounters might enable human women to build entirely new communities with their alien counterparts. Inevitably, this process begins in the classroom, as humans and aliens learn to negotiate their differences for the sake of their children's futures. This is particularly true of Henderson's People stories. Written between 1953 and 1975 and anthologized in a number of collections, the People stories follow the adventures of a psionic starfaring race that is ship-wrecked on Earth in the late nineteenth century.[7] In some respects the People are much like the alien narrator of Emshwiller's "Adapted," permanently displaced from home and forced to survive on a world that fears their talents. Ultimately, however, they are more like Brown's aliens in that they have strong recollections of home (which are, in this case, transmitted to each subsequent generation through racial memory). Not only does this sustain the People over the next two generations as they slowly regroup, but it provides them with the utopian hope that they might some day live amongst humans without giving up their unique identities and talents.

Henderson's stories are also like Brown's in that key meetings between humans and aliens occur in the classroom and its related environs. The People stories are, in essence, Teacher stories organized around a group of women who first meet while pursuing education degrees in college. Some, like Karen, the protagonist of Henderson's earliest stories, are representatives of the People seeking to learn more about humanity by forging new bonds with sympathetic human women. Others, like Melodye Amerson, are humans who long for more than what they are given in the world as it is. Encounters between these women in the liminal spaces of the college dormitory and, later, the primary school classroom enable new caretaking practices that cure homesickness for human and alien alike by putting memory in perspective and using it as a template to forge new hybrid communities.

These themes are closely intertwined in "Pottage" (1955), the third of Henderson's People stories. "Pottage" relates the adventures of Melodye as she discovers a lost group of People in the ghost town of Bendo, Arizona, and helps them reunite with Karen's thriving group in Cougar Canyon. Although all the People have some difficulty adapting to Earth, the Bendo group are particularly traumatized by their disastrous first encounter with humans who mistake their ability to levitate for witchcraft and slaughter the People wholesale. In response, the survivors retreat to the desolation of Bendo and teach

---

7. Anthologies of Zenna Henderson's People stories include: *Pilgrimage: The Book of the People* (1961); *No Different Flesh* (1966); *The People Collection* (1991); and *Ingathering: The Complete People Stories* (1995).

the next two generations of People that they can survive Earth only by stamping out their psionic talents. As a result, the Bendo people become as dry and lifeless as the land they inhabit. As one human outsider puts it, "I've been to Bendo. . . . Sick community. Unhappy people. No interest in anything. Only reason they have a school is because it's the law. Law-abiding, anyway. Not enough interest in anything to break a law, I guess" (76). Much like Emshwiller's alien narrator, the Bendo People illustrate the devastating price of conformity: by repressing their differences they reduce themselves to a shadow of what they should be, thereby further increasing their alienation from their new home.

As in other stories by postwar women writers, the alienation of the extraterrestrial parallels that of the human woman herself. Like the Bendo People, Melodye is defined by her memories of a better home to which she can never return—in this case, the college dorm room she once shared with Karen, who told Melodye stories of the People in Cougar Canyon and consequently inspired her human friend with the utopian longing for something more in life: "I walked over to the Quad and sat down on one of those stone benches I'd never had time to use, those years ago when I was a student here. I looked up at my old dorm window and, for a moment, felt a wild homesickness—not only for years that were gone and hopes that died and dreams that had grim awakenings, but for a special magic I had found in that room. It was a magic—a true magic—that opened such vistas to me that for a while anything seemed possible, anything feasible—if not for me right now, then for Others, Someday" (77). Frustrated by her inability to achieve such magic on her own, Melodye quits her job at the plush suburban school where she has taught for years. At the last minute, however, she agrees to take a much less desirable job at Bendo because it reminds her of her own childhood home and is "about as far back as I could go to get a good running start at things again" (76).

More than a mere retreat to the past, the job at Bendo eventually enables both Melodye and the People she teaches to move into the future—a process that begins in the classroom. Although the Bendo aliens attempt to conceal their extraterrestrial origins from Melodye, she quickly divines who they are and what has happened to them. Inspired by the hope that "if I could break prison for someone else, then perhaps my own bars [would dissolve]," Melodye resolves to help the group by helping their children (90). Accordingly, she devises a series of exercises that teach the children how to put both the good and bad aspects of their past into perspective and recover their psionic skills:

> In one of those flashes of clarity that engrave your mind in a split second, I saw my whole classroom.
> Joel and Matt were chinning themselves on non-existent bars, their heads brushing the high ceiling as they grunted upwards. Abie was swinging in a swing that wasn't there, just missing the stovepipe from the old stove. . . . Miriam was kneeling in a circle with the other girls and they were all coaxing their books up to hover unsupported above the floor, while Timmy *v-roomm-vroomed* two paper jet planes through intricate maneuvers in and out the rows of desks. (99)

By making her classroom a place where they can safely remember their extraterrestrial origins and abilities, Melodye provides the Bendo children with the psychological space they need to stop thinking of themselves as dangerous outsiders. And so her classroom becomes the first true home that the Bendo children experience on Earth.

Melodye's classroom enables the Bendo adults to break the deadly cycle of repression and make themselves at home on Earth as well. When the group elders suddenly burst into Melodye's classroom, they startle Abie out of the air, causing him to crack his head on a cast iron heater and lapse into a deadly coma. At this point Henderson's protagonist reveals her knowledge of the People's heritage and helps the elders tap their powers so they can call Karen's group in Cougar Canyon for help. This simple act radically transforms the Bendo community. As Melodye observes, "in the pause that followed, I was slowly conscious of a new feeling. I couldn't tell you exactly what it was—a kind of unfolding . . . an opening . . . a relaxation. . . . 'They're coming,' [one elder] said, wonderingly. . . . 'We're *not* alone'" (104). And so both Abie and the Bendo People as a whole are saved by reunion with others of their kind—a reunion that could not occur without either the prior friendship of Karen and Melodye or their shared concern for the well-being of all children.

In turn, the People help Melodye create a new home for herself as well. Once again, this process begins in the classroom. After they establish regular contact with the Cougar Canyon group, the People of Bendo blossom rapidly. This transformation prompts mixed emotions in Melodye: "I was surprised at myself for adjusting so easily to all the incredible things done around me by the People, and I was pleased they accepted me so completely. But I always felt a pang when the children escorted me home—with me, they had to walk [rather than fly]" (110). Everything changes, however, at the end of the school year when Karen and the other members of the Cougar Canyon group decide to start a new kind of summer school in which the People will try to pass on their psionic skills to sympathetic humans. Naturally, Karen invites Melodye and her friend Dr. Curtis (the human surgeon who helps save Abie and is therefore privy to the secret of the People) to become her first pupils. Although there is no guarantee that Karen's plan will work, the humans accept eagerly:

> "Look," I said slowly. "If you had a hunger, a great big gnawing-inside hunger and no money and you saw a bakery-shop window—which would you do? Turn your back on it? Or would you press your nose as close as you could against the glass and let at least your eyes feast? I know what I'd do. . . . And you know, you never can tell. The shop door might open a crack, maybe—someday. . . ." (112)

Thus, Henderson ends her story on a hopeful note for all people whose biological origins and social identities place them on the margins of society. Home is not simply a space where such people can safely embrace some original or authentic identity, but one where individuals—much like pupils in the classroom—strive to become something new and better as well.

Housewife Consumers in Postwar Culture

Although caretaking might have been the primary activity that postwar homemakers were expected to undertake, they did not have to go it alone. Instead, women were encouraged to channel their nurturing instincts into a secondary form of domestic labor: family-centered consumption. May explains that the money women spent on household operation and recreation was generally perceived as enhancing domestic security: after all, if husbands and children had everything they needed at home, they would not want to leave it. Such spending was not decadent but a means by which women could "reinforce home life and uphold traditional gender roles" (*Homeward Bound* 166). Spending also enabled women to feel that they were contributing to the American economy. In 1965 *Time* ran a cover story celebrating the fourth straight year of economic expansion in the United States, an expansion that the magazine's editors explicitly attributed to the American consumer who "continued spending like there was no tomorrow" precisely because she knew that "the luxuries of today are the necessities of tomorrow" (qtd. in Cohen 1050). In contrast to turn-of-the-century homemakers who were encouraged to become educated consumers so they could protect their families from market predation, postwar homemakers were lauded for spending freely to protect their families from moral corruption and to bolster the market itself.

But Americans did not just celebrate women's work as consumers in the pages of their favorite magazines; they also celebrated this mode of domestic labor on the global political stage. During their televised tour of the 1959 American National Exhibition in Moscow, Vice President Richard Nixon and Soviet Premier Nikita Khrushchev engaged in what is now known as the "Kitchen Debate." After politely admiring the dazzling array of domestic technologies displayed in the exhibition's model kitchen, Khrushchev noted that Soviet women were content with fewer "gadgets" because, like their male counterparts, they were busy working outside the home for the greater good of the state. Nixon responded—and in the eyes of many Americans, won the Kitchen Debate—by explaining that "what we want to do is make easier the life of our housewives" ("Moscow Kitchen Debate"). For Nixon, American superiority derived from the freedom of American women to *leave* the paid workforce and devote themselves to their families. And American women were ready and willing to do so because they could chose a wide range of new goods and technologies to help them with their work in the home.

Postwar ideas about the necessary relations of homemaking and consumption were perhaps most clearly conveyed through advertising itself. To sell products, advertisers walked a fine line between making housewives feel inept and assuring them that they were already successful women who could regulate and, if they so desired, even transform their lives by buying specific products.[8] Either way, media scholar Bonnie J. Fox notes, mid-century advertising rarely depicted beauty products, household goods, or even automobiles as ways to escape homemaking—after all, such rhetoric "would have

---

8. For analyses of mid-century advertising as playing upon women's fears about their domestic performance, see especially Barbara Ehrenreich and Dierdre English's *For Her Own Good* and Susan Strasser's *Never Done: A History of American Housework*. For discussion of advertising as celebratory of women's domestic accomplishments, see especially Friedan's *The Feminine Mystique,* and, more recently, Marsha Bryant's "Plath, Domesticity, and the Art of Advertising" as well as Laura Scott Holliday's "Kitchen Technologies: Promises and Alibis, 1944–1966."

undermined the campaign to elevate housework's status and define it as serious work; it would have raised the possibility that women's interests might lie outside the confines of domesticity" (33). Instead, advertisements targeted at women emphasized service to the family, the romance of married life in a high-tech era, and the creation of fantastic new worlds at home. For example, a 1953 advertisement for Lava soap urged mothers to "Guard Against 'Dirt Danger' Days! Dirty hands can be dangerous to your children—*clean hands are healthy hands!*" ("Lava Soap"). Invoking the notion of women as domestic cold warriors, this advertisement promised homemakers that they could contain the threat of bacterial invasion in the home and in the bodies of their children by purchasing Procter & Gamble products.

But homemaking was not all hard work and unceasing vigilance. As General Motors assured women in its promotional film *Design for Dreaming* (1956), with the right technologies—and the right man—homemaking could be glamorous and sexy. As Laura Scott Holliday suggests, *Design for Dreaming* "links seduction by commodities to seduction by romance" by following the adventures of a young woman awakened in the middle of the night by a masked, tuxedo-clad man who transforms her pajamas into a ball gown and whisks her away to the Kitchen of Tomorrow (88). Fortunately, the Kitchen of Tomorrow is filled to capacity with labor-saving devices that enable the young woman to continue wearing her evening gown and even change into a dazzling array of other fashionable outfits, thereby indicating how much fun (rather than work) she will have in the modern home. Throughout the film the masked man offers to buy the young woman a number of different cars, and soon after he reveals his identity as her future husband, the couple tumble into their Firebird II prototype car and drive off into tomorrow singing about how "together, together/we'll make the world new" (qtd. in Holliday 91). Thus *Design for Dreaming* holds forth the tantalizing promise that new household technologies will enable women to convert domestic labor into romance and adventure.

Advertising also told women that the home—without or without a man—could be a site of feminine creativity and empowerment. In her survey of postwar women's magazine advertisements, Marsha Bryant concludes that advertisers often relied on surreal images and narratives to better "dramatize domesticity by investing the woman with supernatural powers"—powers that were, of course, inherent within the woman but channeled by the products she used on a daily basis (18). The well-stocked kitchen became a site of fantastic transformation in which the magician housewife (sometimes accompanied by fabulous creatures such as the Wishbone Salad Dressing genie, the Betty Crocker Mix brownie, or the Philco Quick-Chef oven sprite) "could levitate herself by opening a box of River or Carolina rice, . . . fly like a jet if she made Junket fudge ('the world's fastest'), or like an angel if she used Sucaryl artificial sweetner [*sic*]" (20). She also exerted control over other people and objects, turning children into eager beavers with Big Top peanut butter and, in one ad for Gibson appliances, marrying her refrigerator (28). Even more than their counterparts in politics and psychiatry, advertisers were quick to assure women that staying home could be far more exciting than pursuing paid work in the corporate world.

But as with the feminine mystique, not everyone agreed on the meaning and value of consumption in women's lives. Public intellectuals were particularly critical of housewife consumers. For example, Vance Packard and Russell Lynes both argued that homemakers were victims of those advertising and marketing experts who played upon their insecurities to encourage reckless spending.[9] Lynes even opened and closed his bestselling book *The Tastemakers* (1949) with anecdotes about a housewife acquaintance who nearly had a nervous breakdown while trying to decorate her living room in a manner that would impress her friends. The problem, Lynes concluded, was that "taste had become big business" (335). As corporate tastemakers increasingly equated consumption with social status, homemakers such as the one described by Lynes were increasingly diverted from the simple act of enjoying things for their own sake.

Again, however, the most significant challenges to dominant representations of women's work came from women. Although social critics had been making simple distinctions between masculine producers and feminine consumers since the late nineteenth century, women complicated this schema by organizing into consumer groups and forging active alliances with corporations that lasted well through the 1960s. These groups provided corporations with valuable feedback about which domestic products did and did not work for real women engaged in real housework. They also provided design ideals for new technologies that were still in early development stages and suggested practical uses for those without obvious scripts. As women established their expertise at explaining the concerns of private consumers for

9. See especially Packard's bestselling book *The Hidden Persuaders* (1957) and Lynes's equally popular *The Tastemakers* (originally published in 1949 and reprinted in 1953 and 1954).

corporate America, they also forged new career paths. Technology historian Ruth Oldenziel explains that by the 1930s and 1940s women involved with consumer rights movements regularly "entered business and industry in consumer relations, marketing, product development, testing, and demonstration. They acted as self-appointed mediators between consumers and producers while performing a balancing act between selling products and educating consumers now cast as women" ("Man the Maker" 140). Much like their counterparts in the suburban daycare center, these housewife consumer experts were active coproducers of both domestic knowledge and their own destinies.

Although organized consumer activism began as a middle-class endeavor, the general affluence of the postwar era enabled working-class women to impose their own taste on mass-produced objects as well. Cultural historian Shelley Nickles explains that although industrial designers of this period hoped to inculcate housewives with the "less is more" mentality of modernist aesthetic values, working-class women insisted that "more is better" and demanded refrigerators with sparkling chrome details and flatware with intricate Victorian rosebuds (583). These women were aided in their efforts by the editors of *True Story,* a working-class women's magazine that commissioned dozens of studies throughout the 1940s and 1950s to better understand the sociological situation of suburban blue-collar housewives. As editors interpreted these survey results to readers and advertisers, working-class housewives were not the unwitting victims of bad taste but, like their middle-class counterparts, active coproducers of "a new suburban culture where women were reformulating class relations as they shopped, worked, and raised families, forging new commonalities and new distinctions" (607). Rather than simply acceding to middle-class domestic ideals, these women insisted on their own cultural authority as stylists and tastemakers in the home.

Housewife Consumers in Postwar Women's Media Landscape Stories

Like other Americans, SF authors were both alarmed and fascinated by the massive expansion of a national consumer culture based on salesmanship and advertising in the decades following World War II. This interest led to the creation of a unique new science-fictional narrative form: the media landscape story. Set as they were in funhouse worlds "dominated by images of advertising and the popular arts" and run by "all powerful admen," media landscape stories "were never," according to SF scholars David Pringle and Peter Nicholls, "intended to be serious predictions of a possible tomorrow" (792, 793). Instead, postwar novels including Frederik Pohl and C. M. Kornbluth's *The Space Merchants* (1953) and Fritz Leiber's *The Green Millennium* (1953) "exaggerated aspects of the present in order to comment upon . . . the present itself" (794). In essence, media landscape stories were fictional instantiations of the hopes and fears voiced throughout postwar culture by public intellectuals and consumer advocates alike.

Although Leiber addressed the exploitation of feminine images by advertisers in his short piece "The Girl with the Hungry Eyes" (1949), most of the media landscape stories written by men in this period revolved around the exploits of admen and other male characters involved in global networks of production, sales, and distribution. In contrast, women writers told media landscape stories from the perspective of female consumers. These stories generally followed one of two distinct narrative trajectories. Much like Packard and Lynes, some authors imagined that consumer culture might articulate with new domestic technologies to create a surveillance state in which women are judged by their ability to align themselves and their families with the new social and moral orders of the media landscape. Other authors took inspiration from the work of consumer advocates and the promises of advertising itself to recast housewife consumers as critical and creative agents who used truly fantastic domestic technologies to either escape the home or reclaim it as a site of feminine community.

In "Captive Audience," Ann Warren Griffith imagines that new advertising technologies will erode the boundaries between public and private life in dangerous ways. First published in *The Magazine of Fantasy and Science Fiction* in 1953, Griffith's story unfolds in a future America where advertising and consumption have been taken to daring new extremes by the invention of the MV, or Master Ventriloquist, a "miraculous" technology that allows commercials to be "broadcast into thin air and picked up by the tiny discs embedded in the bottle or can or box or whatever wrapping contain[s] the product" in question (198). The impact of MV resonates throughout Griffith's world. Broadcast almost everywhere and timed so that specific kinds of commercials will coincide with specific kinds of personal activities, MV drastically erodes traditional distinctions between the public and private realms.

The new social order engendered by MV is accompanied by a new legal order, too: when concerned citizens take to wearing earplugs, the Supreme Court rules that such behavior is unconstitutional because it encourages an unhealthy and un-American "Restraint of Advertising" (200). The broad ramifications of this new social and legal order are made clear by Griffith's depictions of one woman and her family. "Captive Audience" follows two days in the life of Mavis Bascom, a suburban housewife who is happily married to Fred, a sales executive at the MV Corporation, and unhappily preparing for a visit from her grandmother, an MV protester who has recently been released from jail.

From the opening lines of her story, Griffith makes clear that advertising does indeed transform the family—but only in highly disruptive ways:

> Mavis Bascom read the letter hastily and passed it across the breakfast table to her husband, Fred, who read the first paragraph and exclaimed, "She'll be here this afternoon!" but neither Mavis nor the two children heard him because the cereal box was going "Boom! Boom!" so loudly. Presently it stopped and the bread said urgently, "One good slice deserves another! How about another slice all around, eh, Mother?" Mavis put four slices in the toaster, and then there was a brief silence. Fred wanted to discuss the impending visit. . . . [But the] cigarette package interrupted, "Yessir, time to light up a Chesterfield! Time to enjoy that first mild, satisfying smoke of the day." (197–98)

Rather than bringing the family closer together, in this passage consumer goods—and the incessant advertising that accompanies them—function as agents of divisive change, quite literally forcing Mavis and her family to realign their patterns of interaction in accordance with the demands of these goods themselves.

Although initially this accommodation of people to things might seem quite humorous, elsewhere Griffith insists that it devastates women's lives. The course of Mavis's day is rigidly guided by the MV, which "announced that now it was possible to polish her silverware to a higher, brighter polish than ever before; wondered if she weren't perhaps guilty of 'H.O.—Hair Odor,' and shouldn't perhaps wash her hair before her husband came home; told her at three different times to relax with a glass of cola; suggested that she had been neglecting her nails and might profit from a new coat of enamel; asked her to give a thought to her windows; and reminded her that her home permanent neutralizer would lose its wonderful effectiveness the longer it was kept. By early afternoon . . . she was exhausted" (203–4). Here, Griffith challenges the utopian promise of postwar advertising to liberate the housewife by providing her with new and better tools for the maintenance of home and self. Instead, she insists that new tools enslave women like Mavis, driving them from task to task—and pleasure to pleasure—in a merciless manner.

Griffith also suggests that new advertising techniques make it nearly impossible for women to work effectively as mothers. Although most of "Captive Audience" is told from Mavis's point of view, one crucial scene focuses on her husband, Fred. At almost the exact same time Mavis collapses, Fred learns that one of his pet sales campaigns, a colic medicine for babies, has taken a turn for the worse. Because the advertising chip in the medicine bottle sounds like a crying baby, mothers have been confusing it with the cries of their own children and administering overdoses. Fred's reaction to the news is rather telling: "Dopes! Why didn't they have enough sense to put the [medicine] bottle at the other end of the house from the baby, and then they could tell by the direction the sound came from whether it was a bona fide baby or an advertising baby!" (202). It is little wonder that housewives like Mavis end up sick and exhausted at the end of the day. As Fred's callous response indicates, it is not just that new goods and advertisements are dangerous in and of themselves. Rather, it is that the creators of those advertisements—men who do not understand the logistics of childcare—expect mothers to reorganize sensible patterns of domestic and maternal behavior so they conform to the new economic and social orders of the media landscape.

And indeed, it seems that women who do not conform to these new orders will be treated as criminals by society at large. This becomes particularly clear when Mavis's grandmother comes to visit. A woman who "had never adjusted to MV," Grandmother proudly wears earplugs in public and embraces the jail time she repeatedly earns for this activity because "it's really the only sensible place for me. I have friends there, and it's the quietest place I know" (199, 209). Not surprisingly, although Mavis loves her grandmother, she anticipates her arrival with mixed feelings: "Perhaps it was true, as Fred said, that Grandmother was a bad influence. It wasn't that she was *right*. Mavis believed in Fred, because he was her husband, and believed in the MV Corporation, because it was the largest corporation in the United States. Nevertheless, it upset her when Fred and Grandmother argued, as they almost always did when they were together" (202). Refusing to integrate into the media landscape makes Grandmother more than just a cranky old woman—it marks her as a dangerous criminal. According to the narrative logic of Griffith's story, Grandmother is a public enemy and a private nuisance, one whose very name threatens to further disrupt the fragile routines of the advertising-age family.

Ultimately, however, Griffith's media landscape is so pervasive that it easily contains the threat of Grandmother. Although Mavis and Fred initially fear her influence on their children, their worries are quickly laid to rest: the children are polite to Grandmother, but they are also visibly bored by her stories of pre-MV life, leading their parents to happily conclude that "Grandmother could talk herself cross-eyed but [the children] wouldn't fall for that stuff" (207). In a similar vein, Grandmother is visibly bored by the rhythms of Bascom family life, and after less than a day she decides to don her earplugs and return to jail.

The real triumph of the media landscape is not just that it can contain dissonant elements quickly and easily, but that it turns potential crises into triumphant opportunities. Soon after Grandmother leaves the Bascom house, Fred—ever the brilliant adman—comes to the conclusion that prison exacerbates rather than solves the problem posed by people like Grandmother because "people in jail . . . don't buy any products, so they don't get any MV. Can you imagine what this does to their buying habits?" (210) Inspired by this insight, Fred quickly formulates a plan to sell prisons a new form of MV that blends commercials and public service announcements to "really help prepare them for life on the outside again" (211).

Significantly, this plan does more than promise to contain public enemies such as Grandmother; it also contains the anxieties that these public enemies might engender in private citizens such as Mavis. Upon hearing Fred's idea, Mavis relaxes for the first time in the entire story, proudly telling herself that nobody but Fred "would think right off, first thing, not just of the money-making side, but of the welfare and betterment of all those poor prisoners!" (211) Hence Griffith shows how the new social order of the media landscape inevitably gives rise to a new moral order in which all subjects—be they upstanding citizens or public enemies, admen or housewives—are bound together as a new kind of captive audience.

While Griffith imagines a world where women are put in jail for refusing to adhere to new patterns of advertising and consumption, in "Woman's Work" (1956) Garen Drussaï explores how even the most perfect housewife consumer might become a prisoner in her own home. At first glance the two stories seem quite different. Griffith's housewife heroine is defined by her compliance with MV and other forms of broadcast advertising, but Drussaï's is defined by her ability to do high-tech battle with the legion of traveling salesmen who show up on her doorstep each day. Indeed, Drussaï's story revolves around a single, extended fight between her protagonist, Sheila, and one particularly aggressive salesman who tries to force his way through her front door. The salesman—who appears promptly at 4 a.m.—tries to blind Sheila with a sunshine bubble, distract her with laughing gas, and even literally sweep her off her feet with a portable pneumatic float. In retaliation, Drussaï's intrepid heroine soaks the salesman with an artificial rainstorm, cancels out his laughing gas with a weeping pill, and finally drives him away with a stink bomb. As she retreats into her home to await the next salesman, Sheila crows to herself that "the taste of triumph was sweet and delicious. . . . After all, this was woman's work" (106). As an avatar of the housewife consumer as domestic warrior, Drussaï's protagonist defends her home through careful consumption—which in this case includes learning how to resist indiscriminate spending.

But like any good satirist, Drussaï slowly undermines this ideal over the course of her story. First, she suggests that Sheila does not really control her work as a housewife consumer. Instead, she is often the victim of her own battle weapons. For example, when the salesman turns on his pneumatic float, readers learn that Sheila "activated the Stimulator. Then, instead of seeming to rest on a pneumatic couch, she felt the sharp ridges of a rocky ledge pressing into her flesh. She didn't care. The discomfort of it mattered little if she could win" (105). Much like her counterparts in scores of postwar advertisements for household cleaning products, Sheila is a technoscientific expert who uses domestic products to defend her home (in this case, against unwanted salesmen rather than bacteria). Unlike her advertising counterparts, however, she pays a physical cost for doing so.

Drussaï's heroine cannot escape this situation because—just as public intellectuals such as Packard and Lynes suggested—she is literally conditioned to it. Sheila spurs herself on through battle with the thought that she willingly sacrifices herself for the good of her family: "She thought of Hal lying there in the bedroom—trusting her to do her best. . . . Hal wouldn't forgive her if she let him down. They just couldn't afford to buy one more thing" (105). But Sheila becomes battle-ready only when she is subject to a series of "small electric shocks" from the alarm she wears on her wrist (104). Furthermore, when exhaustion leads her to doubt the value of her work, Drussaï's protagonist comforts herself by dreaming about those few hours in the late afternoon when "she could escape to the shops and shows that made up her day" (106). Thus Drussaï suggests that Sheila is much like one of Pavlov's infamous dogs or any other subject of the behavioral modification programs that were popular at mid-century: a creature trained to duty through a clearly defined system of punishments and rewards.

And as readers learn in the final passages of "Woman's Work," Sheila is indeed the object of pseudoscientific scrutiny by another salesman—her husband, Hal. When she finishes her battle with the traveling salesman and realizes it is already 4:30 a.m., Sheila tries to wake Hal to send him off on his own workday. But Hal does not rush to join his wife in the predawn chill:

> "Don't worry dear. I'm not loafing. I just got a terrific idea this morning. I'm going to let the other guys soften up my prospects at four and five in the morning." He stood looking down on her, a kind of dreamy, gloating look on his face.
>
> "Then, when I give my pitch at about six o'clock—just after they've been through a couple of displays—and just before they've had time for their morning coffee . . . Sheila, my love, they'll be pushovers! . . . Now you watch out Sheila. Watch out for those six o'clock pitches. Don't you fall for them!" (106)

And so it seems that all of Sheila's efforts are for naught: as she works to defend her family from traveling salesmen, she simply provides them with a steady flood of information about how they might perfect their own craft—and get a few extra hours of sleep while they are at it. In a world where housewife consumers literally sleep with their enemies, it seems quite likely that woman's work will never be done.

The media landscape story provided postwar women writers with a powerful new narrative form through which to contest the reduction of women's work to caretaking through consumption. But this story form also enabled a great deal of playful creativity. More specifically, SF authors seem to have been inspired by the surreal logic of advertising to tell tales about women who use truly fantastic household goods to transform their worlds and do battle with the agents of patriarchy. While such characters are not necessarily feminist ones per se, they are not mere reiterations of the conservative gender ideals so central to mid-century thinking, either. Instead, authors such as Margaret St. Clair and Kit Reed treat their protagonists much like those housewives who joined consumer advocacy groups: as active coproducers of their own destinies.

While postwar advertisements such as General Motors's *Design for Dreaming* assured women that they could use new kitchen technologies to infuse their homes with romance and excitement, in "New Ritual" (1953) St. Clair proposes that women might use such technologies to escape from the home into the real site of romance and action: the advertisement itself.[10] "New Ritual" follows the adventures of Marie Bates, an overworked farmwife who chafes at the restraints of living on an old-fashioned apricot farm with her equally old-fashioned husband, Henry, a simple man whose only passion is studying the rituals of his men's lodge. In response, Marie decides to create her own ritual by purchasing one of the miracles of modern home technology: the deep freezer. Spurred on by promises that it will eliminate "messy kitchens [and] scalded fingers" while comforting the housewife with its "soothing, companionable noises" (173, 172), Marie uses her new machine to enact a series of changes that eventually allow her to exchange the drab farm world of the past for a shiny new suburban future. In its broadest dimensions, then, "New Ritual" follows the narrative logic of mid-century advertisement, mapping the personal and social transformation of an average housewife through strategic consumption.

From almost the very beginning of her story, however, St. Clair challenges advertising's promise that new domestic technologies will radically change women's domestic work or their romantic lives. In "New Ritual" the high-tech deep freezer is a fantastic object that literally transmutes the products of Marie's labor, but the results are not at all what she expects. For example, while freezing the seemingly endless supply of apricots that Henry harvests from the farm, Marie idly wishes that she had some blueberries instead because "when they were first married, years ago, [Henry] said that his mother had baked wonderful blueberry pies. That was quite a lot of talk on one subject, for Henry" (160). Much to her surprise, when she next opens the freezer, blueberries have mysteriously replaced the apricots. Rather than question her luck, Marie decides to simply make her pies. But when Henry gobbles them down without comment, Marie's special night ends much like all her others—with Henry in silence and Marie herself in tears as she clears away the remnants of dinner. As Marie

---

10. "New Ritual" first appeared in *The Magazine of Fantasy and Science Fiction* under St. Clair's regular pen name, Idris Seabright.

quickly learns, she cannot simply transform objects and expect people to follow.

Accordingly, St. Clair's protagonist decides to up the ante and transform her own appearance. Soon after the blueberry pie incident, Marie's sister-in-law Bertha chides her for letting go of her looks, reminding Marie that Henry "always liked pretty things" (162). Without thinking twice, Marie once again turns to her new freezer for help, sneaking out of bed in the middle of the night to put her old Sunday clothes in its storage compartment. Sure enough, by morning her rayon church dress has been mysteriously replaced by a "printed black and pink and gray silk dress" that is the height of modern, middle-class good taste (177). Despite feeling "sick" and "half guilty" about her actions, Marie quickly dons the new dress and plans her romantic assault on Henry (178). Seduced as she is by the promise of transformation attending new domestic technologies like her deep freezer, Marie seems to have completely forgotten the disastrous results of her previous experience with this kind of transformation. Indeed, even the sense of physical dis-ease that attends her latest endeavor cannot dissuade her from her intended goals.

Again, however, the results of this transformation vary drastically from what advertising promises the housewife consumer. Just as Marie hopes, Henry is overwhelmed with desire when he sees his wife in her pretty new clothes, showering her with compliments and kisses. Unfortunately, Marie is also overwhelmed by the moment—but not with reciprocal desire. Rather, when she realizes that Henry hasn't even bothered to put in his dentures that day, Marie is gripped by "an almost apocalyptic horror" that immediately shatters her dreams of romance (179). Once again, the evening threatens to end with Marie in tears. As such, it might well seem to St. Clair's readers that the only truly new ritual of the advertising age is the systematic decimation of women's expectations in both the domestic and romantic spheres.

Eventually Marie realizes that the only way to gain control over her life is to transform Henry himself. Still reeling from the horror of his gummy kisses, Marie lures her husband into the kitchen and pushes him into the freezer before climbing in herself. When Bertha visits the farm several days later, the couple have vanished, leaving behind everything including their broken freezer. The only clue that Bertha ever receives regarding the Bates's disappearance comes in the form of a mysterious postcard: "It was a glossy photograph of a man and woman on skis against a winter background and, except that the man was taller and both he and the woman were much younger and better-looking than the missing couple, the pair in the picture bore a remarkable resemblance to Marie and Henry Bates. Neither of them looked a day over thirty. They wore expensive ski clothing and both of them were wreathed in smiles. The postmark on the card was Sun Valley, Idaho. . . . There was no message on the card's back" (180–81). Thus, Marie finally achieves the romance and excitement promised by postwar advertising. But she does not do so by using new domestic technologies to transform the home. Instead, she uses those technologies to escape into the dreamworld of the media landscape itself.

While St. Clair explores how women might use fantastic technologies to avoid domestic entrapment, in "Cynosure" (1964) Kit Reed imagines that women might use such technologies to reclaim the home as a site of feminine community and empowerment. In doing so, she playfully invokes—and seriously revises—the narrative logic of postwar advertisements for high-tech cleaning products that promised to transform helpless housewives into unstoppable domestic warriors. Set in a world much like postwar suburban America, Reed's story revolves around Norma Thayer, a recently divorced young mother who has just moved into a new house and anxiously awaits the approval of her new community: "Norma knew, just as well as anybody on the block, that a house was still a house without a Daddy, and things might even run smoother in the long run without all those cigarette butts and dirty pyjamas to pick up, but she was something of a pioneer, because she was the first in the neighborhood to actually prove it. . . . If all went well, [her neighbors] would look at the sectional couch and the rug of salt-and-pepper tweed (backed with rubber foam) and see that Daddy or no, Norma was just as good as any of the housewives in the magazines, and that her dishtowels were just as clean as any in the neighborhood" (96). For all her brave talk of pioneering, Norma is well aware that a woman without a man is morally suspect in galactic suburbia. Therefore, she hopes to impress her new neighbors by proving her social worth as a picture-perfect housewife instead.

Much like St. Clair's protagonist, however, Norma quickly learns that this ideal is nearly impossible to achieve in the real world. In this case, the problem is not masculine indifference but feminine opprobrium. To participate in the social life of her new community, Reed's protagonist must first pass muster with Clarice Brainerd, unofficial leader of the neighborhood women. Clarice herself is a walking, talking advertisement, proudly flaunting the Sweetheart pin she receives for collecting "labels from the Right Kind of Margarine," while harshly criticizing Norma for her "musty rooms" and "stains that even bleach can't reach" (97). Terrified that Clarice will prevent her from ever becoming part of the community, Norma swallows her pride and obediently purchases the myriad of scouring products that her new mentor recommends. To become the perfect housewife, Norma must not just consume and clean indiscriminately; she must consume and clean in accordance with socially sanctioned standards.

When Clarice proves to be unimpressed with Norma's efforts, Reed's housewife heroine resorts to extreme measures—in this case, by responding to an advertisement that promises to "end household drudgery" and make Norma's house "the cynosure of the neighborhood" (101). Although Norma has no idea what "cynosure" means, she is so moved by the ad's "picture of a spotless and shining lady, sitting in the middle of a spotless and shining living room" that she immediately drains her bank account to purchase the mystery product (101). And when the mystery product turns out to be a "small, lavender enamel-covered machine" that can immobilize and reanimate any living object, Norma rejoices to herself that "expensive or not, it was worth it. She had to admit that none of her household cleaners worked as fast" (101). With the acquisition of this amazing new cleaning technology, it seems that Norma is close to achieving her dream of becoming the housewife she sees in the advertisement.

Accordingly, Norma transforms her house into an advertisement by using the lavender machine to immobilize her pets and her daughter, Polly Ann. Any slight twinge of guilt Norma might feel over freezing her family quickly dissolves when she sees the result of her labor: "They were all arranged very artistically in the living room, the dog and the cat curled next to the sofa, Polly Ann looking just as pretty as life in her maroon velvet dress with the organdy pinafore. Her eyes were a little glassy and her legs did stick out at an unnatural angle, but Norma had thrown an afghan over one end of the couch, where she was sitting, and thought the effect, in the long run, was just as good as anything she'd ever seen on a television commercial, and almost as pretty as some of the pictures she had seen in magazines" (103). Like any other good cleaning product, Norma's fantastic machine gets at the real source of mess in the home. In Reed's world, however, the enemy is not dust or germs but the family itself. Just as her heroine suspects from the start of this story, housewifery is much easier when there is no one to clean up after but the housewife herself.

Eventually Norma finds herself betrayed by the false promises of advertising. When Clarice first sees Norma's frozen family she is so taken with this innovative solution to the problem of household messiness that she finally invites Norma to join the neighborhood coffee circle. However, she immediately rescinds the invitation when she discovers Norma's cake has "that greasy feel" every housewife dreads (105). Faintly protesting that "the commercial *promised*" otherwise, Norma snaps and turns the lavender machine on Clarice herself (105). Driven mad by the impossible standards instilled in her and every other woman living in this particular media landscape, Reed's protagonist ends up destroying what it is she believes she wants most.

However, it is precisely this act of destruction that enables Reed's protagonist to reclaim her mind and her home:

> First [Norma] propped Mrs. Brainerd up in a corner, where she would be uncomfortable. Then she reversed the nozzle action and brought Polly Ann and Puff and Ambrose back to mobility. Then she . . . let Puff rub cat hairs on the furniture and she sent Polly Ann into the back yard for some mud. Ambrose, released, Did It at Mrs. Brainerd's feet.
>
> "So glad you could come, Clarice," Norma said, gratified by the look of horror in Mrs. Brainerd's trapped and frozen face. Then, turning to Polly Ann's laden pinafore, she reached for a handful of mud. (105–6)

Surrounded by the chaos of pets and children, Norma finally rejects identification with Clarice and, by extension, the social and moral order of the media landscape Clarice represents. Instead, she embraces the playfulness of her daughter and, it seems, a more creative approach to homemaking as a whole. Thus Reed concludes her story by suggesting that women do not need to defend their homes against dirt or germs, but against the impossible ideals of advertising itself.

Conclusion: Alienated from the Labor of Love

In this chapter I have shown how women SF writers critically engaged the new understandings and representations of domestic labor that emerged after World War II. Although postwar celebrations of the home and women's work within it might strike contemporary readers as surprisingly Victorian, they were very much responses to the modern world. While politicians invoked the specter of communism to make sense of homemakers as domestic cold warriors whose caretaking and consumer activities were fundamental expressions of American values, psychologists naturalized these activities by invoking the Freudian notion of biology as destiny, especially as it was codified in the rhetoric of the feminine mystique. These new ideas about women's work in the home were reiterated throughout popular culture and were particularly apparent in visual media, including television, film, and print advertising, all of which assured women that homemaking could be an exciting and romantic adventure with the help of the right household product or technology.

Like their male counterparts, postwar women generally assumed that domestic labor was and would continue to be central to women's lives. But they contested the meaning and value of that labor in a number of ways. In their capacity as caretakers, suburban housewives literally reorganized their homes to refuse their roles as cold war surveillance officers and better foster individual privacy and self-expression. They also created cooperative daycare centers to fulfill their desire for feminine community and organized political engagement. As consumers, homemakers used their domestic expertise to form consumer advocacy groups and exert aesthetic authority over industrial designers and other cultural tastemakers. Taken together, such activities demonstrate the diverse ways that women adapted new gender ideals to their individual and collective needs.

As literary critics Catherine Wiley and Fiona Barnes explain, the tension between cultural representations and personal experiences of homemaking is a central theme not just in contemporary women's lives but in their literature as well. As such, writing about home has become an important way for women authors to participate in, contribute to, and even redefine conventionally masculine literary realms. This is certainly true of those postwar women writers who used SF to explore new domestic ideals, especially in relation to science and technology. Much like their counterparts in the suburban home and the daycare center, SF authors Carol Emshwiller, April Smith, Rosel George Brown, and Zenna Henderson sought to reveal the debilitating effects of the feminine mystique on women's work as caretakers and to imagine how women might reclaim that work as a creative and communal activity. They did so by invoking and revising one of SF's oldest tropes: the female alien other. In contrast to those male authors who produced patriarchal fantasies of strong alien women who nobly sacrifice their convictions and their lives for the love of human men, postwar women authors explored how the figure of the female alien might be used as a metaphor for human women's estrangement from patriarchal society and as a symbol for the progressive new communities that women might create when they reach out to one another across the boundaries of family and species.

Women authors also used one of SF's newest narrative forms, the media landscape story, to rethink women's work as consumers. While men including Frederik Pohl, C. M. Kornbluth, and Fritz Leiber generally told stories about media-saturated futures that satirized postwar America from the perspective of male characters involved in advertising and sales, women such as Ann Warren Griffith, Garen Drussaï, Margaret St. Clair, and Kit Reed told such tales from the perspective of housewife consumers. While some of these stories reiterated the concerns of mid-century public intellectuals who treated housewives as victims of capitalist tastemaking, others drew inspiration from the surrealism of advertising itself to imagine what women might do if they could use everyday household products to truly transform their worlds. Although such stories are not feminist ones per se, they cast women as coproducers of their own destinies who use domestic goods and technologies to either escape the home or reclaim it as a source of feminine creativity.

Taken together, the range of SF stories that postwar women wrote about homemaking illustrate both the centrality of domestic labor to modern American women's lives as well as the diverse ways that they understood, engaged in, and represented that labor. But was this the extent of what women had to say about life in galactic suburbia? As I will demonstrate in the next chapter, it most certainly was not. Instead, SF authors often used stories about the future of marriage and motherhood to explore the two of the most pressing political issues of the day: nuclear weapons and civil rights.

CHAPTER THREE

ACTIVISTS

THIS CHAPTER examines how postwar women writers used SF to interrogate some of the most pressing political issues of the cold war. With its emphasis on other worlds and other times, SF was, as Judith Merril recollects, "virtually the only vehicle[s] of political dissent" available to authors interested in commenting on the cultural conservatism of the day ("What Do You Mean" 74). Women's SF was particularly well suited to this task because stories about galactic suburbia seemed to be thoroughly in line with the mid-century glorification of femininity and motherhood. This does not mean, however, that such stories necessarily celebrated postwar culture. Rather, this new mode of SF provided many authors with a narrative space where dearly held beliefs about the sanctity of hearth and home could be invoked to critically assess the emergent scientific and social arrangements of mid-century America as a whole.

As such, women writing SF after World War II both anticipated and extended their activist counterparts' progressive political practices. Conventional wisdom has it that feminism all but vanished during the cold war. Over the past two decades, however, feminist historians have argued for a more nuanced account of women's activities in the McCarthy era.[1] Although mid-century women generally did not identify themselves as feminists, they did contribute their energies to those causes that seemed most pressing at the time, most notably, the reconstruction of prewar peace organizations and the creation of major civil rights coalitions. Activists made sense of their demands for social change by representing themselves in historically specific and culturally charged ways. Rather than resisting the postwar glorification of motherhood and domesticity, progressive women invoked these ideas in the service of what I call domestic patriotism, presenting themselves as private citizens reluctantly moved to public action out of concern for the futures of their children.

Domestic patriotism embodies what scholars often describe as a feminine philosophy of social change. In the past two decades, feminist psychologists have shown that women tend to value connectedness over rugged individualism, communication over stoic silence, cooperation over competition, and mercy over justice. According to Carol Gilligan, these values lead women to prefer moral and ethical systems centered on "obligations to myself and my family and people in general" rather than ones that emphasize separateness and noninterference with the rights of others (21).[2] In the postwar era, such preferences also led progressive women to expand their repertoire of political strategies. As feminist historian Susan Lynn notes, "women in the postwar coalition continued to rely on older voluntary groups to achieve change through education, publicity, and lobbying." At the same time, they increasingly "employed a female ethic specifically to build bridges" across conventional racial, political, and sometimes even economic lines (*Progressive Women* 3–4). Because these new networks of support valorized personal relations, they strongly anticipated one of the central tenets of second-wave feminism as it emerged in the 1960s: that the personal is always already political.

1. See, for instance, Dee Garrison, "'Our Skirts Gave Them Courage': The Civil Defense Protest Movement in New York City, 1955–1961"; Harriet Hyman Alonso, "Mayhem and Moderation: Women Peace Activists During the McCarthy Era"; Eugenia Kaledin, *Mothers and More: American Women in the 1950s;* Susan Lynn, *Progressive Women in Conservative Times: Racial Justice, Peace, and Feminism, 1945 to the 1960s;* and Amy Swerdlow, *Women Strike for Peace: Traditional Motherhood and Radical Politics in the 1960s.*

2. For other groundbreaking discussions of women's developmental and learning patterns, see Nancy Chodorow, *The Reproduction of Mothering: Psychoanalysis and the Sociology of Gender,* and Mary Field Belenky et al., *Women's Ways of Knowing: The Development of Self, Voice, and Mind.*

In the following pages I explore how this ethic informed the domestic patriotism of postwar women's SF as well, especially as authors used the genre to protest nuclear weapons and advocate the cause of civil rights.[3] In the first section of this chapter I briefly review how peace activists presented themselves as mothers united by their common concerns for children living in the shadow of the mushroom cloud—concerns that were, they insisted, comparable to those articulated by respected scientists (and fellow peace activists) Linus Pauling and Albert Einstein. I then examine how similar sentiments were expressed in mid-century women's SF, focusing on stories by Judith Merril, Virginia Cross, Carol Emshwiller, and Mary Armock. The majority of these stories work to raise the consciousness of readers by extrapolating from scientific and activist literature and imagining dystopic futures where nuclear weapons and the cultural logic of nuclear defense destroy the nuclear family, pitting parents against children and husbands against wives in tragic but inevitable ways. At the same time, at least one such story—Merril's *Shadow on the Hearth* (1950)—suggests that women might prevent these scenarios from happening by making alliances with likeminded women and scientists in antiwar and antinuclear activism.

In the second half of this chapter I explore women's civil rights activism in tandem with women's SF stories about race relations. Throughout the postwar period, women drew upon their expertise at managing families and facilitating interpersonal communication in their work as "bridge leaders" for the civil rights movement. In this capacity they organized local political actions, translated the goals of movement leaders to grassroots coalitions, and facilitated private meetings between blacks and whites to ensure the smooth enactment of civil rights legislation in everyday life. Meanwhile, SF authors

3. Of course, feminist SF scholars have already documented a similar ethic in women's utopian and science fiction written during historical periods marked by intense feminist activity. Carol Farley Kessler, Marleen S. Barr, and Robin Roberts all construct histories of feminist speculative fiction that loosely connect utopian writing with first-wave feminism and feminist SF with second- and third-wave feminisms. For the most part, however, they are silent on the issue of women's SF between the establishment of universal suffrage in 1920 and the revival of feminism in the 1960s. Significantly, even Jane L. Donawerth, who writes extensively about women's pulp SF in the 1920s and 1930s, allies this SF with the feminist politics of preceding decades rather than, say, the woman-centered but ultimately nonfeminist politics of "municipal housekeeping" espoused by socialist and New Deal women at this time. For further discussion, see Carol Farley Kessler, *Daring to Dream: Utopian Fiction by United States Women Before 1950;* Marleen S. Barr, *Lost in Space: Probing Feminist Science Fiction and Beyond;* Robin Roberts, *A New Species: Gender and Science in Science Fiction;* and Jane L. Donawerth, "Science Fiction by Women in the Early Pulps, 1926–1930."

including Margaret St. Clair, Kay Rogers, Cornelia Jessey, and Mildred Clingerman merged one of the oldest SF story types, the encounter with the alien other, with one of American literature's newest subgenres, the racial conversion narrative, to espouse the cause of civil rights to their readers. Like their counterparts in the political sphere, these authors embraced a bridge-building philosophy, insisting that communication between individual representatives of different races was essential to the well-being of both—and that the absence or failure of such communication might mean the end of both individual families and humanity as a whole.

Maternalist Politics and Postwar Peace Activism

The onset of the nuclear arms race after World War II sparked heated debates over what it meant to be a patriotic American citizen. Broadly speaking, the participants in these debates identified with one of two positions. Those who saw nuclear war as inevitable advocated a military model of civil defense in which every citizen would be a self-reliant soldier working to maintain social and political order. Those who thought war was *not* inevitable joined various peace organizations, becoming conscientious objectors to all preparations for World War III.

Like their more fatalistic counterparts, peace activists believed that education was key to nuclear-age citizenship. However, they dismissed the military model of citizenship as too prone to fascist interpretation and replaced it with a scientific one based on free inquiry and rational skepticism. Invoking the growing cultural fascination with technological expertise, activists allied themselves with outspoken scientists, including Albert Einstein, who wrote that "there is no defense against atomic bombs, and none is to be expected. Preparedness against atomic warfare is futile and, if attempted, will ruin the structure of the social order" (qtd. in Mechling and Mechling 140). Thus, peace activists imagined that Americans who were educated in the scientific principles of nuclear technologies would naturally conclude that the only way to prepare for atomic war was to ensure it never happened in the first place.

Since participants on both sides of this debate assumed that there were no civilians in the nuclear age, it is not surprising that they attempted to recruit the newest of soldiers—women—to their causes by suggesting strong connections between patriotism and domesticity. After World War II, women were asked by politicians and employers alike to give up their wartime jobs for homecoming male veterans. These requests were couched in the language of civic duty: just as women had been obliged to exchange the private sphere for its public counterpart during the war, now they were obliged to focus their energies on hearth and home.[4] Although women did not always take this advice to heart, rhetorical equations between women's domestic identities as wives and mothers and their national identities as civic-minded Americans became central to the public imagination for the next two decades.

These equations were especially central to advocates of the military model of cold war citizenship. Elaine Tyler May argues that the expert discourses of this period called on women to combine their natural feminine instincts with "professionalized skills to meet the challenges of the modern era" (*Homeward Bound* 102). These challenges included the creeping threat of communism and the associated possibility of nuclear war. For instance, the atomic-age wife was encouraged to express a sexual enthusiasm for her husband that would keep him safe at home and therefore safe from association with unsavory characters. Spurred on by their mutual conjugal satisfaction, women and men would produce more children and provide them with the wholesome family environment necessary to prevent juvenile delinquency and ensure the future of America.

The cold war homemaker was supposed to cultivate her domestic instincts in the name of civil defense as well. In its extensively publicized "Grandma's Pantry" campaign, the Federal Civil Defense Administration encouraged women to be "just as self-sufficient as Grandma was" (May, *Homeward Bound* 105). In addition to performing their regular household duties, American women were encouraged to line their shelves with canned goods and bottled water and to brush up on their nursing skills so they would be prepared for an atomic attack. And so the feminine impulse to nurture others was imagined to be—in combination with modern goods and techniques—the family's first line of defense in the event of a nuclear emergency.[5]

---

4. For further discussion, see Eugenia Kaledin's preface to *Mothers and More: American Women in the 1950s*; chapter 3 of Elaine Tyler May's *Homeward Bound: American Families in the Cold War*; chapter 5 of Annegret Ogden's *The Great American Housewife: From Helpmate to Wage Earner, 1776–1986*; and chapter 2 of Leila J. Rupp and Verta Taylor's *Survival in the Doldrums: The American Women's Rights Movement, 1945 to the 1960s*.

5. For further discussion of how civil defense was naturalized in relation to mid-century ideals of suburban domesticity, see Mechling and Mechling's "The Campaign for

Mid-century peace organizations also invoked specific equations between patriotism and domesticity. Echoing the maternalist politics of their eighteenth- and nineteenth-century predecessors, twentieth-century social activists urged women to join the antinuclear effort because their domestic management skills and moral integrity made them ideal candidates for "municipal housekeeping" (Lynn, "Gender and Progressive Politics" 106). For example, in the early 1950s the Women's International League for Peace and Freedom (WILPF) recruited new members with radio commercials featuring earnest housewives urging their peers to join the peace movement so that "you and I—and all the mothers in the world—can go to sleep without thinking about the terrors of the Atomic Bomb or the H-Bomb" (qtd. in Alonso 131). In 1951 the Los Angeles branch of American Women for Peace began organizing Mother's Day marches to protest the proliferation of nuclear arms (Alonso 147). Much like their civil defense counterparts, peace activists explicitly equated motherhood with civic duty. According to the logic of the latter, however, it was women's civic duty to protest against—rather than acquiesce to—the cold war social and moral order.[6]

Women who saw themselves as political centrists distinct from the left-leaning "old pros" of peace activism were especially attracted to the techniques of maternalist politics. Dee Garrison chronicles the story of Janice Smith and Mary Sharmat, two New York housewives who assumed leadership of the New York City civil defense protest movement in the early 1960s. Intent on mobilizing "nonradical persons" as well as "old pros," Smith and Sharmat combined their considerable personal energies with the political resources of the Catholic Workers and War Resisters League (WRL) to stage what were estimated to be the two largest nonviolent civil defense protests of the era. The success of these protests derived largely from the women's decision to appeal to the public with carefully managed images of protective motherhood: "They made detailed plans to surround themselves with children and toys during the Operation Alert protest, arranging for trucks to bring the heaviest items to the park before the drill began. Plans were made to pass out extra babies and toys to single male activists who would practice civil disobedience alongside the young

---

Civil Defense and the Struggle to Naturalize the Bomb."

6. As Sara Ruddick points out, these strategies are still central to women's peace activism around the world today—most notably, perhaps, in Argentinean and Chilean women's resistance to the military regimes of their respective countries. For further discussion, see chapter 9 of Ruddick's book *Maternal Thinking: Toward a Politics of Peace.*

mothers. All guessed correctly that police would not want to take parents, complete with children, playpens, trikes, and assorted childhood paraphernalia, into custody" (Garrison 215). By bringing children and other accoutrements of domesticity into City Hall Park, Smith and Sharmat created a public space where private citizens could express dissent from the status quo of civil defense.[7]

Mid-century women's peace organizations legitimized such dissent by aligning maternal instinct with scientific knowledge. As early as 1952, WRL distributed pamphlets quoting Albert Einstein about the futility of preparing for a postholocaust future. Later, WRL associates Smith and Sharmat reiterated this sentiment when they proposed that civil defense drills were pointless because "in the event of a nuclear war most of New York City would be incinerated" (Alonso 210). Women Strike for Peace (WSP) made even more direct connections between mothers and scientists. As historian Amy Swerdlow notes, WSP leaders "refused to speak in terms of 'capitalism,' 'imperialism,' 'containment,' 'deterrence,' or even of 'truth to power' because they believed that ideological language obliterated the felt experience of all mothers." They were, however, "given to paraphrasing Albert Einstein's statement that the atom bomb had changed everything but the way we think" (236–37). By framing their concerns in relation to scientific discourse, activists positioned themselves as something other than overwrought women or political radicals. Instead, they emerged as rational beings reluctantly driven to public action by an understanding of nuclear weapons similar to that of scientific experts.

Peace activists also wove together the languages of maternal concern and scientific expertise in their political activities. In early 1962 WSP launched a campaign to enlighten Americans about how dairy products could be contaminated by radioactive fallout from nuclear testing. One prong of the campaign involved the circulation of a "Dear Neighbor" letter encouraging women to boycott dairy delivery services in times of nuclear testing because uncontaminated milk "is of vital health to our children" (Swerdlow 84). The letter assured women that this call to boycott was based on information that WSP had gathered from the Atomic Energy Commission, the U.S. Public Health Service, and the Federal Radiation Council. Thus, WSP activists allied them-

---

7. As Amy Swerdlow argues, these are essentially the same tactics that antiwar groups like Women Strike for Peace (WSP) used so spectacularly in the 1960s. Indeed, Mary Sharmat went on to work closely with WSP for several years after she and Smith staged their New York protests. For more detail, see Swerdlow's *Women Strike for Peace: Traditional Motherhood and Radical Politics in the 1960s.*

selves not just with independent scientists like Einstein but also with institutions established and sanctioned by the U.S. government itself.

Maternalist Politics and Postwar Women's Nuclear Holocaust Narratives

City streets and courtrooms were not the only places where mid-century Americans explored the promises and perils of the dawning atomic age. SF authors had been telling stories about nuclear sciences and technologies long before the advent of World War II; afterward, such authors seemed to be "prophets proven right by the course of events" (Berger 143). For example, in 1944 U.S. security agents debriefed *Astounding Science-Fiction* editor John Campbell for publishing a story with descriptions of a nuclear bomb remarkably similar to the one that was under construction at Los Alamos. After the war ended, government interest in SF was replaced by corporate interest, and several of Campbell's other writers began second careers as popular science writers and industrial consultants.

Even mainstream magazines including *Collier's* and *The Saturday Evening Post* embraced the SF mindset, inviting authors Robert Heinlein and Ray Bradbury to write for them. In 1951 *Collier's* even published a special issue called "Preview of the War We Do Not Want: Russia's Defeat and Occupation, 1952–1960." Although none of the special issue authors (who included Edward R. Murrow, Robert E. Sherwood, and Senator Margaret Chase Smith) had any formal affiliations with SF, the title suggests how indebted the *Collier's* editors were to future-oriented, speculative thinking. The opening editorial column insisted that this special issue was "no careless fantasy or easy invention" but rather a carefully constructed "hypothetical case" built by knowledgeable authors who "proceeded from the factual basis of the world situation today to a logical analysis of what may come" ("Preview" 17). And so the science-fictional spirit of logical extrapolation seemed to be one with the social and political climate of the times.

Women were also on the front lines of nuclear war storytelling. Authors working in the new mode of women's SF that emerged after World War II produced highly innovative and memorable variations on this kind of storytelling by combining two distinct twentieth-century literary traditions: the nuclear holocaust narrative and feminist anti-war writing. As Edward James notes, the nuclear holocaust narrative was one of the most pervasive story types to emerge in postwar SF. Although some authors used this narrative as a kind of "cleansing exercise" to imagine what America could become if certain undesirable elements were conveniently eliminated, most authors took a more thoughtful approach, using nuclear holocaust stories to explore "how societies decline into tribalism or barbarism . . . or develop from barbarism to civilization" (90).

In the hands of women SF authors, nuclear holocaust stories usually showed readers how societies declined into barbarism, especially for women and their families.[8] Such stories often were told from the perspective of what Sara Ruddick calls the *mater dolorosa* or "mother of sorrows," a character type that figures prominently in twentieth-century women's antiwar literature. Typically, the *mater dolorosa* survives war only to find herself faced with a series of dreadful tasks that include rebuilding destroyed homes, tending the wounded, and burying the dead (142). Even more importantly, this figure "reveals a contradiction between mothering and war. Mothering begins in birth and promises life; military thinking justifies organized, deliberate deaths. . . . Mothers protect children who are at risk; the military risks the children mothers protect" (148). As such, the *mater dolorosa* provides authors with an ideal way to explore the contradictory social and moral orders that arise during times of war.

An important part of women's writing about World Wars I and II, the *mater dolorosa* also lent herself quite handily to speculative fictions about World War III. Women SF authors made their appeals to readers by describing in sometimes grisly detail the nightmare fates of forced marriage, reproductive mutation, and familial destruction that awaited those women who managed to survive the actual event of nuclear war. Writ large upon the postnuclear future, such tales both anticipated and extended the progressive sensibilities of the mid-century peace movement. More specifically, stories about the postholocaust *mater dolorosa* enabled women writers to make concrete those "terrors of the Atomic Bomb" that could only be hinted at in peace activist literature.

Postholocaust domestic tragedy is perhaps most memorably illustrated in Judith Merril's short story "That Only a Mother." Published

8. While the impact of nuclear war on the nuclear family was a subject of interest for many women SF authors, it was by no means the only one. Like their male counterparts, such authors also used nuclear holocaust narratives to critique the repression of individualism and progressivism in cold war America. For an excellent discussion of the different ways postwar women approached this SF story type, see Dianne Newell and Victoria Lamont's "Rugged Domesticity: Frontier Mythology in Post-Armageddon Science Fiction by Women."

in 1948, Merril's often-anthologized tale brings together two of the primary fears of the early atomic age: the possibility of mutation from radioactive materials and the probability that an international nuclear war would effectively destroy all humanity (Trachtenberg 355). Set in a near future where exposure to radiation from an ongoing nuclear war has produced a generation of radically mutated children, Merril's tale depicts an insane world populated by sorrowing mothers who struggle to protect their children against fathers who commit infanticide, juries who acquit the men of any wrongdoing, and journalists who report the whole process with tacit approval (346–47, 351). Hence, Merril insists that nuclear war might well lead to the death of all humanity, but in a far more horrifying way than even the most pessimistic scientist might have predicted. In Merril's world, radioactive fallout from nuclear war clearly produces physically mutated children. But even more significantly, it produces a kind of psychological mutation in men as well, leading to a dreadful new mode of fatherhood based on revulsion and murder rather than love and protection—a fatherhood that threatens to wipe out humanity even more effectively than the atomic bomb.

Although such events are initially presented as part of a terrible new moral and social order located specifically in postwar Japan, the land of the enemy other, Merril ultimately suggests that this new world order—much like radioactivity—has no respect for national borders. The majority of "That Only a Mother" follows the story of Margaret and Hank, an American couple that give birth to Henrietta, a "flower-faced child" with stunning intelligence but a limbless body (349). Margaret responds to her child's deformity by retreating into insanity and insisting that "*my baby's fine. Precocious, but normal*" (345, 351; original italics), while Hank—equally horrified by both his child and Margaret's response to her—seems destined to repeat the insanity of his Japanese counterparts as he prepares to kill his child at the close of the story. In this respect, Merril's story effectively anticipates the kind of warning that peace groups like WILPF would issue in the 1950s: that "a bomb doesn't care in the least whether you are wearing a soldier's uniform or a housewife's apron" (qtd. in Alonso 130).

Merril further extends the maternalist logic of mid-century peace activism by using her *mater dolorosa* to demonstrate how motherhood might be reshaped by the exigencies of nuclear war. Initially readers might assume that the tragedy of Merril's tale is Margaret's insanity. Early in the story Margaret tries to alleviate her worries about her unborn child by visiting a psychologist who tells her that she is "probably the unstable type"; later, she dismisses news reports about genetic mutation by telling herself over and over that *"my baby's fine. Precocious, but normal"* (345, 351). When the story shifts to Hank's perspective in the final passages, it seems that Margaret has been deluding herself about Henrietta all along and that the baby is—as the title of the story suggests—a child "that only a mother" could love.

Of course, if Margaret is insane, Merril makes clear that she has been driven to this state by the madness of her entire society. Throughout her story Merril links descriptions of Margaret's mental condition with newspaper reports of wartime atrocity. Margaret's initial depiction of herself as "the unstable type" is juxtaposed with the tales of American juries who refuse to prosecute fathers for infanticide; later, her frantic refrain concerning Henrietta's normalcy is interspersed with increasingly grim facts concerning the rate of genetic mutation in newborns from Hiroshima and Nagasaki—a litany that ends with the observation that "only two or three percent of those guilty of infanticide are being captured and punished in Japan today" (351). Therefore, the chain reaction of the atom bomb extends even further than we might already think: the insanity of nuclear war leads to an insane mode of fatherhood based on militaristic thinking about "organized, deliberate death" rather than love and protection. This, in turn, leads to a literal insanity "that only a mother" can fully experience or understand.

The story of Merril's *mater dolorosa* illustrates how the conflict between mothering and militarism provokes a final mutation, tragically altering the relations among married couples. In theory, modern war is waged between national and ideological enemies. In Merril's story, however, war is ultimately waged between men and women. Fathers from all nations "do it" to their mutant children; little wonder that when Hank first comes home Margaret can only perceive him as "a khaki uniform" topped off by "a stranger's pale face." Although Margaret tries to reassert normal relations with Hank by grasping his hand and telling herself that, "for the moment that was enough," her subsequent actions indicate otherwise (351). Instead, her passive attempts to distract Hank from the unsettling reality of Henrietta's body suggest that, for Margaret at least, the war has just begun.

Framed as this homecoming scene is by descriptions of khaki uniforms and strangers' faces, one cannot help but read it as a narrative of invasion and occupation. In this case, Merril's heroine emerges a desperate woman protecting her child against the real enemy: her husband. As such, "That Only a Mother" challenges dominant cold war assumptions about nuclear weapons and the nuclear family. Rather than preserving the domestic relations that are supposedly at the heart of the American way of life, nuclear weapons engender a new social and moral order that threatens to destroy those same relations, turning parent against child and husband against wife.

Virginia Cross's "Adversity" (1955) also merges contemporary understandings of nuclear war with the maternalist sensibilities of women's peace activism. By the middle of the 1950s many Americans had exchanged their earlier convictions about the apocalyptic nature of the bomb for the new belief that a limited nuclear war was fightable and that society would simply have to adjust to this new reality (Trachtenberg 355). In Cross's story, readers learn just what this adaptation might entail. "Adversity" follows the story of Eileen Rankin, an average housewife and mother who is "neither brave nor cowardly, stupid nor very imaginative, ignorant or well-educated" (90). Much like Merril's Margaret, Eileen is clearly meant to be a kind of Everywoman with whom readers can identify and sympathize.

However, while Merril's heroine survives World War III in relative physical comfort, Eileen must negotiate a far more treacherous postholocaust world. Although the countryside and some green spaces within major cities continue to flourish after World War III, the only animals to survive are those that hid underground during the actual war. As far as Eileen can tell, she is the last human left alive—and pregnant to boot. In addition to avoiding radioactive hot spots and scavenging enough supplies for herself and her unborn child, Eileen also must contend with the shadowy presence of "Kelly," an eight-foot-tall "amphibian type of life freakishly left over from the Carboniferous Era" (84). Although Eileen knows Kelly's past from visits to the zoo where he was previously imprisoned, she has no idea how he survived the war or what his intentions toward her might be.

Much like the *maters dolorosae* of other antiwar stories—and in accordance with the sentiment of mid-century America—Eileen does manage to adjust and even thrive in the postholocaust world. Driven by the conviction that there is "no hope of relief except that her baby might live," Eileen begins to pick up the pieces of her world and knit them into new patterns, teaching herself to fish and scavenging enough canned goods to keep herself and the forthcoming baby fed for years. She also strikes up a tentative friendship with Kelly, whose peaceful demeanor and "obvious intelligence" lead her to wonder, "who knows how long ago his personal world ended, with the loss of his own kind? Centuries? Eras? Or only at his capture in '85? Had there been a lost mate? Puzzled, fretful children left behind there [when he was captured by humans]?" (85, 86). And so Eileen's maternal sensibilities, combined with her experience as a holocaust survivor, enable her to connect with the one individual left in her world who has undergone experiences much like her own.

Kelly affirms Eileen's belief in his inherent kindness when he delivers her baby and builds a warm shelter for mother and child. As a result, Eileen gains new perspective on postholocaust life: she is still a mother and "He was not longer It, the Kelly-Thing . . . He was He, Kelly . . . definite, organized, an entity. Companion" (91). In apparent contrast to the isolated mothers, fearful father, and broken families of Merril's world, in "Adversity" nuclear war seems to lead to the reconsolidation of the nuclear family.

Or does it? On the one hand, Cross clearly casts Kelly in the role of the father, designating the creature as male and describing his efforts to feed and shelter his new family in affectionate terms. At the same time, she never actually names him as such. Instead, at the end of the story, his identity is firmly fixed as that of the implicitly asexual "companion." This is, of course, entirely appropriate. As a sympathetic alien other, Kelly can help Eileen and her child survive, but he cannot have any children of his own, nor is it at all likely that he and Eileen will be able to produce offspring together; at best, they have cobbled together a temporary postnuclear living unit. In the end, Cross's story ultimately reinforces the primary message of midcentury peace activism: no amount of "adjustment" can hide the grim fact that nuclear war will lead to the end of the nuclear family and, eventually, all sentient life.

Finally, Carol Emshwiller's "Day at the Beach" (1959) and Mary Armock's "First Born" (1960) explore the consequences of nuclear war for future generations in even more direct and unsettling ways. Expert discourses and public polls of the late 1950s continued to reflect the belief that America could (and should) fight a limited nuclear war if the situation arose (Trachtenberg 354). At the same time, public concern about nuclear fallout continued to grow, especially as reports about unexpected illnesses filtered in from the Nevada Test Site, which began testing atom bombs in 1945, and from the Marshall Islands, where H-bomb tests had been performed since 1954 (Hafemeister 437–38).

Perhaps not surprisingly, the late 1950s and early 1960s saw the publication of numerous books that reflected this new public concern (A. Stone 192). Nevil Shute's *On the Beach* (1957), which was made into a major motion picture starring Gregory Peck, Ava Gardner, and Fred Astaire in 1959, explores the fate of a group of Australians who learn that nuclear war has wiped out all life in the Northern Hemisphere — and that they, too, will eventually be killed by the fallout of a war that they neither asked for nor participated in. Meanwhile, Walter Miller's *A Canticle for Leibowitz* (1959) imagines what might happen to Americans in the millennia following a nuclear holocaust. If possible, Miller's book is even more pessimistic than Shute's: a few shreds of humanity manage to survive ignorance and disease and even to slowly rebuild civilization — only to wipe it out once again with yet another nuclear war.

Emshwiller and Armock also insist that nuclear war may not immediately kill all life on Earth, but that in time the literal and psychological fallout from such a war will most certainly do so. In contrast to their male counterparts, however, they do not focus outward on the grand sweep of history, imagining the rise and fall of entire civilizations. Instead, these authors look inward, linking the death of humanity to reproductive tragedies within individual families.

In "Day at the Beach," Emshwiller depicts a world that extends the most terrifying elements of those postholocaust futures created by women writers before her. For example, much like Virginia Cross, Emshwiller imagines that some fragments of humanity might adjust to the reality of nuclear war, or at least to its aftermath, and that the cost of such adjustment might be much stranger than we think. In "Day at the Beach," World War III has been over for four years and all public institutions have vanished, but individual families still scratch out lives on the postnuclear frontier. Adults who survive the war, like Emshwiller's protagonists Myra and Ben, are pink, toothless, and bald; children born after the war, such as Myra and Ben's Littleboy, are small and feral, complete with sharp teeth and masses of black hair that seem to grow "too far down" their spines to be considered quite normal (277). Nonetheless, heroic parents like Myra and Ben struggle to maintain a sense of normality by religiously following their prewar domestic routines: Myra cooks and cares for Littleboy at home, Ben commutes to work five days a week, and the whole family enjoys, as the title of the story suggests, occasional outings together such as a weekend day at the beach.

Of course, as Emshwiller's readers soon realize, the abnormal situation wrought by nuclear war affects even the most seemingly normal of daily routines. Littleboy expresses affection for Myra by biting a "half-inch piece" of flesh from her neck (277); Ben's "work" is to quite literally put food on his family's table by scavenging it from the burnt-out remains of the city (and to fight off the other "commuting" fathers who would gladly steal it from him); and "a good day" at the beach is one in which the family picnics, swims, and successfully kills the marauding vagabond who tries to murder them for their gasoline (284). For Emshwiller, adaptation to the postholocaust world is a grotesque affair underscored by the grotesque nature of the postnuclear family's rituals.

This grotesquerie is further underscored by Emshwiller's depiction of Myra as a *mater dolorosa* consumed by her efforts to negotiate the unbearable contradictions that nuclear war has wrought upon her family. Even more than Merril's protagonist, Emshwiller's heroine is clearly torn between husband and child. Although the silent and savage Littleboy seems to be the exact opposite of the charmingly civilized (if physically limited) Henrietta, both mutant children threaten the unity of the family. When Ben threatens to swat Littleboy for throwing his food on the floor and biting Myra, Myra quickly assures her husband that "three is a hard age. . . . It says so in the books" (277). Privately, Myra admits to herself that these same books "really said that three was a beginning to be cooperative age," but, in the interest of protecting her child, she chooses to tell Ben a few white lies (277). Here, of course, the tension between husband and wife is nowhere nearly as pronounced as it is in Merril's tale; Myra defends her child but is not blind to his differences, and Ben's desire to punish Littleboy for bad behavior is certainly a far cry from wanting to kill him for his strangeness. Nonetheless, as this sequence of events makes clear, the nuclear war that threatens to destroy the family from without also initiates—in however muted a form—a potentially deadly chain reaction from within as well, triggering a series of physical and psychological transformations that can pit parent against child and wife against husband at a moment's notice.

Ultimately, of course, Myra loves Ben, Ben loves Myra, and both love Littleboy—and this is the tragedy of Emshwiller's story. Alone with her family at the seaside, Myra seems to articulate precisely that dream of moral cleansing driving so many postapocalyptic narratives, noting to Ben that the scenario on the beach is "like Adam and Eve . . . just you and me and our baby" (280). And yet, when Ben eagerly interprets Myra's observation as an invitation to engage in the sexual activities they have abstained from since Littleboy's birth three years earlier, Myra quickly stops him by pointing out that "I don't even know a doctor since Press Smith was killed by those robbing kids and I'd be scared" (280). Before the couple (or the reader) can even begin to sort out the implications of this exchange, Emshwiller abruptly shifts tone, and the "real" action of the story begins with the appearance of the marauding vagabond and the subsequent deadly fight over the gasoline for Ben and Myra's car.

Despite the exciting nature of the battle between the family and the marauder, I would argue that the brief conversation preceding it is the real heart of Emshwiller's story. Although the dominant discourses of mid-century America celebrated the nuclear family as the natural result of an evolutionary biology predicated on heterosexual reproduction, Emshwiller suggests that in a postholocaust world, nuclear families can only survive—and even then only for a limited time—by avoiding reproduction altogether. As Myra's comment about her doctor's death implies, pregnancy and childbirth on the nuclear frontier are hardly events to romanticize, since the birth of a new child might well mean the death of its mother.

At the same time, readers realize that Myra and Ben are essentially damned if they do and damned if they don't—after all, if they give in to their desire for one another, they run the risk of Myra becoming pregnant and dying in childbirth, thereby depriving the nuclear family of its central figure, the woman as wife and mother. And yet if they hold fast to their resolve and do not have sex, they ensure the immediate survival of their family but jeopardize its future: without more children, there can be no more family whatsoever. Emshwiller conveys her antinuclear message by inviting readers to logically extrapolate the consequences of biological reproduction in a postholocaust world. In doing so, she destabilizes the mid-century fantasy of nuclear war as a necessary evil that strong people can adjust to and even survive. Instead, it becomes quite clear that, rather than paving the way for a brave new world based on a new (or, in this case, very, very old) social and moral order, nuclear war shatters all order to such an extent that neither God, family, nor even biology can be taken for granted any longer.

Finally, while other nuclear holocaust narratives written by mid-century women treat reproductive tragedy and the death of the human race indirectly, Mary Armock's "First Born" (1960) presents this possibility in a chillingly forthright way. Extending those themes first introduced by Merril, Armock imagines a postholocaust world ruled by quasi-military "Copdocs" who carefully monitor all women of childbearing age because "we have to be absolutely sure. . . . Have to keep the race pure, you know" (85). Meanwhile, civilian husbands justify this invasion into their wives' reproductive privacy by insisting that compliance with the Copdocs is simply part of being a "responsible citizen" in the postnuclear age (87). In keeping with the grim nature of Armock's world, "First Born" specifically follows the adventures of one unnamed *mater dolorosa* and her doomed attempt to defy the Copdocs and preserve the life of her young mutant son, David, with whom she shares a close telepathic connection.

Armock's plain-speaking heroine further underscores the frankly dystopian nature of her postholocaust world. When her husband refuses to acknowledge his son's mutation, suggesting instead that his wife is simply hysterical due to an unexpected visit from the Copdocs, our *mater dolorosa* sharply retorts, "I loved [David] and watched him grow and learn and. . . . now he's going to die because he's a mutant. He's going to die before he lived. . . . We nearly blew the whole world into this many pieces. Now we've settled on individual worlds" (87). And when he tries to comfort her with the possibility of another (presumably normal) child, Armock's heroine crushes her husband's belief in the system he has so long defended by bluntly revealing the fate of all women who bear mutant children: "they're sterilized" (88). In contrast to those earlier science-fictional sorrowing mothers who testified mutely to the contradictions of nuclear-age motherhood through their actions, Armock's sorrowing mother clearly articulates the horrifying transformations wrought upon women and children's lives by World War III.

Armock gives her story one more turn of the screw by granting a voice to the *mater dolorosa*'s mutant child himself. While other mid-century women's nuclear holocaust stories are told by a seemingly omniscient third-person narrator, the events of "First Born" are filtered through the imperfect understanding of David. At the beginning of Armock's story David seems to be a happy, loving child secure in his small world with his mother and eager to go "Outside" with his father when he is a little bit older. As the story progresses and the intrusive visits by the Copdocs lead to David and his mother's commitment in a mysterious hospital, he becomes increasingly fearful and disoriented. In the final passages of the story, a terrified David tries frantically to reach the mind of his drugged mother:

> I can't reach her at all. All there is is a little bubble way down deep inside her mind that keeps saying, "No . . . no . . ." Just like crying, only worse. I wish I could talk to Mother once more before I'm born so she could love away this frightened thing that's shaking inside me.

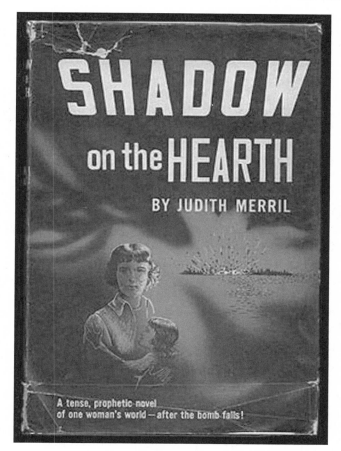

Figure 4. Original cover of Judith Merril's *Shadow on the Hearth* (1950). Merril disliked both the title Doubleday chose for her novel and the artwork itself. She found the former to be "dismaying" and the latter to be cowardly: "it could have been [an illustration for] a gothic novel, or basically anything" (Merril and Pohl-Weary 99). It does, however, capture the spirit of radical motherhood projected by Merril's antinuclear activist counterparts.

Mother . . .? What is a mutant . . .? Mother, *why* can't an X-ray show love? (89)

It is only at the very end of Armock's story that we finally realize David is a fetus about to be aborted against his mother's will for what, at this point, can only seem like a cruelly abstract notion of racial purity. Much like those housewife heroine SF authors before her, Armock makes concrete those "terrors of the Atomic Bomb" that haunted so many postwar mothers' nightmares. Indeed, "First Born" makes those terrors all the more terrifying by putting them, quite literally, in the mouth of babes.

As all of the above stories demonstrate, SF provided mid-century women writers with a powerful narrative form through which to explore what might happen to women and their families if America continued down the path it seemed to have set for itself at the beginning of the cold war. But how might women prevent these nightmare futures from happening? What other futures might be available to women and their families?

Judith Merril's *Shadow on the Hearth* (1950) answers these questions in a manner that would have been familiar to postwar peace activists: women can prevent these nightmare futures from happening by connecting with other women and with scientists to build an antiwar community. Although *Shadow on the Hearth* has not received much critical attention in retrospect, at the time of its publication it was remarkably well received: the *New York Times* compared it to the cautionary works of H. G. Wells and George Orwell, and *Motorola TV Hour* broadcast a dramatic version of it in 1954 under the title "Atomic Attack" (Merril and Pohl-Weary 99–100) (see figure 4).

Like other nuclear holocaust narratives written by women, *Shadow on the Hearth* appeals to the antiwar sensibilities of women readers based on their common situation as mothers haunted by "the terrors of the Atomic Bomb." Merril's novel follows the story of Gladys Mitchell, a Westchester housewife and mother of three. Gladys is the epitome of mid-century domesticity, dispensing nuggets of wisdom about the effects of French toast on cranky children while struggling with her conscience about whether or not she should abandon the laundry to attend a neighborhood luncheon (87). With the advent of World War III, Gladys's life turns upside down: her husband Jon is presumed dead in New York City, her daughters Barbara and Ginny are exposed to radioactive rain at school, and her son Tom, a freshman at Texas Tech, seems to have vanished off the face of the planet.

In Merril's story nuclear war shatters readers' certainty about what it might mean to be a wife and mother in the atomic era. At first, Gladys tries to imagine what her husband would do in her situation. However, she soon gives this up because

Jon wasn't there. For more than two days Jon hadn't been there. The

other time, the other war, it was different. Then she wrote him cheerful, encouraging letters, telling him all the little troubles that came up
each day, the little things he customarily solved, that she had learned
to cope with. But these were not little problems now, nor were they
the kind that anyone customarily solved.

What would Jon do?

That was the old formula, the way it had worked in the last war. She'd
ask herself and get the answer. Now there was no answer. (188)

As Merril's heroine realizes, the formula for gender relations that
made sense in World War II has little or no bearing on the radically different situation of World War III. This insight challenges the rhetoric
of civil defense as it was expressed in official government documents
such as the "Grandma's Pantry" pamphlet. Rather than looking to the
past for models of appropriate feminine behavior that will make sense
of a frightening new present, Merril's readers must acknowledge that
shifting modes of technology create new social realities that demand
new modes of relations between women and men as well.

In contrast to many of the short nuclear holocaust narratives written by women (including her own "That Only a Mother"), *Shadow on
the Hearth* is more than just a warning about the tragedy of domestic life in the nuclear age. Instead, it is an appeal to readers to help
prevent that tragedy. Accordingly, Merril devotes the majority of her
novel to Gladys's transformation from helpless housewife and *mater
dolorosa* to educated mother and activist citizen. The course of Gladys's
transformation is marked by her engagement with three distinctive
ways of knowing the world—what feminist psychologists Mary Field
Belenky et al. call "received knowledge," "subjective knowledge,"
and "constructed knowledge." In essence, received knowers rely on
external (and usually male) authorities "for direction as well as information" about how to act appropriately (40). Conversely, subjective
knowers—who often admit to having been deeply disappointed by
male authorities—depend on their personal experiences and inner-
most feelings both to intuit the truth of any given situation and to
derive a course of action based on that subjective truth (54). Finally,
women who operate from the position of constructed knowledge create new and stronger personal identities "by attempting to *integrate*
knowledge that they [feel] intuitively . . . with the knowledge that
they [have] learned from others" (134). Although these three kinds of
knowing are not entirely distinct from one another, they do indicate

the broad developmental trajectory that characterizes women's development as socially and politically engaged subjects.[9]

In *Shadow on the Hearth*, Gladys's engagement with different ways of knowing lead her toward an increasingly critical conception of masculine authority as it informs the rhetoric and practice of civil defense. At first Gladys is a received knower who uncritically accepts official government statements claiming that nobody in her neighborhood has been exposed to dangerous levels of radiation. She accordingly dismisses her youngest daughter Ginny's crankiness as an understandably childish reaction to the frightening events unfolding around them. However, when Ginny's hair begins to fall out, Gladys finally convinces the local doctors to examine her for radiation poisoning. At this point the doctors admit that Gladys's growing suspicions are correct and that Ginny has fallen ill from playing with her favorite stuffed animal, which was left out in the rain when the bombs first fell. Although they assure Gladys that Ginny will live through the initial bout of radiation sickness, the doctors cannot predict her future health. Shocked by the extent to which official knowledge has undermined her parenting abilities, Gladys wonders, "Isn't anything safe? Not the rain or the house? Not even a little blue horse? . . . Would anything ever be safe again?" (275). The answer to these questions seems to be a resounding "no": after World War III women might retain the instinct to protect their children, but instinct itself might be tragically compromised by inept masculine authority.

Gladys reacts to her disappointment with male authority by embracing a mode of subjective knowledge that enables her to make connections with other women. When local civil defense officials attempt to arrest her housekeeper, Veda Klopac, as a communist spy, Gladys refuses to cooperate, dismissing the whole idea as ludicrous because, as she knows from personal experience, Veda "couldn't possibly be an enemy agent. She just works too hard [and] wouldn't have

9. Belenky and her coauthors identify two more ways of knowing the world: through silence (perhaps the simplest way of knowing the world, and one that is experienced primarily by very young and/or very socially, economically, and educationally deprived women) and through procedural knowledge (the kind of formal knowledge that women tend to acquire in college or in other complex learning experiences, such as family therapy). Moreover, as scientists working in the fuzzy domain of human development, they are quick to point out that women rarely experience these ways of knowing the world separately or in a strict logical sequence. Of course, Merril is writing fiction rather than transcribing real life, and she has a particular goal in doing so: to introduce readers to the habits of thinking associated with peace activism. Therefore it should come as no surprise that her depiction of women's psychological development is relatively simple and linear.

the time" (93). Later Merril's heroine also opens her home to Edie Crowell, an aristocratic neighbor who has been exposed to radiation and is in need of medical treatment. Indeed, Gladys decides to care for Edie herself because masculine authority has betrayed them both: as Edie rather dramatically (but nonetheless accurately) announces to everyone who will listen, "I told you I was [sick]. I told you . . . and I told them, and nobody would believe me!" (114). In turn, both Veda and Edie draw upon their respective skills to help Gladys preserve her family: Veda takes charge of the family's daily activities while Edie uses her sharp tongue to fend off the civil defense officers who hope to break up the household and regain control over the women.[10] Thus, Gladys, Veda, and Edie create a quasi-utopian community of women who work together—however temporarily—to protect themselves and their children from the dangerous new social and moral orders that threaten them.[11]

Eventually Gladys learns how to become an even more critically engaged subject in her brave new world by combining received knowledge with personal experience. First she learns how to read between the lines of official government radio broadcasts by checking them against the information she gleans from her son Tom's physics books and her own experience in the home: "The news all sounded so good, [Gladys] reflected, things seemed to be improving every hour. Then it occurred to her that nothing had been said about the imminent failure of the gas supply or about the possible discontinuance of telephone service. . . . It wasn't all quite as good as it sounded

10. This largely positive depiction of communal living may well have stemmed from Merril's own experience of the same. Throughout the late 1930s and early 1940s many of the male Futurians lived together to minimize their expenses and maximize their creative output. When their husbands were sent overseas during WWII, Merril and Virginia Kidd set up their own communal household. As Merril recollects, "Living with Virginia was lots of fun against the backdrop of great intellectual stimulation, caring for children, coping with relationships, buying groceries, and all those things that are part of everyday life as a single working mother" (Merril and Pohl-Weary 56). Given that Merril's fictional heroines are also housewives who have been transformed into single mothers by the exigencies of war, it is not surprising that they also cope with their changed circumstances by pooling their intellectual and domestic resources.

11. This household utopia is temporary, of course, because Merril refuses romantic notions of rugged individualism. No suburban household can be magically transformed into a self-sustaining fiefdom, and the women must maintain contact with the outside world to get food and medical attention for Gladys's daughters and Edie Crowell (all of whom have been exposed to radioactive dust and rain). Nonetheless, the tenor of their dealings with the outside world does change radically once Merril's heroines realize that they can rely on themselves to take care of many of the problems they have traditionally delegated to men, like fixing gas leaks and defending themselves against burglars.

after all; maybe the other part, the big news about the whole country [surviving the war without any major damage], was weeded out in the same way" (162). Later Gladys learns how to successfully challenge blind authority as well. When civil defense officials order her to leave home because of a gas leak, Gladys refuses to comply. Instead, she dons her husband's pants and marches into the basement to fix the problem herself (122). Thus, Merril suggests that modern women can and must prepare for the exigencies of the atomic age by developing contextualized ways of knowing the world that combine subjective, domestic instincts with the more objective skills of rational inquiry and technological know-how.

Of course, it is not enough that Gladys simply establish herself as a capable mother. She also must ally herself with one of two distinct models for atomic-age social order: the military model of uncritical compliance or the scientific model of rational skepticism. Gladys's relationship to these contrasting models of social order is expressed in terms of her relationship to the two men who personify them: Jim Turner, her neighbor turned civil defense official, and Garson Levy, a nuclear physicist turned math teacher under surveillance by the U.S. government for his highly publicized peace activism. Merril asks her readers to evaluate the merit of these men and the competing models of social order they embody based on whether or not they foster con-structed ways of knowing the world, especially as they enable what Belenky et al. call "connected and caring" relations to others (142).

In *Shadow on the Hearth*, the military model of social relations fails spectacularly on all counts. Jim Turner initially seems to be an avatar of efficiency and organization, a confident man with "a big sound-ing masculine laugh that made [Gladys's] worries seem silly" (51). Unfortunately, Turner is also a petty tyrant who delights in playing soldier, bullying the men assigned to his work detail while bragging to their wives about his importance in the new scheme of things. More to the point, Turner's rage for order makes him intolerant of anyone who questions that order. When Gladys asks a series of eminently sen-sible questions about how to ensure the safety of her house and chil-dren, Turner impatiently warns her that "you don't have to go looking for extra work, Miz Mitchell. You'll have plenty to do, just following instructions" (55). As this exchange suggests, civil defense practices may ensure a certain kind of social order, but only if they successfully convince private citizens to acquiesce to a largely untested public authority that embodies the rigid, hierarchical relations of received knowledge.

Later developments in the novel demonstrate the danger of this authority when Turner tries to extract sexual favors from Gladys. Preying on her desire for information, Turner takes up the habit of stopping by Gladys's house to tell her what he knows about the latest developments in local government war planning—and to make passes at her when she least expects it. When plans to evacuate Westchester County are announced, Turner becomes even more overtly aggressive, telling Gladys that he could secure priority transportation and shelter for her family "if we got to know each other a little" (185). When Gladys resists his advances on the grounds that her husband might still be alive, Turner dismisses her as a "damn fool" (269). More than mere melodrama, Merril here uses the trope of the sexually persecuted woman to underscore how all citizens might be objectified by the practices of civil defense. By emphasizing Gladys's devotion to her husband and revulsion for Turner, Merril insists that the new social order mandated by civil defense must be resisted because it undermines all normative understandings of moral order as well.

Even more to the point, Merril indicates that the military model of social order is directly at odds with maternal instinct. When Gladys offers to take in several war orphans, Turner throws out her application and tells her, "I don't think that's such a good idea, Gladys. They sent me a form to check off whether your house was okay. Of course I know it would be nice for the kids here, but you got to remember what I told you before. It wouldn't make things any easier to have a couple of extra kids here" (186). Turner's words certainly sound sympathetic, but by this point in the novel discerning readers can hardly help but wonder: isn't the real problem here that a few extra children "wouldn't make things any easier" for *Turner* in either his rage for unquestioned order or his pursuit of Gladys's affections?

Turner's monstrous selfishness—and, by extension, the monstrosity of the entire system he represents—is more than confirmed by his final exchange with Gladys. After Ginny becomes sick with radiation poisoning, Turner orders Gladys to take the child to the hospital. Gladys refuses, pointing out that she has already been to the hospital with Ginny once and that she will not return to what has become a charnel house overflowing with the victims of the New York City bombing. In a horrifyingly misguided attempt to placate her, Turner insists that Gladys must be wrong. Although he has never actually visited the hospital, the civil defense official knows it must be fine because "I had to send my own wife and baby there, on account of not having anybody to take care of them at home. They didn't even get exposed, but. . . . [They're] better off at the hospital" (268). Not surprisingly, this scene marks the pinnacle of Gladys's disgust with Turner, who is perfectly willing to abandon his own family so he can play soldier with impunity. Hence, Merril suggests that the cultural logic of the nuclear age, especially as expressed through the quasi-military procedures of civil defense, transforms all women and children into structural if not literal victims of the bomb.

By way of contrast, physicist and peace activist Garson Levy embodies a model of scientific knowledge and political practice that is highly compatible with the contextual, connected ways of knowing that Gladys herself increasingly values. Unlike Turner, the first impression that Levy gives off is one of astounding ordinariness: "he didn't look like a madman, or a hero either. He looked like a scholarly middle-aged man who never remembered to have his suit pressed" (143). Nonetheless, Merril's scientist turns out to be anything but ordinary, escaping from his government-imposed house arrest to make sure that his students' families are warned about the radiation that they were exposed to during the first wave of bombings and taking time to explain radiation test results when civil authorities like Jim Turner refuse to do so. Impressed with both Levy's concern for his students and his cheerful willingness to explain scientific and medical concepts to laypeople, Gladys invites the scientist to stay with them for the duration of the war, even if it means harboring a public enemy.

Merril further encourages readers to sympathize with Levy by demonstrating how he helps Gladys make informed decisions about her family and home. For example, when civil defense authorities try to convince our heroine that her family is not in danger because there have been no explosions near Westchester County, Gladys "remembers that Dr. Levy had said something about bombs directly overhead" and demands that her children be tested for the kinds of radiation poisoning that most closely match the symptoms she has already observed in them (151). Reluctantly impressed by Gladys's carefully detailed argument, the civil defense workers agree to run the tests. Unlike the military model of social relations which sacrifices women's concerns for the sake of public order, the scientific model enables women to connect their concerns with larger events occurring beyond the home. This, in turn, enables them to protect their families as effectively as possible.

The scientific model of social order does more than simply enable maternal authority; for Merril it also acknowledges this authority as a valid mode of perception in and of itself. For example, although she successfully stops the gas leak in her basement, it is only when Levy arrives that Gladys can fully diagnose the problem and safely turn the gas back on. Levy is more than willing to give credit where credit is due, telling Gladys that he could not have solved the problem by himself either, but that he depended upon "the way you described your trouble with the stove" (157). Once again, domestic experience proves to be highly compatible with scientific authority in Merril's world. Of course, the relationship between physicist and housewife is not an entirely equal one: after all, Levy possesses more formal knowledge than Gladys. Nonetheless, he recognizes the importance of close observation and detailed description as skills that are essential to scientists and mothers alike.

Finally, Merril invites readers to sympathize with Levy's antiwar agenda by linking the scientist's peace activism to the creation of family and preservation of moral order. Although Levy is nominally a bachelor, his years of political activism have earned him an extensive network of devoted friends and followers. This network includes Peter Spinelli, the young Westchester doctor who becomes part of Jim Turner's civil defense team. Spinelli is the only civil defense worker to defy Turner's bullying and rage for procedural order, taking extra time after his official rounds to help neighborhood women prepare for life after the bomb. The similarities between Spinelli and Levy are no coincidence, as the young doctor tells Gladys upon discovering Levy's presence in her home, "I was a high school senior, a science major in Year One of the atom bomb. . . . I heard [Garson Levy] talk several times and I gave money to his committees. . . . The money I gave and the petitions I signed were largely responsible for making me a doctor. . . . It means a lot to me, knowing that somebody took him in. He's important" (236–37). In addition to inspiring filial devotion amongst his followers, Levy reproduces himself (or at least the political and moral agendas he embodies) by virtue of the example he sets for them. Accordingly, he becomes the nexus for a model community of scientists, doctors, and mothers who are bound together by a shared concern for the terrors of the atom bomb and a mutual desire to protect future generations from its devastating legacy.[12]

For Merril, however, the scientific model of social order is at best an only partial solution to the problem of nuclear war. Although

12. Unlike Jim Turner, neither Levy nor Spinelli abuses his authority to extract sexual favors from women. Indeed from almost the very beginning, Gladys and Levy simply treat each other as old friends.

Gladys, Levy, and Spinelli do preserve the family unit, its survival is far from guaranteed: Ginny's health is still in jeopardy; Gladys's son Tom is located but much to her horror has been drafted into the army; her husband, Jon, returns from New York City but is wracked with radiation burns and gunshot wounds that prevent him from asserting his place as the head of the family; and Levy himself is diagnosed with a potentially fatal strain of radiation poisoning.[13] This ambivalence is key to Merril's project: if she depicts a postholocaust future where scientists can solve all the problems associated with nuclear war, then there would be no reason to protest that kind of war in the first place. Of course, that is not her project. The goal of *Shadow on the Hearth* is twofold: to alert readers to the devastating effects of nuclear war and to investigate what models of social order are most likely to address women's concerns about the nuclear age. By demonstrating the moral similarities between mothers and scientists, Merril makes a strong case for models of social order that treat individuals as rational subjects of a high-tech era rather than irrational objects of modern military strategy. And by demonstrating how even the natural sympathies of women and scientists might not be enough to guarantee survival in a postnuclear future, she also makes a strong case for peace activism in the present.

Building Bridges between Worlds in the Civil Rights Movement

Although nuclear weapons might have been the most pressing technological issue for women involved in mid-century political activism, it was certainly not the only one that captured their interest. Many turned their attention to what was undoubtedly the most pressing social issue of the day: the struggle to secure equal social and political rights for African Americans. Indeed, the two issues were inextricably intertwined in some minds. As activist Elizabeth Waring put it to the Charleston press in 1950, to southern whites the civil rights movement was "like the atom bomb which they are afraid we will use to destroy their selfish and savage white supremacy way of life" (qtd. in Synnott 194). Consequently, the earth-shattering potential of nuclear weapons

---

13. The original ending of the novel—which Doubleday refused to publish—was even more pessimistic. In Merril's final draft, Gladys's husband survives the horrors of postholocaust New York only to be shot to death by civil defense officials in his own backyard (Merril and Pohl-Weary 100).

quickly became a metaphor for the paradigm-shattering social changes that might be wrought by racial integration in America.

Of course, most civil rights activists usually dispensed with such
drastic metaphors, choosing instead to equate racial integration with
American democracy. For instance, when African American Pauli
Murray's application to graduate school at the all white University
of South Carolina was rejected in 1938, she immediately wrote the
president of the university to ask "how much longer . . . is the South
going to withhold elementary human rights from its black citizens?
How can Negroes, the economic backbone of the South for so many
centuries, defend our institutions against the threats of fascism and
barbarism if we too are treated the same as the Jews in Germany?"
(qtd. in Gilmore 62). In the 1940s and 1950s, civil rights organizations
including the National Association for the Advancement of Colored
People (NAACP) and the Congress of Racial Equality (CORE) specifically invoked the rhetoric of the cold war, positioning themselves as a
necessary part of America's effort to combat communism and spread
democracy and social justice throughout the world (Lynn, "Gender
and Progressive Politics" 108).

Civil rights organizations took a two-pronged approach to the task
of ensuring democracy for all, working to secure racial integration
at the levels of both the state and the neighborhood. The efforts that
occurred at the first level are those that have been most thoroughly
recorded by historians: the struggle to integrate public schools as
mandated by the Supreme Court's landmark 1954 decision *Brown
v. Board of Education of Topeka, Kansas* (which firmly rejected the
"separate but equal" doctrine that had governed U.S. policymaking
since the 1890s); the year-long Montgomery bus boycott organized
by Martin Luther King Jr. after Rosa Parks was arrested for refusing
to give up her bus seat to a white man in 1955; and, of course, the
massive, nonviolent demonstrations initiated by King and other black
leaders in the late 1950s and early 1960s (Kaledin 150–55). All these
activities were carefully planned efforts to secure equal rights for all
Americans through the regular channels of participatory and representative democracy.[14]

14. Although men like Thurgood Marshall (who represented the NAACP in *Brown v.
Board of Education*) and Martin Luther King Jr. are the people most commonly associated with the mid-century civil rights movement, black women were also important
leaders in efforts to secure civil rights legislation. For further discussion, see Jacqueline
Jones's "The Political Implications of Black and White Southern Women's Work in the
South, 1890–1965" and Eugenia Kaledin's *Mothers and More: American Women in the
1950s*.

But this is, quite literally, only half the story. As feminist and civil rights historians increasingly note, the success of the civil rights movement depended on both those very public actions undertaken by male leaders such as King and the diverse array of communal and interpersonal efforts initiated by women. As Charles M. Payne puts it, "men led, but women organized" (156). More specifically, Kathryn L. Nasstrom suggests that men and women occupied different kinds of leadership positions that loosely reflected postwar assumptions about gendered expertise. As public spokespersons with positions of formal authority, men "interpreted strategies and goals to constituencies beyond the movement itself" (114). Meanwhile, women took on informal roles as "bridge leaders," drawing on their family management skills and ties to community groups to "develop the potential for reflection and action in others" and to "involve as many participants as possible in the decision-making that shaped the movement's direction" (114). Because they worked primarily behind the scenes in traditionally feminine spaces such as the home, the classroom, and the neighborhood, the American public rarely recognized the significance of bridge leaders. Nonetheless, their efforts to foster dialogue amongst those parties most immediately impacted by civil rights legislation were key to its actual implementation.

The strategies that bridge leaders used to enhance communication and build community consensus depended on individual leaders' race and class positions. For example, black women involved with the massive voter registration drives that took place in Atlanta, Georgia, in 1946 utilized traditional volunteer and social groups to spread their political messages. Declaring 1946 to be a "Woman's Year," the genteel leaders of the National Council of Negro Women pledged to ring doorbells, canvass neighborhoods, and work with other civic and professional groups to ensure black voter registration. In a similar spirit, leaders of the Negro Cultural League, a labor organization for the domestic workers who comprised two-thirds of Atlanta's black female population, rechristened themselves the League of Negro Women Voters and vowed to ensure "that every woman and girl who becomes of age is registered" (qtd. in Nasstrom 125). Finally, the schoolteachers of Atlanta's MRS club used their positions as cultural authorities to register students of voting age as well as their parents, organizing both classroom lessons and extracurricular lectures to ensure the civic education of the entire community. Much like their counterparts in the peace movement, bridge leaders in the civil rights movement capitalized on culturally specific feminine identities and relations—as philanthropists, domestics, and teachers—to do the radical work of social change.[15]

Although southern white women rarely organized in favor of civil rights in the 1950s, those who did so employed similar tactics.[16] After the governor of Arkansas closed down the entire state school system to prevent the integration of Little Rock Central High in 1957, over 2,000 concerned women joined the Women's Emergency Committee to Open Our Schools (WEC). Led by socialites Vivion Lenon Brewer and Adolphine Fletcher Terry, the WEC co-opted key politicians to their cause by invoking the southern lady's prerogative to manipulate men as long as they did not directly challenge their power. For example, Terry advised women to forego business meetings with state leaders in favor of elaborate dinner parties because "southern gentlemen have been taught to be courteous to their hostesses, so when you give men food to eat they cannot be impolite to you and they must do a favor in return" (qtd. in Jacoway 277). In essence, the WEC women succeeded in changing conservative southern notions of proper race relations by playing upon equally conservative notions of gendered etiquette.

Finally, as feminist historian Susan Lynn explains, progressive interracial women's organizations such as the Young Women's Christian Organization (YWCA) were instrumental in lobbying for civil rights legislation. What has been less often recognized, however,

15. Much like their counterparts in the peace movement, civil rights movement women also drew upon their moral authority as mothers to make sense of their demands for social change. However, they were less likely to rely exclusively on this strategy than peace activists. As Elizabeth Jacoway notes, Americans—especially white southern Americans—have traditionally defined the moral superiority of motherhood as a white and middle- or upper-class prerogative (273). Because women involved with the early civil rights movement were more interested in reforming race than gender relations, they typically worked within, rather than against, such definitions.

16. Of course, a number of individual white southern women—including Lillian Smith, Frances Freeborn Pauly, Sarah Patton Boyle, Alice Norwood Spearman Wright, Virginia Durr, Anne Braden, and Katherine Du Pre Lumpkin—worked extensively with interracial civil rights groups. At the same time, it is important to note that many other white southern women were virulently opposed to racial integration; as such, they lent their efforts to the Ku Klux Klan or, more commonly, drew upon their authority in the home to terrorize black servants suspected of civil rights activism. For further discussion of progressive southern white women, see especially Vicki L. Crawford, Jacqueline Anne Rouse, and Barbara Woods, eds., *Women in the Civil Rights Movement: Trailblazers and Torchbearers, 1941–1965;* for further discussion of white women's opposition to the civil rights movement, see Lauren F. Winner, "Cooking, Tending the Garden, and Being a Good Hostess: A Domestic History of White Women's Opposition to the Freedom Movement in Mississippi."

is they were also central in developing new strategies for integration that "emphasized a female ethic as central to creating social change, particularly by building friendships across racial lines" ("Gender and Progressive Politics" 112). These strategies included the development of antiracist literature, lecture series, and, most centrally, summer conferences where black and white girls worked and lived together for months at a time. Hundreds of girls attended these conferences, and hundreds left testimonials reporting that the most important part of the conferences for them was the realization that "in hundreds of little ways we felt the same whether our skin was dark or light" (qtd. in "Gender and Progressive Politics" 113). Much like other civil rights organizations, the YWCA built consensus for racial integration by encouraging interpersonal dialogue between groups of people who might otherwise never speak to one another.

Interracial groups of women built bridges between adults as well. Throughout the 1950s women allied with the American Friends Service Committee (AFSC), a co-ed group founded by Quaker activists in 1917, and worked closely with local NAACP leaders to ensure that the *Brown v. Board of Education* decision would be enacted as smoothly as possible. These women enacted the feminine ethos of social change by facilitating meetings between black and white parents, students, school boards, and community leaders (Lynn, *Progressive Women* 73–80). More than mere auxiliary to the rest of the civil rights movement, this new mode of social change—like those modes enacted by black and white women activists elsewhere—became central to the daily implementation of civil rights legislation.[17]

Building Bridges between Worlds in Postwar Women's Encounter with the Alien Other Stories

Of course, the struggle to register black voters and integrate public schools hardly seems to be the stuff of SF. And it is true that stories featuring protagonists of color and extended meditations on race relations were not regular features of the genre until African American

17. Susan Lynn's essay "Gender and Progressive Politics: A Bridge to Social Activism of the 1960s" and her book *Progressive Women in Conservative Times: Racial Justice, Peace, and Feminism, 1945 to the 1960s* are the definitive works in this subject. For other discussions about race relations and progressive politics, see Jacqueline Jones, "The Political Implications of Black and White Southern Women's Work in the South, 1890–1965" and Leila J. Rupp and Verta Taylor, *Survival in the Doldrums: The American Women's Rights Movement, 1945 to the 1960s.*

authors such as Samuel Delany, Charles Saunders, and Octavia Butler entered the field in the 1960s and 1970s. For the most part, postwar SF authors either focused on the adventures of white characters or, following the example set by Robert Heinlein in *Starship Troopers*, imagined futures worlds marked by relative racial harmony. In such worlds individuals might retain ethnic names, but all other cultural differences seem to have been dissolved by the advent of a global society that looked much like white, middle-class America.[18]

At the same time, a small but significant number of writers did use SF to explore the changing nature of race relations in postwar America. Once again, women who wrote SF were on the front lines of such storytelling. Such women made powerful statements about the necessity of the civil rights movement through tales that combined elements of one very old story type, SF's "encounter with the alien other," and one very new one, the emergent southern literary sub-genre of the "racial conversion narrative."

As Brian Stableford notes, writers have long used encounter with the alien other stories to explore what might happen when cultures collide. Influenced by Darwinian theory, early SF stories ranging from H. G. Wells's *The Time Machine* (1898) to Edmond Hamilton's "Thundering Worlds" (1934) depicted alien others as the natural enemies of mankind. By the middle of the twentieth century, however, most SF authors had turned to more nuanced investigations of "the problems of establishing fruitful communications with alien races" ("Aliens" 16). As such, the postwar encounter with the alien other narrative lent itself quite easily to authors interested in telling allegorical stories about bridge-building activities between human races in the present.

Racial conversion narratives emphasized similar themes. As a literary form that first emerged in the 1940s with the publication of Lillian Smith's *Killers of the Dream* (1949) and Katharine Du Pre Lumpkin's *The Making of a Southerner* (1947), the racial conversion narrative enabled conscientious white authors, as literary critic Fred Hobson puts it, to talk about "coming up from racism and embracing racial brotherhood and sisterhood" (205). Racial conversion narratives tend to follow a very specific pattern, beginning with descriptions of the author's childhood inculcation into racist attitudes and chronicling the author's "racial awakening" as he or she comes to know

---

18. For specific discussion of postwar SF stories about race that never actually featured anyone but white people, see Sheree R. Thomas's introduction to *Dark Matters: A Century of Speculative Fiction from the African Diaspora*.

African Americans on a personal basis and is forced to confront his or her own racial biases (Hobson 211). The narrator's awakening almost always occurs within black communities or institutions such as the church. Here, the narrator experiences new forms of communication—usually singing, preaching, or speech making—that seem "extracultural, beyond the normal limits of American culture" and that lead him or her to imagine a new, more egalitarian world order based on "the power of love" (Hobson 214). Upon returning to his or her home community, the narrator inevitably experiences a profound "alienation from [white] society" and its racist values (Hobson 220). Finally, the narrator channels his or her newly politicized understanding of America into aesthetic activity—the writing of the racial conversion narrative.[19]

Women's racial conversion narratives are often organized around a female ethic of social change much like the one embraced by progressive women in the civil rights movement. Karen Ramsay Johnson and Diantha Daniels Kesling identify three characteristics of women's conversion narratives that demonstrate this clearly. First, women consistently link their racial conversions to gendered events such as the birth of a child or the ritual of dressing for a dinner party. These events lead racial conversion narrators to think about larger patterns of racial injustice, such as the different ways that black and white women are treated during pregnancy or the implicitly white standards of beauty that permeate black women's lives (509–10). Second, women writers tend to define activism as both doing and listening (510). As such, their narratives are most likely to focus on those (primarily female) activists who contributed to the civil rights movement by facilitating communication or otherwise acting as bridge leaders. Finally, the authors of women's racial conversion narratives position themselves as "mediating between the worlds of their activist work and those of their contemporary readers" (512). In turn, the act of writing becomes a kind of bridge building in and of itself.

19. It is interesting to note that racial conversion narratives follow a pattern of cognitive estrangement on the part of the narrator that is very similar to the one experienced by the protagonist of many SF and utopian stories: in essence, a person much like ourselves travels to a strange world, learns the superior ways of that world, and then finds him- or herself completely alienated from his or her own society. Furthermore, the racial conversion narrative—much like its science-fictional and utopian counterparts—provides readers with a logical explanation of how that alternate world came to be (in this case, through the American institution of slavery) and how a better world might evolve (through sustained political education and action). Little wonder, then, that this narrative form lent itself so handily to postwar SF authors.

The similarities between SF's encounter with the alien other story and mainstream literature's racial conversion narrative are particularly apparent in postwar women's SF. Although authors including Margaret St. Clair, Kay Rogers, Cornelia Jessey, and Mildred Clingerman typically reference legal decisions, social demonstrations, and other public events associated with the civil rights movement to build their fictional worlds, the actual plots of their stories revolve primarily around the promises and perils of cross-cultural communication between individuals in the private sphere. Moreover, these SF authors both anticipate and extend the practices of their mainstream literary counterparts by specifically linking racial conversion to conventionally feminine interests such as the pursuit of romance or domesticity.

As such, these stories also function much like postwar women's nuclear war narratives: as warnings about the nightmare future America might create for its private citizens given current social arrangements. Mid-century women's alien encounter narratives also resemble their nuclear war counterparts in that both refuse the apolitical, ahistorical "love conquers all" mentality that dominated so many other forms of contemporary popular culture. Instead, they show how private relations between individuals are always already conditioned by historical and material factors, and how reformation of these relations can be meaningful only if accompanied by a similar reformation of their institutional counterparts.

One of the primary concerns of women's alien encounter narratives from the early 1950s is the difficulty of enacting legislation to secure genuine racial justice. Although President Harry Truman established the first Civil Rights Commission in 1946 and ordered the desegregation of the U.S. military in 1948, he restrained from enforcing any more specific legislation at the time for fear of alienating white southern voters (Chafe 91). It is not surprising, therefore, that stories such as Margaret St. Clair's "Brightness Falls from the Air" (1951) imagined that even the most successful examples of interracial communication would fail in the face of an entrenched bureaucracy. St. Clair's story depicts a far future where humans have ruthlessly taken over every habitable planet they can find, leaving indigenous peoples to starve and die unless they are willing to participate in the deadly battle sports that have become the conquering race's favorite distraction. When sympathetic humans try to help "exteys" they are stoned to death by their fellow humans (162).

True to the pattern established elsewhere in postwar women's political fictions, "Brightness Falls from the Air" explores the impact of this dystopic future on two star-crossed lovers. Kerr is a minor human bureaucrat who, from the very beginning of the story, acknowledges his people's wrongdoings but shrugs them off as "a particular instance of the general cruelty and stupidity" that he believes characterizes all peoples in all times (162). He is forced to revise this opinion when he meets Rhysha, a beautiful bird woman from the planet Ngayir with whom he promptly falls in love. Kerr's kindness intrigues Rhysha as well, and the two soon exchange personal histories. When Kerr learns that the battle sports his people love are actually perversions of the dignified leadership rituals that once structured life on Rhysha's world, Kerr vows to help the Ngayir escape extinction by sponsoring their immigration to a new world. As in other conversion narratives, bonding and communication between individuals of different races leads the protagonist of the dominant race to a new understanding of larger patterns of racial injustice—and to a new determination to change those patterns.

Unfortunately, all is for naught. When the arbitrator who rules on colonization matters learns that Kerr's colonization request is for an alien race rather than one of Earth's indigenous peoples, he pigeon-holes Kerr as a kindly but misguided "conservationist" and dismisses his petition because "immigration is restricted by executive order to terrestrials" (164). Soon afterward Kerr falls gravely ill; when he recovers, it is only to learn that Rhysha has sacrificed herself in the battle sports arena to secure food for her family. Noble as it may seem, St. Clair warns that even this extreme individual sacrifice cannot change the tide of history.

As "Brightness" concludes, Kerr finds himself alone with Rhysha's body, listening to an advertisement for a new kind of alien battle game and "the bloodiest combats ever televised" (165). Played by a new alien race even more desperate than the bird people, this game seems to seal the doom of Ngayir as a whole. Thus, St. Clair insists that the power of love might lead individuals of different races to new understandings of one another. However, even the most committed of these individuals cannot withstand the intransigency of public institutions.

A similar pessimism informs Kay Rogers's short story "Experiment" (1953), where humans have been enslaved by the snakelike Venusians who are a cold-blooded race with limited emotional capabilities. Unlike the wildly passionate humans of St. Clair's story, Rogers's Venusians are a gravely intellectual people who approach even the seemingly most intimate of relations in a detached manner. For example, when a human accuses her captor of being unable to love his fellow Venusians, he immediately dismisses her complaint as "Terran nonsense" because "his people did not sentimentalize reproduction. One [simply] went to the mating clinics as required" (97). This does not mean, however, that Rogers's Venusians behave toward their conquered races any more kindly than do St. Clair's humans. Although they do not treat humans as objects of entertainment, Venusians do use them as test subjects for their scientific experiments. Much like slave owners of the antebellum South, Venusians consider their slaves to be bright but difficult animals, keeping men and women together just long enough to breed them and then breaking up families and parceling them out to interested scientist owners.

Once again, the encounter with the alien other is a decidedly personal one. Rogers's story follows the adventures of Cobr, a Venusian scientist who decides to investigate the "emotional aberration" that humans call love. Accordingly, he rescues a "not unusual, perhaps, but adequate" human woman from his slave pens and installs her in his own household with all the comforts that his people usually accord one another (97). Upon learning that she was a performer in her former life, Cobr promptly secures a guitar for his human subject and encourages her to sing for him because "he had read that women used their voices thus to beguile and he was pleased he might subject himself to such sounds" (97). Here then cross-cultural love begins not as a happy accident but as a carefully planned event.

The outcome, however, is much the same, as Cobr finds himself transformed by an alien mode of communication beyond anything he has ever experienced before:

> He had forgotten the pens, listening to the slave's plaintive, smoky voice. How unlike the labor hymns and battle chants of his own people! The slave's songs told only of regretted or baffled matings. Strange, useless music!
>
> As strange as the mistake he had made regarding the slave's beauty. She was not merely adequate, but an extraordinarily beautiful specimen of her race. . . . So now he admired her? Yes, Cobr decided, it was true. (98)

As in standard conversion narratives, Cobr's racial awakening hinges on experiencing a new mode of communication that transcends cultural barriers, prompting him to reconsider his racial biases and to rethink his relations with the alien other.

Much like St. Clair, however, Rogers insists that the power of love is not enough and that interracial romance cannot flourish in a world where public sentiment does not change at the same pace as private emotion. Although Cobr's human admits that she might be able to return her captor's feelings someday, this possibility is crushed by a Venusian plague that sweeps through the country and kills her. When a servant delivers this news and offers to find another test subject, Cobr, who is strangely moved by the "empty sound" of the singer's guitar, abruptly ends the experiment because "I do not wish another singing one" (99). And so Rogers's protagonist is alienated from both his society and himself, caught in the grip of a newfound emotion that he cannot even properly name.

As the civil rights movement gained momentum in the middle of the 1950s with landmark legal decisions such as *Brown v. Board of Education* and social actions such as the Montgomery bus boycott, women's SF stories began to treat the problem of civil rights in more forthright ways. For example, Rogers's "Command Performance" (1954), written just two years after "Experiment," imagines what America might become if it fails to enact positive social change through education. "Command Performance" takes place in a far future where humans have conquered the solar system and "put the Golden Rule on a cash basis," taxing racial discrimination against Jews, diasporic Africans, and Martians (the only other sentient race in the solar system besides humans) equally (73). The new taxes are enforced by an elaborate surveillance system composed of miniature camera recorders that minorities are encouraged to wear on their wrists at all times. When the Martians suggest that education might be a better way to prevent racial strife, humans "indulgently" dismiss them for failing to recognize the "cynical" reality of modern humanity (71).

Rogers demonstrates the impossibility of achieving racial equality through this kind of legislation with the domestic drama of a single Martian family as it struggles to adjust to life on Earth. Bix and his mother are grateful to be rescued from the chaotic relocation center where they have spent several years, but they are skeptical when their landlord insists that they will not need to wear their camera recorders in his apartment building because "I like my Unit to be one big family" (74). As Bix's mother privately warns her son, "I don't care what he said. . . . I want you to wear that thing. I don't think anyone will say or do anything, there's the law, but—the law forbids against discrimination in word and deed. But things like that take time. Education would be better, it seems to me. So don't expect too much" (71). From the outset of her story, Rogers suggests that laws designed to regulate public behavior in punitive ways are likely to fail. Instead, they must be replaced by laws that encourage intellectual growth and psychological change from within.

And so the only racial awakening that occurs in "Command Performance" is that of the alien other who experiences the new forms of discrimination engendered by prejudice tax laws. When Bix tries to make friends with Sam Clay, a neighborhood boy about his own age, he is rebuffed in a number of ways. For example, when they first meet, Sam tells Bix that he "looks funny"—and then noticing Bix's camera recorder, immediately amends his comment to suggest that Bix looks funny because Sam is hanging upside down from his toy antigravity belt (72). Eyes still fastened on Bix's recording device, Sam offers to let the Martian child play with his belt—only to quickly conclude, "Ma says I'm not to let anybody take it unless I'm around. And I gotta go in now" (72). This sly cruelty drives Bix back into his apartment while Sam continues to play outside with his toy. For Rogers, the failure to educate children about race relations will inevitably thwart (rather than foster) interracial communication.

But Rogers suggests that public legislation is only half the problem and that the other half is rooted in the private sphere of the home. Soon after the Martian family moves into his apartment building, the landlord arranges for Mrs. Clay to take Sam and Bix to see a rocket launch. Although Mrs. Clay greets Bix cordially enough, she cannot keep her eyes off Bix's camera recorder. Loudly declaring that "it ain't hard for me to remember [to be polite to Martians] but it's awful hard for some folks," Mrs. Bix launches into a story about a fine her daughter Mary incurred for swearing at a Martian girl (75). After a lengthy recital that casts Mary as a "poor lamb" provoked to unthinking behavior by a "young chit" who dared to try on a skirt that Mary and her friends wanted to purchase, Mrs. Clay concludes by offering Sam a burnt cookie and asking if he really wants to go with them to the rocket launch (75–76). Inevitably, Bix declines and slinks back to his apartment. Like other postwar SF authors, Rogers uses motherhood as a register for the promises and perils of larger social arrangements. In the case of "Command Performance," the perversions of a legal system that fails to adequately address the needs of a multiracial populace are reflected in the perversions of mothers who fail to properly educate and care for the children around them.

While authors such as St. Clair and Rogers use the encounter with the alien other to explore the real need for positive civil rights legislation in America, Cornelia Jessey's "Put Out the Light" (1955) explores the hatreds and fears that encouraged many Americans, especially southern Americans, to oppose the civil rights movement. Jessey's story follows the adventures of an unnamed public relations man for a senior senator from the Deep South who has just lost his campaign for reelection. The story begins with Jessey's protagonist bitterly reflecting on the election results: "What was the use of hanging on? The senior senator had lost, no matter how many little outlying counties were heard from. The city voters had beaten him. The city precincts with their foreign agitators, nigger-loving yankees, yankee-loving southerners, traitors to their own kind—the city precincts had beaten the senior senator" (18). Given the effectiveness of the massive black voter education and registration campaigns that swept the American South after World War II, the opening beats of "Put Out the Light" hardly seem science fictional at all. Rather, Jessey's story closely resembles the realist racial conversion narrative, beginning as it does with this brief but vivid glimpse of a country—much like postwar America—on the cusp of radical social change.

To a certain extent "Put Out the Light" might be considered a reverse racial narrative because it begins, rather than ends, with its protagonist's alienation from society. Mocked by the northern press as "the senior senator's running dog," the PR man soon learns that southerners are even more dismissive of him (20). When Jessey's protagonist receives the opportunity to ghostwrite the biography of a famous southern colonel, he jumps at the chance because "it was the height of his ambition, to be part and parcel of that world of old plantations, old colonial homes, old families" (21). As the story unfolds, however, it becomes painfully clear that he is not part of this world. Upon arriving at the colonel's house and witnessing the internment of an old black woman in the colonel's family plot, the horrified PR man accuses his hero of moral degeneracy. The colonel immediately fires him because "this old nigger happens to be my mammy, suh, and I'll thank you to keep your trap shut. . . . I've [even] made arrangements in my will to be buried next to my black mammy. That's for your information and good day to you. Cheap white trash!" (21) Thus the PR man is revealed to be a person out of time who cannot communicate with anyone because he has been displaced from both the race relations of an emergent future he fears and those of a distant past he does not fully understand.

At this point Jessey's story shifts to a more fantastic mode, and the PR man experiences a rather peculiar racial conversion. Driven to despair by the senator's loss and the colonel's rejection, the PR man wills himself to die, hoping that his afterlife will somehow make up for the disappointments of the mortal world. When Gabriel's horn awak-

Figure 5. Original illustration for Cornelia Jessey's "Put Out the Light" (1955). Artist Naaman Peterson previews the very literal racial conversion experienced by Jessey's protagonist by shading the main figure's head with black ink while leaving his hands white.

ens him in heaven, he is puzzled to find himself surrounded by black people who lovingly address him as "son." In a desperate attempt to make sense of the new world around him, the PR man swings back and forth between the joyful conviction that he has become a southern aristocrat complete with his own black mammies and pappies and the paralyzing fear that he has been buried in a black cemetery and condemned to a black hell (23). Thoroughly alienated from the two mixed-race communities he encountered in the course of his life, the PR man cannot even begin to fathom an afterlife populated solely by those men and women whom he has always dreaded as the dangerous racial other.

In the end, it literally takes an act of God to complete the PR man's racial conversion. As Gabriel's horn trumpets one last time, the PR man finally looks into the "pitch black" face of the heavenly father who has been holding his hand and realizes that "the wind [of

Gabriel's horn] had blown everything right out of his mind, all the old hatreds, all the convictions, all the despair—everything—swept it clean and empty. He felt his hand being released and the presence moving away from him. Timidly, humbly, he looked down at his hand knowing already that it was black" (24). One the one hand, Jessey's story powerfully echoes and extends the hope inherent in many mainstream racial conversion narratives: that white Americans might find a solution to their own social alienation in the new modes of community offered by their black counterparts. On the other hand, it reiterates the pessimism characteristic of many encounters with the alien other stories, concluding that the only real change possible is that which might occur in the hereafter (see figure 5).

As widespread public demonstrations both for and against the civil rights movement gained momentum in the late 1950s and early 1960s, Americans from all parts of the nation found themselves caught up in what, just a few years earlier, had seemed to be a regional problem that might be resolved by a few enlightened legislative measures. Not surprisingly, women's SF stories from this period reflect both the increased urgency of the civil rights movement at this time and an increased awareness of the difficulties inherent in massive, protracted social reform.

This is particularly apparent in Mildred Clingerman's 1956 short story, "Mr. Sakrison's Halt." Much like Jessey, Clingerman uses SF's encounter with the alien other story to show how the most alien of all encounters are those that occur between humans. In "Mr. Sakrison's Halt" the encounter with the alien other takes the form of a romantic encounter between the southern belle Mattie Compton and the northern liberal Mr. Sakrison. Although she initially dismisses him as a "Yankee beast," Miss Mattie soon falls in love with the gentle man and his vision of a better world: "I'd never heard anybody speak so sadly about the nigras. . . . He put words to the little sick feelings I'd had at times, and I began to catch his vision" (39, 40). Clingerman's story begins much like a mainstream racial conversion narrative, where the white protagonist meets someone of a different cultural background and then, prompted by the power of love, begins to grapple with her own complicity in racist practices.

At the same time, Clingerman echoes the skepticism of St. Clair and Rogers concerning the transformative power of love. Fueled by a vision of themselves as crusaders for racial justice, Miss Mattie and Mr. Sakrison decide to migrate north, where they will marry and begin the good fight among like-minded people. However, their plans collapse when their train makes an unexpected stop in an unnamed town where beautifully dressed people of various races peacefully mingle "all mixed in together" (41). Mr. Sakrison immediately gets off the train and is welcomed by a distinguished-looking black man; Miss Mattie, overcome by a flash of prejudicial anger and fear, hangs back—and loses her chance for happiness when the train starts up and barrels on without her fiancé. As a kind of penance, Miss Mattie spends the next forty years of her life riding the Jim Crow cars of the same train, desperately searching for the mysterious town where her beloved vanished. For Clingerman, interpersonal communication in the guise of romantic love may be the first important step toward the elimination of racial prejudice in America, but it is by no means enough to eliminate such prejudice altogether.

This is not, however, the end of "Mr. Sakrison's Halt." Clingerman goes beyond her predecessors to explore how social change might derive from more mundane but effective kinds of activism, such as storytelling and sympathetic listening. Clingerman's tale is actually narrated by an anonymous young woman born in Miss Mattie's home-town but raised in the north. To counteract the hostility she feels as an outsider when visiting her birth town, the narrator makes friends with the only other person who does "too much traveling around": Miss Mattie (38). In contrast to the other townsfolk, Clingerman's narrator does not simply dismiss Miss Mattie's tale as the product of a lovesick mind. Instead, she cherishes Miss Mattie precisely because the old woman's story provides her with an imaginative bridge between the world of what America is and what it might have—or might yet—become.

Accordingly, Clingerman's narrator is given the privilege of wit-nessing both the happy conclusion of Miss Mattie's story and this other America. During their last train ride together the narrator spots the mysterious stop that Miss Mattie has described so many times before. This time Miss Mattie does not hesitate to get off the train, and she is rewarded almost immediately with the return of both her youth and Mr. Sakrison. Hence, it would seem that with patience and continued communication between sympathetic individuals, there might be a future in which love—between individuals and between races—could prevail.

Like Miss Mattie and the protagonists of many other racial con-version narratives written by women, Clingerman's narrator also mediates between two worlds: the one of social reform to which she has been a witness and the one of her readers. In using her narrator this way, Clingerman underscores the very real gulf that still exists between these worlds. Miss Mattie and her lover are only reunited in a magical, alternative America that the narrator glimpses but can never find again, trapped as she is in a world of "fiery crosses" and white supremacist rage (43). The narrator's closing observation further underscores the difference between these two Americas: "The Katy local was retired years ago. There's a fine highway now to the city. . . . I hear everything has changed. But I read in my newspaper last week how they've locked the doors to the schoolhouse and barred with guns and flaring anger the way to the hill, and I realize how terribly far [my birth town] still is from Mr. Sakrison's halt" (43–44). More than mere apocalyptic imagination, this final image encapsulates some of the most dreadful headlines of Clingerman's day: after all, "Mr. Sakrison's Halt" appeared in print just one year before the Arkansas governor shut down the entire state school system to prevent the integration of Little Rock Central High School. And much the same thing can be said of Clingerman's story. With all its twists and turns, the narrative structure of "Mr. Sakrison's Halt" closely mirrors the hopes and fears attending the civil rights movement in America. Although Clingerman's narrator—and by extension, Clingerman's readers—might have been able to catch glimpses of the brave new world imagined by civil rights activists and their sympathizers, in the American South of 1956 it might well have felt as if that dream was still impossibly far away.

Conclusion: The Many Faces of Domestic Patriotism

In this chapter I have examined how postwar women used SF stories to interrogate the social arrangements of cold war America. In accordance with the new spirit of political conservatism and cultural conformity that swept the nation, the dominant discourses of the era encouraged women to become domestic patriots by exchanging paid work in the public sphere for childbearing and housekeeping in the privacy of the new suburbs. More than mere helpmeets to their men, postwar homemakers were figured as cold warriors responsible for ensuring familial order in the home and, by extension, moral order throughout the democratic state.

While many women no doubt took such exhortations to heart, others enacted a different kind of domestic patriotism on America's streets and in its courtrooms. Invoking the rhetoric of feminine moral authority and social facilitation, politically progressive women enacted a female ethic of social change to advance a variety of causes including protest against nuclear weapons and advocacy of the civil rights movement. Such women exploited the instability inherent in postwar discourses of gender. By playing on American beliefs about the sanctity of hearth and home, mid-century women made persuasive arguments against a cold war status quo that threatened the very existence of the family in particular and democracy in general.

SF authors espoused their own brand of domestic patriotism to readers who might not otherwise have thought extensively about how their cold war world came to be—or what it might become if left unchecked. Judith Merril, Virginia Cross, Carol Emshwiller, and Mary Armock set the feminist antiwar figure of the *mater dolorosa* wandering in the blasted landscape of SF's nuclear holocaust narrative. In doing so, they made concrete peace activists' warnings about the devastating effect of nuclear war on the nuclear family. Additionally, Merril tried to think beyond the disastrous ending of the nuclear war narrative by transforming the *mater dolorosa* into a *mater scientifica*, a figure that makes connections to other progressive mothers and scientists in an effort to build new communities based on logic and love rather than hysteria and fear. Consequently, peace activists became models for a new kind of science-fictional heroine.

Margaret St. Clair, Kay Rogers, Cornelia Jessey, and Mildred Clingerman used similar strategies in their stories about American race relations, inflecting SF's encounter with the alien other story with elements drawn from southern literature's racial conversion narrative. Translating the bridge-building work of their civil rights activist counterparts into fiction, these authors illustrated how both cross-cultural communication and positive legislation were necessary to ensure the dream of democracy for all. Although these authors seemed relatively pessimistic about the possibility of egalitarian race relations in present-day America, both Jessey and Clingerman clung, however faintly, to the utopian dream of racial harmony in other worlds and other times.

Clearly postwar women writers used SF stories about women and children as focusing lenses through which to examine widespread scientific and social change in contemporary America. But what did such authors have to say about the impact of marriage and motherhood on women's work in the fields of science and technology themselves? The next chapter answers this question by examining SF stories that feature women as scientists, engineers, and astronauts.

CHAPTER FOUR

SCIENTISTS

IN *THE* preceding chapters of this book I have examined how postwar women writers used SF to examine the impact of new sciences and technologies on women's work in the home. In this final chapter I explore how such authors helped shape new representations of women's work in the fields of science and technology as well. For the most part, postwar Americans seemed reluctant to accept women as professional scientists, engineers, and astronauts. This reluctance is clearly conveyed by the character of Dr. Maureen Robinson from the popular early 1960s television series *Lost in Space*. At the beginning of the first episode, Maureen Robinson seems to have it all: in her techno-cultural position as a space explorer on the generation ship *Jupiter 2*, she is valued as both a biochemist and a mother. Unfortunately, when Dr. Smith destroys the *Jupiter 2*, he also destroys this pro-tofeminist dream. Once the Robinsons are marooned, the show becomes a frontier narrative and characters take on the traditional gender roles of the pioneer family. Before the first episode even ends, Dr. Robinson has already become Mrs. Robinson—a transformation that all the characters including Robinson herself seem to find perfectly natural.

And indeed, this kind of transformation probably did seem perfectly natural to many viewers. As feminist Betty Friedan argues, postwar American investment in the ideology of feminine mystique fostered specific ideas about appropriate kinds of work for women. The mystique defined women in terms of their sexual and maternal drives; accordingly, it dictated that women would be most fulfilled by the domestic labor of marriage and motherhood. Although women might make significant contributions to society by pursuing careers outside the home, in doing so they condemned themselves to lives of unmarried loneliness. Thus, the conservative gender ideals of postwar America "spelled out a choice—love, home, and children, or other goals and purposes in life" (183). For Friedan, this choice was a mistaken one because advocates of the feminine mystique never considered the possibility that women, like men, might combine domestic and professional labor throughout their lives.

Although figures such as Maureen Robinson may well have embodied widespread conservative attitudes towards women's work in science and technology, they were by no means the only ones available to postwar Americans. In the first part of this chapter I briefly review postwar American attitudes toward science, technology, and gender. Historians generally agree that while the decades following World War II constituted a golden age of American science, prevailing convictions about the feminine mystique prevented scientifically and technologically inclined women from reaping the same benefits as their male counterparts. In an era when women's work in the home was seen as the first line of defense against the encroachment of communism onto American soil, women scientists were often represented in the mainstream media as unnatural and unpatriotic.

Yet, women continued to study and practice science and technology in record numbers. Moreover, the advent of the Space Race suggested that America truly needed them to do so. Accordingly, new initiatives such as the National Defense Education Act of 1958 provided scholarships to scientifically inclined boys and girls alike, while new programs such as NASA's short-lived Women in Space Early (WISE) program showcased the technical skills that many American women already possessed. Although these initiatives did not produce results for years, the publicity materials they generated provided mid-century Americans with striking new images of women who seemed to be equally at home in laundry rooms, laboratories, and launch pads.

In the second part of this chapter I show how women in the

postwar SF community incorporated changing ideas about science, technology, and gender into both their science and SF writing. As contributors to major SF magazines such as *Amazing Stories* and *Fantastic Adventures*, authors including June Lurie, Sylvia Jacobs, and Kathleen Downe wrote hundreds of articles on topics ranging from the historic foundations of mythology and superstition to new developments in deep sea diving and atomic energy. Following the conventions established by women science writers of the eighteenth, nineteenth, and early twentieth centuries, these columnists represented themselves as trained educators or scientific wives whose education, close observation skills, and first-hand experience of science and technology empowered them to critically assess the discoveries made by male scientists and engineers. And so these authors claimed places for themselves as essential members of the scientific community.

Fiction writers addressed the issue of women's scientific authority even more directly. Authors including Marion Zimmer Bradley, Judith Merril, Katharine MacLean, Doris Pitkin Buck, and Anne McCaffrey all wrote stories of scientific discovery and adventure extrapolated from changing ideas about the nature of women's work in a high-tech world. In such stories, the choice between family and career is more than a mistaken one for women; it is downright deadly because it destroys individual families and undermines human progress as a whole. But these authors also rewrote masculinist myths about science and technology to imagine future worlds where women might combine their professional and personal lives, thereby creating utopian new modes of technoscientific labor. The protagonists of such stories escape the fate of Maureen Robinson. They are not unhappy housewife heroines lost in space but compassionate and consummate professionals who lead their people to the stars.

Scientist Mothers and Lady Astronauts in the Golden Age of American Science

The postwar era was a difficult period for American women interested in science and engineering. As science historian Margaret Rossiter explains, American science experienced a "golden age" as cold war anxieties spurred a "period of record growth in almost every aspect of American science that one could count—money spent, persons trained, jobs created, articles published, even Nobel prizes won" (xv). However, women did not share in the gains of this golden age.

Although they had been courted by industry, academia, and even the military during the technical manpower shortages of World War II, that courtship came to a sudden end after the war.[1] Over the course of the next two decades, women comprised less than 7 percent of all science and engineering professionals (Rossiter 98). Meanwhile, the number of women receiving science PhDs dropped from a postwar high of 9.35 percent in 1947 to a low of 6.16 percent in 1954 (Rossiter 80). Such trends seemed to confirm what advocates of the feminine mystique had argued all along: women naturally preferred domestic labor in the home to paid work in the laboratory.

Given the prevalence of this belief, it is not surprising that women who pursued professional technoscientific work faced a variety of obstacles in both academia and industry. The GI Bill enabled returning veterans to enroll at the colleges and universities of their choice in unprecedented numbers. In doing so, they displaced female applicants—and eventually female staff and faculty members—in unprecedented numbers as well (Rossiter 27). Women were further marginalized in academia by the reinstatement of the antinepotism rules that had been lifted during wartime. For example, when the award-winning physicist Maria Goeppert Mayer sought academic employment after World War II, the University of Chicago granted her husband a tenured position in chemistry but insisted it could not offer Mayer an equivalent position. Instead, officials created the new category of "volunteer professor" for her at the university's Institute for Nuclear Studies. Although this enabled Mayer to continue what would become her Nobel Prize–winning research, it did not provide her with a salary or any of the other formal benefits that her husband and other male colleagues enjoyed (Rose 154).

Women scientists and engineers faced even greater challenges outside academia. As one woman succinctly put it, "when I graduated, industry informed me that they were not interested in hiring a woman engineer" (qtd. in Mack 156). Of course, women could secure industrial employment if they were willing to take on low-paying, low-prestige jobs as librarians, editors, and research assistants where they provided "the largely invisible and highly feminized infrastructure"

---

1. For further discussion of changing ideas about women's work during and immediately after World War II, see the opening chapters of Kathleen Broome Williams's *Improbable Warriors: Women Scientists and the U.S. Navy in World War II* and Margaret Rossiter's *Women Scientists in America Before Affirmative Action, 1940–1972,* as well as the concluding chapters of Jenny Wosk's *Women and the Machine: Representations from the Spinning Wheel to the Electronic Age.*

that supported the work of their more highly paid male colleagues (Rossiter 29). In this respect, women were considered valuable members of the postwar scientific community. However, the labor for which they were most prized was that which most closely resembled women's traditional work in the home.

Even women in customarily feminine scientific professions lost authority to their male counterparts after World War II. For example, as home economics expanded to include new theories of childcare management, the women who created this field at the turn of the century—including Lillian Gilbreth, whose work inspired the Hollywood films *Cheaper by the Dozen* and *Belles on Their Toes*—found themselves eclipsed in the public eye by male experts such as Dr. Benjamin Spock. Moreover, male university administrators often cited the fact that "old" women such as Gilbreth still dominated home economics as clear evidence that such disciplines were outdated. As these women reached retirement age, administrators "seized upon the opportunity to reshape this formerly female bastion into the somewhat more gender neutral subjects of 'nutritional sciences,' 'human development,' or 'human ecology,'" replacing female deans and faculty with men who received higher salaries, better laboratories, and greater publishing opportunities (Rossiter 184). Similar transformations occurred across the country at the hundreds of teachers' colleges, junior colleges, and women's colleges that had previously trained and hired significant numbers of female scientists and technicians. As a result, masculinization became the preeminent sign of modernization for many institutions.

For the most part, postwar Americans seem to have accepted the marginalization of women's technoscientific labor as a necessary and natural phenomenon. Cultural historian Jenny Wosk notes that even before World War II ended, employers made clear to women that while it was their patriotic duty to take on men's work during times of national emergency, "they were expected to return to their domestic duties as housewives and mothers after the war" (198). As the war drew to a close, glossy magazines such as *Life* and *The Saturday Evening Post* replaced pictures of women at work with new images of them comfortably ensconced in high-tech homes where they enjoyed "the same kind of efficiency . . . as they have found in the factory or business office" (qtd. in Wosk 227). These images did not challenge women's technoscientific skills. Rather, they suggested that truly patriotic women would apply those skills wherever they were most needed to preserve the American way of life—and of course, with the advent of the cold war, it seemed that these skills were most desperately needed in the home to prevent the encroachment of communism onto American soil.[2]

The feminine mystique further reinforced the notion that women were naturally more suited to work in the home than in the laboratory. Most Americans conceded that "old maids" had to work to support themselves, but married women who continued their professional careers into the cold war were criticized for failing to follow their biological drives—and do their duty for America—by bearing children. Public opprobrium was heaped even more thoroughly on women who tried to have both family and career since, as Rossiter puts it, "every reader of Dr. Benjamin Spock knew that a normal child needed the full-time attention of his (or in later editions, her) loving mother" (41). And so the rhetoric of domestic patriotism blended effortlessly with that of the feminine mystique, reinforcing what so many Americans already thought they knew: women might have either family and career, but to sacrifice the former for the latter was unpatriotic and to combine the two was profoundly unnatural.

Scientist mothers were singled out as particularly dangerous to both science and society. Writing for a 1948 issue of *Hygeia* (a popular health magazine featured prominently in many pediatricians' offices), California housewife and educator Olive Lewis insisted that scientist mothers threatened America in two interrelated ways. As professional women who left their homes for extended periods each day, such women were by definition negligent wives and mothers. And as wives and mothers who were (Lewis assumed) preoccupied by the domestic problems that their absence from home caused, such women were bound to be bad scientists as well, unable to "do much good work of their own and even often upset[ting] other scientists' experiments" (Rossiter 41). Even as textbook authors continued to celebrate early-twentieth-century scientist mothers such as Marie and Irene Curie, mid-century Americans seemed all too willing to believe that such women were exceptions to the general rule.[3]

Widespread assumptions about the feminine mystique and women's natural affinity for domestic labor were reflected in the new secondary school curricula devised by proponents of "life adjustment

2. For further discussion of mid-century homemakers and cold war domestic patriotism, see Elaine Tyler May's *Homeward Bound: American Families in the Cold War Era*. For further discussion concerning science-fictional representations of (and challenges to) domestic patriotism, see chapters 2 and 3 of this book.

3. Sally Gregory Kohlstedt provides an excellent discussion of exceptionalism and its impact on women scientists in her essay "Sustaining Gains: Reflections on Women in Science and Technology in the Twentieth-Century United States."

education." Kim Tolley explains that teachers and administrators who favored this mode of education were determined to "make schooling more practical and useful" for students by creating courses that would "socialize individuals for their future careers as homemakers, workers, or citizens" (199–200). Accordingly, girls—who presumably would grow up to be homemakers or workers in traditionally feminine fields such as nursing or elementary education—were directed toward basic biology and home economics classes but away from specialized college preparatory courses in chemistry and physics. Textbook authors reinforced this gender stereotyping by juxtaposing images of famous scientific men with those of anonymous homemakers, nurses, and medical technicians and presenting students with photo montages in which "boys built models of machines and made a collection of minerals, whereas the girls raised house plants and applied first aid" (200). Thus, girls were guided toward domestic rather than professional careers before they were even in a position to make a choice—mistaken or not—between the two.

Despite these obstacles, postwar women pursued technoscientific degrees and careers in record numbers. Rossiter notes that the number of women working in scientific and technological fields nearly doubled after the war, and even the most conservative of "available statistics are sufficient to show that there were tens of thousands of women scientists in the United States in the 1950s and 1960s" (96). Women even made gains in the hypermasculine field of engineering, as previously all-male schools like Clemson University and the Georgia Institute of Technology opened their doors to women.[4] The number of women enrolled in undergraduate engineering programs nearly tripled between 1951 and 1957 (rising from 561 to 1,661), while the number of women who received their engineering degrees quadrupled (rising from 37 in 1952–53 to 145 in 1959–60) (Rossiter 55). If these numbers failed to register with the American public, it was no doubt because postwar men engaged in technoscientific endeavors in record numbers as well, causing the overall percentage of female scientists and engineers to remain statistically low.

Scientific women also employed a variety of strategies to ensure their professional success. Many strove to minimize the fact of their gender because they were acutely conscious of their status as lone women in hypermasculine workplaces. As one engineering graph-

---

4. For further discussion concerning the professionalization and masculinization of engineering at the turn of the century, see Ruth Oldenziel's *Making Technology Masculine: Men, Women, and Machines, 1880–1945.*

ics designer from this period remembers, although she was often propositioned at work, "I just ignored it. . . . [Perhaps if women] had been more aware of each other—networked—advances in combating sexual harassment could have occurred sooner" (qtd. in Mack 158–59). Women who were aware of one another did just that, banding together in independent societies to make themselves visible as professional women with specific goals. For example, when Beatrice Hicks founded the Society for Women Engineers (SWE) in 1950, fewer than sixty other women joined her for the first meeting (Kaledin 204). But by 1958, the SWE had over 500 members and had established regular meetings and awards (Mack 156). Much like the professional organizations that feminists created in the first part of the twentieth century, these postwar societies were dedicated to highlighting the accomplishments of women already involved in the technoscientific professions while actively recruiting a new generation to join them.

Still other scientific women sidestepped the twin problems of isolation and discrimination by pursuing types of work that were less attractive to men. Feminist historian Eugenia Kaledin notes that women regularly excelled in "new fields where tradition had not yet solidified," including crystallography, solar energy research, and computer engineering (203–4).[5] Women were also welcome in federal government agencies that dealt with traditionally feminine issues including home economics, women's labor, and public and child health as well as nonprofit organizations of all types (many of which they created themselves). These agencies and organizations were "frequently characterized by short promotional ladders, flexible work styles, and admittedly low (and in some cases non-existent) salaries." Nonetheless, they "provided titles and positions, allowed women to accept grants and hire others, and sometimes lived on beyond" the women who worked in them, providing such women with a certain degree of long-term institutional recognition (Rossiter 235).

A few women scientists even rose to national prominence during the cold war. In doing so, they complicated the myth of the feminine mystique. Both of the women who won Nobel Prizes in this period— Gerty Cori, who shared the prize in biochemistry with her husband in 1947, and Maria Goeppert Mayer, who won the prize in physics in 1963—were depicted in the press as good scientists *and* good mothers.

---

5. Kohlstedt rightly points out that women scientists sometimes found themselves at distinct disadvantages in even the most open of new fields, as when Rosalind Franklin's DNA photographs were surreptitiously previewed by James Watson and Frances Crick, who then used Franklin's imagery to complete their own work on the double helix.

Indeed, newspaper and magazine editors often seemed to emphasize these scientists' gender over their professional accomplishments, as in the *San Diego Evening Tribune* headline about Mayer that read "S.D. Mother Wins Nobel Physics Prize" (Rossiter 330). Although such representations might seem belittling to contemporary readers, in the context of their times they might have provided powerful antidotes to antifeminists' claims that women could not successfully combine their personal and professional lives.[6]

Two of the most popular postwar women scientists even made family and familial metaphors central to their professional work. As a firm believer in the equality of sexes and races, anthropologist Margaret Mead used both her own and other anthropologists' work on human adaptability in other cultures to support equal opportunity legislation in America. Meanwhile, oceanographer Rachel Carson encouraged Americans to rethink their relation to a rapidly vanishing nature in bestselling books such as *The Sea Around Us* (1951) and *Silent Spring* (1962). Significantly enough, both women presented themselves as successfully blending their professional and personal lives. Kaledin explains that as the working mother of one child, "Mead herself seemed to thrive on the kind of adaptation she believed essential to ensure women's contribution to the melting-pot ideal" (205). Meanwhile, Carson regularly cited her own mother as inspiration for her professional work while encouraging her readers to imagine themselves as a family united by their evolutionary debt to "mother sea" and "mother earth" (Kaledin 206). Rather than allowing their domestic commitments to undermine their scientific work, Mead and Carson demonstrated that women could enjoy rich personal lives while advancing the state of human knowledge.[7]

6. For further discussion concerning the ambivalent representation of women scientists in particular and women professionals in general at this time, see Marcel C. Lafollette's "Eyes on the Stars: Images of Women Scientists in Popular Magazines" and Joanne Meyerowitz's "Beyond the Feminine Mystique: A Reassessment of Postwar Mass Culture, 1946–1958." Lafollette argues that mass media representations of scientist mothers played into the feminine mystique because they created false expectations that only a few rare superwomen could manage work and family with any semblance of success. By way of contrast, Meyerowitz argues that such representations alleviated postwar anxieties about working women precisely because they proved that women could pursue professional careers and retain their femininity. Although such representations certainly preserved cold war gender ideals, they challenged the popular belief that women must choose between work and family, and that they would naturally choose the latter over the former.

7. Kaledin notes that when Carson first published her critique of the pesticide and herbicide industries in *Silent Spring*, her detractors immediately invoked the feminine mystique to dismiss her as a hysterical old maid (206). Significantly, these accusations

But perhaps the most significant event that provided new opportunities for women in science and technology was the advent of the Space Race. From the very start of the cold war, a few scientific institutions and government agencies warned that the United States would eventually find itself at a grave disadvantage if it failed to follow the Soviet Union's lead in training men and women alike for technoscientific careers. As early as 1951 *The Bulletin of Atomic Scientists* and *Newsweek* magazine both proposed that America could avoid future technical manpower shortages by drawing on "scientific womanpower." *Bulletin* editor Eugene Rabinowitch even argued that the federal government should create new fellowships for women interested in studying science and engineering (Rossiter 52). The 1957 National Manpower Council report *Womanpower* made similar claims, arguing that since the number of working women continued to rise despite back-to-the-home movements, schools should provide women with better academic counseling and flexible study programs while industry should consider part-time work and daycare programs (Rossiter 59).

The surprise launch of the Soviet satellite *Sputnik* in October 1957—months in advance of its American counterpart—seemed to confirm the need for American scientific womanpower. It also provided the occasion for the most extensive legislation directed at women in science to date: the 1958 National Defense Education Act (NDEA). Asserting that "the Nation requires the fullest development of the mental resources and technical skills of its young men and women," the NDEA provided fellowships for all students who showed promise in mathematics, science, foreign languages, and other defense-related areas of research (qtd. in Rossiter 63). Although the NDEA was not designed to counteract gender discrimination in either academia or industry, this turned out to be one of its long-term effects. Between 1963 and 1973 (when the act was dismantled), American women accounted for 22.54 percent of all NDEA scholarship holders (Rossiter 76). As women flooded the nation's top university programs, they became increasingly less willing to accept the economic and sexual discrimination that their foremothers had experienced. Inspired by the revitalized feminist movement on the 1960s, many female NDEA recipients went on to become scientific innovators and reformers.[8]

---

do not seem to have had much impact on the public reception of Carson's book—perhaps because, as Carson pointed out, all an average person had to do was look at his or her own backyard to see the immediate effects of industrial chemicals.

8. For further discussion concerning the relations of the NDEA to second-wave feminism and disciplinary reform in the sciences and engineering, see Kohlstedt's

Changing attitudes toward women in science were perhaps most evident in the creation of NASA's Women in Space Early (WISE) program. Shortly after the *Sputnik* launch, hydrogen bomb inventor Edward Teller testified to Congress that America should try to regain the lead in the Space Race by sending astronauts into space as soon as possible—and that those astronauts should be women because "they weigh less and have more sense" (qtd. in Kevles 7). By 1959 scientific teams from the United States, Canada, and Great Britain had all run tests showing that women functioned better than men in cramped spaces and endured loneliness better for longer periods of time—two criteria that were thought to be central to the well-being of humans in space. Little wonder that NASA began contracting civilian scientists to run similar tests for them while journalists and laypeople alike began wondering, "Why not a woman?"[9]

Unfortunately, the WISE program only lasted a few brief years. Initially NASA officials allowed Dr. Randolph Lovelace (who oversaw performance tests for the male Mercury 7 astronauts) to administer WISE from his private clinic in New Mexico. Inspired by his work with female aviators during World War II, Lovelace invited award-winning civilian test pilot Jerrie Cobb and twelve other similarly qualified women to New Mexico for the battery of exams that would enable them to participate in WISE. When the Russians again scooped their American counterparts in April 1960 by making Yuri Gagarin the first man in space, however, NASA officially ended WISE and redoubled its efforts to get the Mercury 7 men into space as soon as possible. At this point, Cobb herself took over, renaming her colleagues the Fellow Lady Astronaut Trainees (FLATs) and attempting to enlist everyone from rocket scientist Werner von Braun to Vice President Lyndon Johnson in her cause. Although Cobb's efforts earned her an appointment as special consultant to NASA and even got the FLATs a hearing in the 1962 Special Subcommittee on the Selection of Astronauts, the government refused to resume training women for space at that time, citing everything from the need for further testing to the feminine mystique itself as grounds for its decision (Kevles 16).[10]

"Sustaining Gains: Reflections on Women in Science and Technology in the Twentieth-Century United States" and Rossiter's *Women Scientists in America Before Affirmative Action, 1940–1972*.

9. The phrase "Why not a woman?" is from Kathleen Downe's 1955 article for *Authentic Science Fiction Monthly*, which I discuss in the following section of this chapter.

10. Kevles succinctly relates the history of WISE and the FLATs as a prelude to the larger story of women in space in the twentieth century. For another excellent history in this vein, see Pamela Freni's *Space for Women: A History of Women with the Right Stuff*. For studies that focus exclusively on the history of WISE and the FLATs, see especially

Although Lovelace and Cobb never got the FLATs into space, they provided a generation of Americans with powerful new images of women's work in a high-tech world. In February 1960 *Look* magazine ran a cover article on Betty Skelton, a three-time national aerobatic champion who trained with NASA's male astronauts (Nolen 92). Six months later, *Life* magazine published an equally extensive article on Cobb (Freni 53). Not surprisingly, these first female astronauts were always carefully photographed in accordance with postwar standards of feminine beauty. But otherwise they were depicted much like their male counterparts, spinning in centrifuges, floating in buoyancy tanks, and proudly looking off into the distant horizon as they climbed into their jets. Suddenly, it seemed the future was wide open and that women might someday be at home everywhere from the laundry room to the launch pad.

Why Not a Woman? Engendering Authority in Women's Science Fiction Magazine Science Writing

Women involved with the postwar SF community certainly thought this was the case, and a number of them demonstrated their own technoscientific authority in the science columns they wrote for prominent SF magazines. As such, these authors can be seen as participating in a centuries-old tradition of Anglophone women's science popularization. Science historians Barbara T. Gates and Ann B. Shteir explain that this tradition began with the Enlightenment, when women first participated in the scientific community as audience members. With the publication of Eliza Haywood's *The Female Spectator* in 1744, women began to write about science for one another. As the century progressed and femininity was defined increasingly in terms of maternal and familial labor, women writers "crossed the threshold into direct expositions of science by writing introductory books for children and parents" (7). By the end of the nineteenth century, children regularly received natural history education at school rather than in the home. Accordingly, women science writers—who were "more well-informed, original and creative popularizers" than ever—started to write for adults (16). In doing so, they began to rival male scientists for audiences.

Martha Ackmann's *The Mercury 13: The Untold Story of Thirteen American Women and the Dream of Space Flight* and Stephanie Nolen's *Promised the Moon: The Untold Story of the First Women in the Space Race.*

Over the course of this period, women created distinctly feminine modes of scientific authority. Eighteenth- and nineteenth-century thinkers generally assumed that although women were not intellectually equipped to grapple with the mysteries of the physical sciences, they were both better observers of nature and more inherently moral than their male counterparts. Accordingly, women had a specific place in the scientific community: they were ideally suited to study natural history and explain its relation to natural theology to children and other women in the home. Eighteenth-century women capitalized on this belief by writing science books that revolved around the figure of "the Scientific Mother" who explores the grounds outside her home with her children so they may better understand the wonders of nature and the wonders of God. Thus, the Scientific Mother (and the author herself) became "an exemplar of female knowledge and intellectual authority" for children and adults alike (Gates and Shteir 9).

As science professionalized in the nineteenth century, women writers exchanged the persona of the Scientific Mother for that of "the trained educator." As someone with either a formal science education of her own or an informal one derived from domestic life with a male scientist, the educator was uniquely qualified to "carefully explain new views of the physical and natural world to women, children, and the working classes" (Gates and Shteir 10). Much like the Scientific Mother, the trained educator provided readers with both scientific and moral lessons drawn from daily activities in the home. However, this latter figure derived authority not just from her role as a clear-sighted, morally pure mother but also from her personal and professional connections to the greater scientific community.[11]

In the late nineteenth and early twentieth centuries women writ-

---

11. As women developed more sophisticated writing personas, they also expanded the repertoire of narrative strategies by which they conveyed their authority. Authors who used the figure of the Scientific Mother to teach science generally employed the familiar format of letters and conversations to create "a pedagogy of interpersonal connection [and] a teaching climate that modeled a new style of family practice" (Gates and Shteir 9). Meanwhile, those who wrote from the position of the trained educator gravitated toward the more formal narrative form of the scientific dialogue, which established women as scientific authorities who translated professional jargon into the vernacular. Eventually women writers replaced the scientific conservation with the journey narrative, in which the educator and her young companion exchanged the comforts of home for the intellectual stimulation of travel. Gates and Shteir suggest that the journey was a particularly compelling narrative form because it preserved the spirit of cooperative learning that characterized earlier kinds of women's science writing while demonstrating that women—like men—could garner scientific authority by "becoming pioneers and going beyond British borders" to present readers with "new vantage points" on science and society alike (13).

ers developed distinctly *feminist* modes of scientific authority. At the turn of the century American suffragette Eliza Burt Gamble and her British counterpart, Arabella Buckley, both wrote evolutionary narratives that challenged Darwin by emphasizing the traditionally feminine qualities of cooperation and altruism over the traditionally masculine qualities of competition and control.[12] Furthermore, as Susan Merrill Squier demonstrates in her work on modernist women's science writing, the varieties of feminist science writing that flourished in this period reflected the range of feminist viewpoints themselves. For example, Charlotte Haldane and Naomi Mitchison—women who were related to one another by marriage and further connected by a mutual interest in improving women's lives—had wildly divergent views on gender and science. Haldane espoused an essentialist feminism that valorized women's roles as mothers and affirmed the workings of normal science. In contrast, Mitchison advocated a "proto-postmodern" feminism that celebrated "the multiplicity of women's biological and social possibilities" while challenging readers to "expand [their] notions of both scientific practice and scientists" ("Conflicting Scientific Feminisms" 181). Much like their predecessors, these feminist authors assumed that women were uniquely qualified to translate science to laypeople. However, they did so by connecting science to political rather than moral insight.

Women were also instrumental in the development of what would become the twentieth century's premier mode of science writing: science journalism. Media historian James C. Foust explains that when E. W. Scripps established the first professional science news service in 1921, he did so with the intent of giving scientists "an interpreter who can translate their language into plain United States that the people can understand" (qtd. in Foust 59). Accordingly, he encouraged his Science Service writers to strike a balance between "romance and scientific fact" by beginning with sensational headlines and then following through with clear explanations of scientific theories and developments that readers could connect to their daily lives (61). Given the similarities between Scripps's goals for science journalism and the methods employed by popular women science writers, it is no surprise that from the outset Science Service employed a number

---

12. Some early feminist science writers directly challenged scientific authorities in their writing. For further discussion, see especially Rosemary Jann's "Revising the Descent of Woman: Eliza Burt Gamble" and Barbara Gates's "Revisioning Darwin with Sympathy: Arabella Buckley," both available in Barbara Gates and Ann Shteir's edited anthology, *Natural Eloquence: Women Reinscribe Nature*.

of women who would go on to become prominent science journalists. These journalists included medical writer Jane Stafford, who founded the National Association of Science Writers in 1945 and served as president of the Women's National Press Club from 1949 to 1950, and psychology writer Marjorie Van de Water, whose groundbreaking work on the psychology of war appeared in science journals, in mainstream newspapers, and on the popular radio program "Adventures in Science" throughout the 1940s and 1950s (Tressider n.p.).[13]

After World War II, women science writers updated the literary conventions established by their predecessors to address contemporary issues. The most famous author to do so was Rachel Carson. Between 1941 and 1955 Carson published three books about the sea that are, as Rebecca Raglon notes, classic examples of nature writing in which Carson joyfully demonstrates the interconnectedness of all life to "mother sea" by "mingling . . . romantic rapture with an unmediated or scientific viewpoint" (197). Much like eighteenth- and nineteenth-century women writers, Carson established her scientific authority by deploying her naturally keen observation skills and scientific training within a quasidomestic setting (figured as the entire family of Earth). And much like late-nineteenth- and early-twentieth-century feminist authors, she used her science writing to impart secular rather than moral lessons. In particular, Carson encouraged readers to study nature so they might better appreciate the complexity of the world of which they were an intimate part.

Carson's growing concern about the destruction of nature led her to develop a new kind of science writing: what M. Jimmie Killingsworth and Jacqueline S. Palmer call "the apocalyptic nature narrative." In her international best seller *Silent Spring* (1962) Carson challenges American faith in scientific progress by synthesizing technical journal reports, anecdotal evidence, and expert correspondence to help readers understand how unregulated pesticide and herbicide use might herald the end of nature and, by extension, humanity itself. In tune with the temper of her times, Carson underscores the urgency of this situation by using "the imagery of nuclear disaster explicitly in [her] critique of the 'chemical death bombs' and 'biocides' of the

---

13. Other women correspondents for the Science Service included Frances Denmore, one of the first ethnologists to study American Indian music; Emma Reh, an archeological journalist who wrote extensively about Mexican history and culture; and Marjorie MacDill Breit, who wrote about "topics that ranged from zoology and entomology to toys and bottled milk" for Science Service (Tressider n.p.). For further discussion, see Mary Tressider's "Women and Science at Science Service."

industries [she] condemns" (186).[14] But the solution she proposes is one that hearkens back to the history of women's scientific practice, as she encourages readers to scrutinize their own backyards for signs of impending ecological disaster (Raglon 207). It is only by taking matters into their own, naturally capable hands, Carson suggests, that laypeople will be able to save themselves and create more egalitarian and ecologically sound forms of community.[15]

Although Carson may be the most famous postwar woman science writer, she was hardly the only one. In the decades following World War II scores of other women established their own technoscientific authority in the science pages of SF magazines.[16] Indeed, two of the most prominent magazines from this period, *Amazing Stories* and its sister publication, *Fantastic Adventures,* featured regular contributions by female science writers including June Lurie, Mildred Murdoch, and Rita Glanzman.[17] Meanwhile, dozens of other magazines (including both established periodicals such as *Astounding Science Fiction* and new ones such as *Slant*) regularly included science essays, editorials, and letters by women such as Bernice J. Peterson, Alma McCormick, and Kathleen Downe. While a few SF science popularizers such as Lurie and Sylvia Jacobs also wrote science fiction, most devoted themselves to nonfiction prose. Much like their fiction-writing counterparts, the women who wrote science nonfiction for the mid-century SF community comprised a discrete group of authors who employed specific narrative strategies to authoritatively comment on a diverse range of scientific and social topics.[18]

14. For further discussion of cold war imagery in Carson's nature writing, see Craig Waddell's excellent anthology *And No Birds Sing: Rhetorical Analyses of Rachel Carson's Silent Spring.*

15. Readers might note that Carson's prescription for saving the earth from ecological disaster parallels those arguments employed by mid-century peace and civil rights activists as described in chapter 3 of this book.

16. Stephen T. Miller and William G. Contento's *Locus Science Fiction, Fantasy, and Weird Magazine Index (1890–2001)* lists fifty-seven women science journalists who wrote for postwar SF magazines.

17. Both *Amazing Stories* and *Fantastic Adventures* (which merged with *Fantastic* in 1954) were owned by Ziff-Davis Publishing at this time, and both were edited by Raymond A. Palmer (1939–49); Howard Browne (1950–56); Paul W. Fairman (1956–58); and Cele Goldsmith Lalli (1958–65). This may explain why these two SF magazines featured regular science columnists, many of whom wrote for both publications. For more details, see Miller and Contento's *Locus Science Fiction, Fantasy, and Weird Magazine Index (1890–2001).*

18. Lafollette contends that that women science journalists, much like women scientists, were largely marginalized throughout the first half of the twentieth century. Fewer than 10 percent of all the popular science articles published between 1910 and 1955 were written by women, and those that were focused on traditionally soft or feminine

Women who wrote about science for *Amazing* and *Fantastic Adventures* generally followed the formula established by science journalists just a few decades earlier. Lurie, a prolific author who published over one hundred science articles between 1946 and 1953, was particularly skilled at this mode of writing. For example, "Icy Cold-War" (1950) reviews the difficulties that passenger ships and freighters encounter in the North Atlantic; "Artificial Universe" (1950) describes how scientists at Notre Dame have created sterile chambers to better study germs; and "Bacteria with Brains!" (1951) explains the process by which some bacteria produce sulfur. While Lurie's headlines were often even more sensational than the titles of the SF stories they accompanied, her columns were just the opposite. Consider, for example, this description of the sterile chamber created by Notre Dame scientists: "This startling innovation in biological technique is made possible by constructing a large metal chamber sealed and gasketed thoroughly against the contamination of the outside air. It resembles in some respects one of those huge cylindrical chambers used in the decompression of deep-sea divers. Entry to it is through an airlock. Built along side it and connecting with it is a second chamber—a half sterile room that serves as a preparation tank" ("Bacteria with Brains!" n.p.). Much like her counterparts at E. W. Scripps's Science Service, Lurie writes in "plain United States," providing readers with a concise description of the scientific invention under consideration—the sterile chamber—and comparing it to something with which readers might have more familiarity: the deep sea decompression chamber. In this respect, Lurie's science writing fulfills the ideals embraced by both Scripps and *Amazing* founder Hugo Gernsback: that authors who wrote about science and technology should balance romance and fact in such a way as to inspire a sense of wonder in readers.[19]

SF science writers also induced this sense of wonder by celebrating scientific progress and technocratic ideals. These ideals were

areas of inquiry. As Lafollette puts it, "In over 3300 magazine issues published over this 45 year period, no woman, either scientist or journalist, was listed as the author of an article on mathematics, astronomy, archaeology, or paleontology, despite the fact that women were actively engaged in research in these fields. Women tended to write about research in the social or biological sciences" (264). Of course, his study only examined mainstream magazines such as *Atlantic Monthly*, *Collier's*, and *The Saturday Evening Post*. As I demonstrate in this chapter, women accounted for a much higher percentage of science journalists featured in SF magazines, and the articles they published there explored new developments in both the hard and soft sciences.

19. For an excellent discussion of Gernsback's ideas about instilling a sense of wonder in SF readers and the impact of those ideas on the development of SF as a literary genre, see Gary Westfahl's *The Mechanics of Wonder: The Creation of the Idea of Science Fiction*.

particularly central to Mildred Murdoch's science history articles, which often addressed the changing relations of mythology, super-stition, and scientific explanation over time. In "Superstitions of the Sea" (1947), Murdoch sympathetically notes, "it is not strange in ages past there were a great number and variety of superstitions rampant among men who roamed the seas. The wonder is that anyone would venture out of sight of land at all" (23). She then points out that "some of the superstitions engendered by the fears of long ago remain to this day [but] many of them have faded away as ignorance and surmise have given way to knowledge" (23). As evidence of this, Murdoch goes on to explain how ancient tales about fearsome beings that ruled the north derived from limited understandings of Iceland's geysers and volcanoes, while legends about sirens, mermaids, and the Flying Dutchman grew from misunderstandings of St. Elmo's fire. Although Murdoch encourages readers to celebrate those ancient sailors "who dared to venture into a realm so beset with perils and terror and uncertainty," she also makes clear that many of these dangers have been drastically reduced—if not banished altogether—by the scientific explanations that replaced maritime superstition.

Of course, women science popularizers were not always so seri-ous. If anything, they seem to have been acutely aware that they were writing to both instruct and entertain their audiences who were, presumably, adolescent males just beginning to take an interest in all things biological as well as mechanical. For example, in "Machines Make the Money" (1952), Rita Glanzman carefully describes how automatic machinery—including the still relatively novel comput-er—might eventually transform office work. Like other science writ-ers, she explains how these new technologies have already changed daily life (by streamlining sorting processes at the U.S. Post Office) and even cites cyberneticist Norbert Weiner on the benefits of using machines to release people from "boring routine tasks" (93). In con-clusion, however, Glanzman breaks with the sober format of scientific journalism to cheerfully assure readers that "there is only one excep-tion to this general rule: the beautiful secretary can't be replaced by the machine—not because she can work as well, but because . . ." (93). As postwar science popularizers like Glanzman developed worldly authorial voices, they seemed to have evolved well past their literary predecessors.

But mid-century SF magazines also regularly featured letters and columns by women who employed the narrative strategies of ear-lier women science writers to establish feminine modes of scientific authority. Such authority is implicit in the title of Bernice J. Peterson's "What Man Can Imagine . . . [A] Cure for Infantile Paralysis?" (1946), which relates how one woman—the author's grandmother—may have found such a cure. Peterson writes that her grandmother, a practical nurse, once observed a poor child with infantile paralysis play daily in dried manure until "in a few weeks, to my grandmother's amazement, the girl grew stronger and stronger. Then she was walking and later running. She was completely cured and not a cripple" (152).

Like any good scientist, Peterson's grandmother responds to this unusual event by developing a hypothesis (that sunshine triggered a restorative chemical in the dried manure), and then testing it on a paralyzed chicken and, when he contracts infantile paralysis, on her own grandson. Much to her grandmother's satisfaction, both animal and child are restored to health—a fact that leads Peterson to "hope [and] pray . . . that medical science will just try this cure" (153). Peterson invokes the authority of the trained educator in complex ways, attributing a distinctly feminine scientific expertise to her grandmother who, in her role as a nurse, uses both close observation and scientific reason to solve the mysteries of the world around her. Meanwhile, Peterson herself takes on the literary task of the trained educator, explaining her grandmother's discovery to readers in a clear, approachable manner while politely challenging the predominantly male medical community to account for and build upon this unique female discovery.

Other women science writers challenged masculine authority more directly. In "Hold That Helium!" (1955), Sylvia Jacobs rebukes rocket scientist and SF author Willy Ley for using outdated diving analogies in his depictions of space exploration and synthetic atmospheres: "In all due humility, I must first explain that I do not by any means profess to be an authority on space problems in general. . . . But when these specialists draw analogies from diving theory to practice, when, for instance, they compare the orientation and propulsion methods of a weightless spaceman with those of a diver at near-neutral buoyancy, they get beyond their depth. In fact, they come way, way down to my level! . . . [The problem is that] science-fictioneers are living back in 1921, with a preconceived and since thoroughly disproved theory" (135). After explaining how the oxygen-helium environments usually depicted in SF would actually kill space explorers, Jacobs cites a number of Navy and civilian diving manuals and draws examples from her own experience as a diver to illustrate how SF authors might extrapolate from the current state of diving knowledge to depict space exploration more accurately.

Much like Peterson, Jacobs takes on the persona of the trained educator to establish herself as part of the scientific community. By citing a range of scientific authorities in combination with descriptions of her own diving experience, Jacobs positions herself as a force to be reckoned with, one who, much like her nineteenth-century predecessors, impresses readers with "self as well as science" (Gates and Shteir 12). At the same time, she is careful not to disrupt traditional gender roles too greatly, balancing her more aggressive pronouncements about male authors and scientists with deprecating asides in which she describes herself as "a very un-athletic and fortyish female" and an author whose "name carries no weight at all" (143, 146). Finally, Jacobs concludes that authors such as Ley should be forgiven for their fictional errors because "not many writers of science fiction are the wives of divers" (149). Thus, Jacobs minimizes the extent of her own diving experience and completely erases the fact that, as a published SF author in her own right, her name might well carry weight for *Astounding* readers.[20] Instead, she opts for the more traditional persona of the scientist's wife. While this narrative choice might seem to undercut Jacobs's authority in a male-dominated community, it preserves another central tenet of SF: that anyone with reasonable intelligence and experience can participate in scientific dialogue—even a housewife.

Still other women writers used their authority as educators to chastise male authors for failures of social extrapolation. In "A Chat with the Editor" (1954), Alma McCormick takes Philip K. Dick to task for writing stories that assume humans and mutants would naturally attempt to eliminate one another to ensure the survival of their own species. "Now really!" an indignant McCormick writes, "I'm a teacher . . . of exceptional children. This semester they are mentally retarded children, as far below the abilities of normal children as *homo sapiens* would be to *homo superior*. They cannot and never will be able to take care of themselves, but we carefully teach them all they *can* learn. . . . We don't, and never expect the rest of the world to, compete with them. They're certainly not being 'cold-decked' from the start" (2). The problem for McCormick is clear. While Dick extrapolates from scientific theories about evolutionary biology to create dramatic stories, he fails to account for social reality—in this case,

20. Prior to the publication of "Hold That Helium!" in 1955, Sylvia Jacobs had published one novella, two novelettes, and two short stories in SF magazines including *Astounding, Galaxy, Universe,* and *Vortex Science Fiction.*

the way that humans have already transcended biology by creating institutional support systems for people with different intellectual abilities. As such, Dick creates xenophobic fantasies that fail to fulfill one of the primary dictates of postwar SF: that authors should put a truly human face on science and technology.

McCormick also draws upon her experience as an educator to challenge scientific theory itself. Although she clearly enjoys all aspects of her work, McCormick reserves her most glowing praise for intellectually gifted children who can be "a bit difficult to handle" but who are "a joy to teach" because they learn quickly and inspire "merely average children . . . to catch fire from them and do better work on their own" (3). This leads McCormack to conclude that "[f]rom my experience with the superior child, and from the kudos our world hands such men as Einstein, Oppenheimer, etc., I think we would merely be *more* impressed and even happier with a truly new race, a truly superior race. Rather than Cro Magnon killing off all the Neanderthal, isn't it possible that their taking over was a matter of natural selection plus absorption? If mutants arrived, it seems more likely to me that homo sapiens would be absorbed gradually. . . . And those of us who lived a full lifetime (as perhaps the Neanderthal did) would live it admiring and accepting the leadership of the superior race" (3). Thus, McCormick does more than simply invoke the harmonious mixed-intelligence classroom to contest science-fictional notions of human-mutant intolerance. Additionally—and perhaps more surprisingly—she uses it to rethink the entire concept of interspecies competition and human evolution. In this respect, she echoes early feminist science writers Arabella Buckley and Eliza Burt Gamble.

Postwar SF science columnists updated the work of their predecessors by replacing religious sentiment with social and political didacticism. In fact, regular contributors such as Lurie and Glanzman rarely missed an opportunity to do so. Lurie's staunch patriotism is particularly apparent in "Red Atoms" (1950): "The international aspects of science are beautifully—if unfortunately—shown by the recent Russian development of the atomic bomb. . . . It will probably be a long time before we know the details of the Russian undertaking, perhaps never, and it will be fascinating to see how they did the trick. Anyone who has read the Smythe report knows what a job it was, to build the first atomic bomb. Presumably, the Russians, with the advance knowledge, had less difficulty. Furthermore, they didn't work with the handicap of not knowing whether or not it could be done. We did" (127). Lurie's words seem carefully chosen to direct readers' attention away the terrifying implications of a bilateral nuclear arms race and toward the heroic skill of the American scientists who developed nuclear weapons first. This enables her to preserve the technophilic ideals central to the SF community to which both she and her audience belong. Moreover, by shifting pronouns from "they" to "we," Lurie invites readers to envision themselves as proud members of the American scientific community, ones who might someday (if they are young readers) grow up to become democratic cold warriors themselves.

In a very different vein, Glanzman's science writing shows how some scientific discoveries might lead to more enlightened social relations. More than just startling scientific fact, Glanzman's "The Bantus with the Brains" (1951) is a surprisingly sophisticated and slyly humorous plea for racial tolerance. Citing a series of anthropological studies on indigenous Australian and African people, Glanzman admonishes readers not to assume that "so-called 'primitive' peoples" are unintelligent simply because they do not have the same formal education or cultural experiences as Americans and Europeans. Quite the contrary, she insists, "intelligence is a common denominator among all human beings, be they Hottentots or Eskimos—or the product of our finest universities" (55). Glanzman then notes that some indigenous peoples seem to be even smarter than their Western counterparts: "It has been reported that the [Bantus of South Africa], for example, will demonstrate the utmost impatience with the white man's conversation because it is so slow! Very often, before the speech is completed, the Bushman will already have grasped the intent of the speaker" (55).

Glanzman's call for better intercultural understanding on the part of Americans was particularly timely as it coincided with the U.S. ascendancy to a position of world leadership. It was also timely in another, more immediate way. The 1950s marked the beginning of a new era for American civil rights activists, as legal decisions such as *Brown v. Board of Education* paved the way for increased racial integration. And so Glanzman's essay anticipates the pleas for better interracial understanding that would become central to political activists on the domestic front as well.[21]

Glanzman's writing often reflected her fine sense of audience, and "Bantus with the Brains" is no exception. After demonstrating the unscientific nature of racism, she concludes in a manner that is guar-

21. As I discuss in chapter 3 of this book, pleas for better interracial and intercultural understanding were central to many of the encounter with the alien other stories that postwar women SF authors published at this time.

anteed to capture the attention of even the most politically apathetic reader: "The point of the whole matter is, of course, that some day men may come into contact with a far stranger species whose minds may operate on levels far beyond our own. Most scientists and writers on interplanetary travel assume an anthropocentric view of things, suggesting that the existence of intelligent life elsewhere—whatever the form—is hardly to be expected. This is surely not a sound supposition. The outward manifestations of their culture do not necessarily reflect the intelligence or military potential of an alien race" (55). Like the women science popularizers who came before her, Glanzman makes new scientific findings relevant to her audience by connecting them to readers' daily lives—or in this case, readers' everyday interest in SF. In doing so, she playfully echoes and updates the moralizing that marked earlier modes of women's science writing. Rather than leading readers to better understand the wonders of nature so they will better understand the wonders of God, Glanzman encourages readers to better understand the wonders of humanity so they may be better prepared to someday deal with the wonders of the larger universe.

And finally, a few women even used SF magazines as forums in which to revise common-sense assumptions about science, technology, and gender. Perhaps the most powerful example of this is Kathleen's Downe's "Why Not a Woman?" (1955). (See figure 6.) Downe begins her essay with the declaration: "there is no reason why a woman should not be the first person to pilot a space ship," because the history of emancipation shows "it doesn't matter two hoots whether the brain has a male or female body" (101). However, she continues, bodies do matter when it comes to space exploration—and this is precisely why women should be the first space pilots: their light bodies would need fewer resources and their quick reaction times (which, she notes, are often mistakenly dismissed as mere "intuition") would enable them to manipulate ship instruments more easily than men. Moreover, women possess a physical toughness that would be a real asset in the event of space emergency because "it is a well known fact that women can stand far more severe pain for longer periods of time than men. . . . Their fortitude is perhaps more striking since it is generally not, as is often the case with men, occasioned by discipline and military training" (102). Thus, Downe anticipates the arguments put forward by Richard Lovelace and other sympathetic NASA officials by nearly half a decade concerning the scientific and cultural reasons why women should lead humanity into space.

When It comes to piloting spaceships—

Why not a WOMAN?

asks Kathleen Downe

THERE IS NO REASON WHY A woman should not be the first person to pilot a spaceship! The emancipation of women is far from complete, but bearing in mind the great strides which have been made along this path in the past fifty years the next fifty will see even greater changes. As our standards of living rise, those women who show marked intellectual acumen will have more opportunity to continue their valuable work, for really good brains will be needed more and more, and the world will soon realise that it doesn't matter two hoots whether the brain has a male or female body. That is, unless the brain is needed to pilot a spaceship.

This will be one time when weight will be a very important consideration. Of two brains of equal keenness, that of the woman will give the best power-weight ratio.

A lighter body means less food, less oxygen, less room to move in, so that the overall advantage would be considerable.

Excessive physical strength would not necessarily be a prerequisite for a space pilot, but quick reaction time, high powers of physical endurance and brilliant intelligence will be essential.

The hardest part of the pilot's flight from a physical point of view would be the strain of acceleration during take-off. This strain has been grossly exaggerated in the past. It is only in the initial stages that a fairly high acceleration would be required, perhaps as much as three g's in a course in which the ship rose vertically for the first fifty miles, then turned eastward and continued in a horizontal direction until escape velocity had been reached.

On this principle, it has been calculated that the pilot of a spaceship would feel four times his—or her—own weight, as gravity is adding its own force. This four g drag would only be felt for about a couple of minutes.

Raising an arm from the lying prone position under four gravities would require about as much strength as is required to lift 10 lbs. of potatoes, a load of washing—or the baby—as very many women do in everyday life.

Most science fiction films and stories tend to dramatise the strain of reaching controls during take-off. Much of the difficulty is enhanced by bad layout of the controls on the screen set. In reality, scientists will, of course, place the controls in the most easily accessible position, and any necessary arm raising will be assisted by the use of counter-balancing mechanisms. Further, it is already current practice for guided missiles to be operated by remote control during take-off, so that the pilot would have nothing to do until after the ascent.

However, should physical strength be needed, a woman could meet the requirements of a spaceship crew member. It is not so very long ago that women were driving three-ton lorries and firing heavy guns. It is as well to remember that, unlike men, women have not been trained to increase their muscular strength, and expert training would increase their capabilities in this direction. Of all the qualities which a space pilot must possess, physical strength will be one of the least important.

A woman does possess the essential qualifications. The Second World War showed them every bit as capable as men at manipulating delicate scientific instruments, and, when it comes to precision work, they are in many cases superior to men. By that peculiar quirk of nature commonly known as "intuition" they have been known to arrive at the solution to some problem which has been baffling a man.

Their quick reaction would be in-

valuable in the handling of a spaceship as would their greater ability to stand up to prolonged strain and tension.

It is a well-known fact that women can stand far more severe pain for longer periods than men, and through the ages they have shown courage, resourcefulness and determination, and these would be essential qualities in the event of any emergency during the flight. Their fortitude is perhaps more striking since it is generally not, as is often the case with men, occasioned by discipline and military training. With such an important and vital task to do these qualities would become even more pronounced.

A woman does not give up hope easily and, provided she is properly trained, she is not likely to be beaten by a problem.

It was Madame Curie who kept on when Pierre would have given in, and after his death she still held on with her work and research until her own death.

In any event, if man is to conquer the stars, woman must accompany him one day. Is it uncharitable to suppose that only his desire to win the glory for himself, covered by an excuse that it is "too dangerous a task for a woman," will prevent a woman being on the first ship?

Women, being the perverse creatures they are, will twist their menfolk round their little fingers so that when the time comes for the first piloted ship to blast off, if the person with the right weight, possessing all the other necessary qualities, happens to be a woman, then a woman will be the first "man on the moon!"

The idea is, after all, not so very far-fetched!

101

102

Figure 6. The SF science column as political commentary: Kathleen Downe's "Why Not a Woman?" (1955). Downe's arguments for training women astronauts anticipated those put forth by NASA scientists and administrators by nearly half a decade.

Much like Lurie and Glanzman, Downe seems well aware of her audience and its needs. Accordingly, she shifts to a much lighter tone in the final paragraphs of her article, suggesting that when men claim space is too dangerous for women, they do so because "they desire to win all the glory" for themselves (102). But of course this will never happen because "[w]omen, being the perverse creatures they are, will twist their menfolk round their little fingers so that when the time comes for the first piloted ship to blast off, if the person with the right brain and the right weight, possessing all the other necessary qualities, happens to be a woman, then a woman will be the first 'man on the moon!'" (102). Although this last-minute retreat to gender stereotyping might be unsettling to contemporary readers, in the context of Downe's historical moment it may well have been a strategic move that enabled her to convey her argument in a manner that would be familiar to SF readers. As Justine Larbalestier explains in *The Battle of the Sexes in Science Fiction*, male and female fans alike have always used SF magazine letters, pages, and open forums to engage in heated debates over the necessary relations of gender, science, and SF (104). By invoking the battle of the sexes in her own article, Downe demonstrates her familiarity with this discourse community as well as her authority to speak to it. And she may have even convinced a few readers that women's participation in space exploration was desirable as well.

Daughters of Earth: Imagining Scientific Utopia in Postwar Women's Science Fiction

While postwar women science popularizers updated the narrative strategies of their literary predecessors to claim a traditional kind of feminine scientific authority within the SF community, SF authors imagined that women might stake out other kinds of scientific authority for themselves on a global and sometimes even intergalactic scale. As such, the tales they wrote about fantastic women who solve medical mysteries, design space ships, and colonize strange new worlds pay tribute to women scientists of their own historical moment.[22] Given that authors including Marion Zimmer Bradley, Judith Merril, Katherine MacLean, Doris Pitkin Buck, and Anne McCaffrey were among the first to extrapolate from postwar American scientific, social, and gendered relations, it is not surprising that their stories tend to engage the rhetoric of the feminine mystique and follow one of two broad narrative trajectories. They either warn about the disasters that will ensue if women are forced to choose between home and career, or they celebrate the magnificent discoveries that will emerge when women combine family and science as their individual natures dictate.

As such, these stories anticipate one of the central concerns of feminist SF as it took shape in the 1960s and 1970s. Robin Roberts explains:

> Even through [many new scientific narratives] are narratives about women, women usually do not write these stories. Women cannot control scientific narratives because, although they are frequently its subject, they are largely excluded from the practice of science. Through feminist science fiction, however, women can write narra-

22. For discussion of the similarities between postwar women's science writing and science fiction, see Dianne Newell's "Judith Merril and Rachel Carson: Reflections on Their 'Potent Fictions' of Science."

tives about science. With its imaginative possibilities, science fiction
provides women opportunities denied them in the real world. In their
revisions of traditional myths, feminist writers can use science fiction
to create the feminist fairy tales that are needed to counteract the
misogynistic stories of our culture. (*A New Species* 6)

Although the situation described by Roberts may, thirty years after
the revival of American feminism, seem more pressing than ever
before, is not unique to the current moment. Many contemporary
sciences and scientific narratives first emerged in the wake of World
War II, and postwar women writers were quick to intervene into
them. In an era when the feminine mystique was regularly invoked
to justify the marginalization of women in scientific and technological
professions, such interventions must have felt all the more urgent to
progressive women.

Furthermore, although many postwar women authors either did
not have access to or chose not to employ the language of feminism
in their storytelling, they nonetheless used narrative strategies much
like those of their feminist counterparts to evaluate the relations of
gender and science. Jane L. Donawerth argues that feminist stories
about science and technology usually imagine "women's participation
in science as subjects not objects, revised definitions and discourse of
science, inclusion in science of women's issues, treatment of science
as an origin story that has been feminized, a conception of humans'
relation to nature as partnership not domination, and an ideal of science as subjective, relational holistic, and complex" (*Frankenstein's
Daughters* 2). Engaged as they were in what was essentially a collective project to debunk the feminine mystique, postwar women SF
authors regularly employed the strategies identified by Donawerth to
propose that progress could occur only when domestic relations were
made central to the practice of science and technology itself.

Of course, postwar women's SF was also very much part of its
own historical moment, and women writers enacted their assess-
ments of science, society, and gender by appropriating and revising
those myths that were most important to the mid-century SF community. Like other Americans, members of this community were often
profoundly ambivalent about cold war sciences and technologies.
However, as Brian Stableford notes, "genre-SF writers mostly responded to the widespread popular opinion that technology had got out of
hand by putting the blame on machine-*users* rather than machine-
makers, claiming that it was not mad scientists but mad generals and

mad politicians who were the problem . . . scientists were often represented as isolated paragons of sanity locked into a political and military matrix that threatened the destruction of the world" ("Scientists" 1077). Prominent authors including C. M. Kornbluth, Algis Budrys, and Kurt Vonnegut all produced stories that explored what seemed to be the inevitable conflict between scientific interest, military security, and social need, focusing particularly on "the difficulty of making scientific discoveries in such circumstances" ("Scientists" 1077). For these authors, the real problem was not the unilateral impact of dangerous new scientific developments on society but the emergence of a deadly new social matrix that perverted even the most benevolent scientific and technological research.

Postwar women writers refashioned this SF myth to explore the perils faced by women scientists trapped in a distinctly patriarchal social matrix that threatens to thwart their research and destroy their worlds.[23] This is particularly apparent in Marion Zimmer Bradley's "The Wind People" (1959), which illustrates how rigid investment in the feminine mystique combined with an equally rigid adherence to normal science might literally drive the woman scientist mad. "The Wind People" revolves around Dr. Helen Murray, a space officer who becomes pregnant four years into her ship's ten-year cruise. Convinced that a baby cannot survive hyperdrive, Helen's captain gives her a choice. She can either do her duty as an officer by euthanizing her son and resuming her place on the ship, or she can follow her instincts as a mother, desert her ship, and raise her child on the uninhabited alien planet that the crew has been mining for nearly a year.

Faced with an extreme version of a choice that would have been familiar to female readers—the choice between work and family—Helen decides to stay on the alien planet with her son, Robin. Captain Merrihew immediately denounces Helen's choice as "insane," to which the doctor soberly replies, "even if I'm sane now, I wouldn't be long if I had to abandon Robin" (16). From the very outset Bradley suggests it is not a mother's love for her child that is insane but those

23. As I have argued elsewhere, postwar women SF authors also protested vehemently against the proliferation of nuclear weapons and the rise of the security state. However, because they were primarily interested in exploring the effects of nuclear war on laypeople and their families (rather than on scientists and scientific development), they generally used a different SF story type, the nuclear holocaust narrative, to convey their sentiments. For further discussion, see my essays "Unhappy Housewife Heroines, Galactic Suburbia, and Nuclear War: A New History of Midcentury Women's Science Fiction" and "Stories 'That Only a Mother' Could Write: Midcentury Peace Activism, Maternalist Politics, and Judith Merril's Early Fiction" as well as chapter 3 of this book.

IT HAD been a long layover for the *Starholm's* crew, hunting heavy elements for fuel—eight months, on an idyllic green paradise of a planet: a soft, windy, whispering world, inhabited only by trees and winds. But in the end it presented its own unique problem.

Specifically, it presented Captain Merrihew with the problem of Robin: male, father unknown, who had been born the day before, and a month prematurely, to Dr. Helen Murray.

Merrihew found her lying abed in the laboratory shelter, pale and calm, with the child beside her.

The little shelter, constructed roughly of green planks, looked out on the clearing which the *Starholm* had used as a base of operations during the layover; a beautiful place at the bottom of a wide valley, in the curve of a broad, deepflowing river. The crew, tired of being shipbound, had built half a dozen such huts and shacks in these eight months.

Merrihew glared down at Helen. He snorted, "This is a fine situation. You, of all the people in the whole damned crew—the ship's doctor! It's—it's—" Inarticulate with rage, he fell back on a ridiculously inadequate phrase. "It's—criminal carelessness!"

"I know." Helen Murray, too young and far too lovely for a ship's officer on a ten-year cruise, still looked weak and white, and her voice was a gentle shadow of its crisp self. "I'm afraid four years in space made me careless."

Merrihew brooded, looking down at her. Something about ship-gravity conditions, while not affecting potency, made conception impossible; no child had ever been conceived in space and none ever would. On planet layovers, the effect wore off very slowly; only after three months aground had Dr. Murray started routine administration of anticeptin to the twenty-two women of the crew, herself included. At that time she had been still unaware that she was already carrying a child.

Outside, the leafy forest whispered and rustled, and Merrihew knew Helen had forgotten his existence again. The day-old child was tucked up in one of her rolled coveralls at her side. To Merrihew, he looked like a skinned monkey, but Helen's eyes smoldered as her hands moved gently over the tiny round head.

He stood and listened to the winds and said at random, "These shacks will fall to pieces in another month. It doesn't matter, we'll have

15

THE WIND PEOPLE

BY MARION ZIMMER BRADLEY

Figure 7. Original illustration for Marion Zimmer Bradley's "The Wind People" (1959). The tagline previews the most sensational aspect of this tale: the possibility of incest between mother and son. It also hints at the protagonist's struggle to rewrite patriarchal origin myths to encompass feminist futures.

patriarchal social and military orders that tell women they must (in this case literally) sacrifice their children if they wish to retain their status as professional scientists.

Bradley underscores the madness of this situation by demonstrating how the mistaken choice between work and family destroys the family itself. When the ship takes off without Helen and her child, technician Colin Reynolds—Helen's occasional lover and Robin's presumed father—commits a spectacularly messy suicide by slitting his throat in freefall, leaving behind no explanation other than "an incoherent note" that Merrihew quickly throws away. Meanwhile, although Helen and Robin physically thrive in the benign atmosphere of their Edenic new world, they, too, encounter tragedy when Robin turns sixteen and tries to initiate sex with Helen. Convinced that "this world has driven us both insane," Helen fights off her son and rushes out of their cabin to determine how she might resolve this situation

(17). Thus Bradley suggests that the mistaken choice between work and family is no choice at all, and that by forcing Helen to leave his ship Merrihew has unwittingly triggered a chain of events destined to end in incest and death (see figure 7).

Toward the end of her story Bradley suggests there might be one way for Helen to escape this madness: since the cultural taboos of Earth have no real bearing on her current situation, she can choose to simply abandon them: "But what now? Robin was sixteen; she was not yet forty. Helen caught at the vanishing memories of society; taboos so deeply rooted that for Helen they were instinctual and impregnable. Yet for Robin nothing existed except this little patch of forest and Helen herself—the only person in his world, more specifically at the moment the only woman in his world. *So much,* she thought bitterly, *for instinct. But have I the right to begin this all over again? Worse; have I the right to deny its existence and when I die, leave Robin alone?"* (26). While Helen is hardly the empowered utopian scientist that Donawerth associates with feminist SF, she does experience a literal and psychological distancing from Earth that prompts her to think about Robin and the world around her in newly "subjective, relational, holistic, and complex" ways. For a brief moment, it seems she might avoid the tragic consequences of the choice between work and family forced on her a decade and a half earlier.

But ultimately, Helen cannot escape the scientific paradigms that have organized her adult life. Although "Merrihew's men had pronounced the world uninhabited," readers eventually learn that Helen and Robin actually share their planet with the wind people of the story's title, an elusive group of beings who are nearly invisible to the human eye (21). Bradley also leads her readers to suspect that Robin's biological father is a wind person, since the boy sometimes sees and hears the wind people and Helen vaguely remembers making love with a wind man. However, she tries desperately to repress this memory because "Helen thought of herself as a scientist, without room for fantasies, and that was why she called [her encounter with the wind man], fiercely, a dream: a dream born of some undiagnosed conflict within her" (20). Rather than acknowledging that there might be a very real conflict between what Merrihew's men tell her and what she experiences, Helen clings to the last scraps of her old identity and belief systems, even at the expense of pathologizing herself.

In doing so, Bradley's protagonist unwittingly assures the complete and utter destruction of her family. Helen lets her shipmates believe that Colin is Robin's father because she is "too ashamed to speak" about her fantastic encounter with the wind man (20). At the same time, she refuses to let the young technician stay planetside with her and the baby. It is precisely this unbearable contradiction, Bradley suggests, that drives Colin to suicide. This same shame also leads Helen to convince Robin that "there are no other people, just us" (22). This, in turn, drives the desperately lonely boy into Helen's arms for both maternal and sexual comfort. If Helen and Robin have been driven mad, it is not because of their world but because Helen refuses to trust her own perceptions of it.

This leads to the death of the woman scientist herself. Just as Helen begins to realize that she might salvage the situation between herself and Robin by abandoning the cultural taboos that have no bearing on their lives, she finds herself standing face to face with the wind person who is probably Robin's father. In conclusion, Bradley writes, "the horror of incest, the son the father the lover suddenly melting into one, overwhelmed [Helen's] reeling brain and she fled insanely to the brink [of the river]. . . . She flung herself down the steep bank, to slip and hurl downward and whirl around in the raging current to spinning oblivion and death" (81). Much as Merrihew predicts at the beginning of the story, Helen finally goes insane. But she does so precisely because Merrihew has forced her to make a choice that destroys her career, undermines her ability to mother, and ultimately claims her life.

Judith Merril's "Dead Center" (1954) also revises the "sane scientist in a mad world" story to critique those patriarchal scientific and social systems that do not take into account lived experience and interpersonal relations. However, Merril goes beyond Bradley to warn that these systems might even thwart the progress engendered by protofeminist modes of scientific practice as well. "Dead Center"—which initially appeared in *The Magazine of Fantasy and Science Fiction* in 1954 and was the first SF story ever featured in the critically acclaimed *Best American Short Stories* series—tells the story of Ruth Kruger, a rocket ship engineer married to astronaut Jock Kruger. Driven by their fierce love and intense intellectual respect for one another, Ruth and Jock have (with the help of their equally brilliant design team) catapulted Earth's space program decades ahead of its original schedule.

It is precisely the Krugers' commitment to one another that enables this achievement. As Ruth notes to herself, "when a man knows his wife's faith is *unshakeable*, he can't help coming back" from even the most dangerous space mission (169). And of course her faith is unshakeable because Ruth, who was a famous rocket designer long before she married Jock, works closely with her team to oversee every aspect of her ships' design and construction. In direct contrast to postwar antifeminists such as Olive Lewis who claimed that marriage and motherhood were incompatible with good science, Merril proposes that real progress might well derive from the woman scientist's ability to incorporate her personal passions into her professional life.

Merril also proposes that without this kind of passion there may be no progress at all. When the Rocket Corps decides to put Jock in charge of the first manned moon landing, they also decide to replace Ruth with Andy Argent, an engineer who claims atmospheric landings as his area of theoretical expertise—even though Ruth has already established her practical expertise with six other rockets. When she is reminded that Rocket Corps funding depends on public goodwill and that the public does not want to know about dissent among scientists, Ruth agrees to the substitution, despite an inner conviction that "something's wrong" with Argent's ship (169). Although Ruth tries to dismiss her concern as mere jealousy, she seems to have good reason for it, since Argent turns out to be an autocrat who destroys the camaraderie of the rocket design team. As the lead Rocket Corps publicist diplomatically puts it, "with somebody new—well, you know what a ruckus we had until Sue got used to Argent's blueprints, and how Ben's pencil notes used to drive Andy wild" (177). More than mere pettiness, Argent's rage for order turns out to be downright perilous for everyone involved. Due to a flaw in Argent's plans (which the demoralized rocket team fails to catch), Jock is thrown off course and forced to use all his fuel to make an emergency landing on the dark side of the moon, where it seems likely that he will die.

But this is only the first half of Merril's story. Appalled by the prospect of bad publicity that will permanently end space exploration, Earth's military and corporate leaders join forces to build an unmanned rescue ship, this time wisely putting Ruth in charge. But no one remembers to explain the situation to Ruth and Jock's young son, Toby, in the whirlwind of activity that ensues. With impeccable childish logic, Toby decides that his father has abandoned him and that his mother will do the same once the new ship is completed:

> She'd come back for him, he told himself. The other times, when Daddy went some place—like when they first came here to live, and Daddy went first, then Mommy, and then they came back to get him, and some other time, he didn't remember just what—but when Daddy

went away, Mommy always went to stay with him, and then they always came to get him too.

It wasn't any different from Mommy going to be with Daddy at a party or something, instead of staying in his room to talk to him when she put him to bed. It didn't feel any worse than that, he told himself.

Only he didn't believe himself. (181–82)

Accordingly, Toby decides to stow away on the ship and confront his parents when he reaches the moon. But the child's weight is just great enough to throw off Ruth's careful calculations and, as a horrified world looks on, the rescue ship explodes while leaving Earth's atmosphere. Thus Merril suggests that a truly viable science must account for both the subjectivity of the scientist *and* the subjectivity of everyone to whom she is connected. If it does not, both individual lives and human progress as a whole are doomed.

And, as in Bradley's story, so is the woman scientist herself. When Ruth learns that the explosion has killed her son and her husband has died of starvation on the moon, she takes her own life in a fit of grief. The Rocket Corps publicity team manages to salvage the situation by "keeping the sleeping-pill story down to a tiny back-page notice in most of the papers" (185). Moreover, in the final lines of the story we learn that "they made an international shrine of the house, and the garden where the three graves lay. Now they are talking of making an interplanetary shrine of the lonely rocket on the wrong side of the moon" (186). Touching as this might seem, Merril leaves readers with more questions than she answers: if Earth's best rocket designer and pilot are dead—killed, albeit inadvertently, by the man who was supposed to be second best—who exactly will build that interplanetary shrine on the moon? And how will they get there anyway? "They" may talk all they want, Merril implies, but when experienced female scientists such as Ruth Kruger are asked to defer to an untried masculine authority, then the hope that humanity might someday reach the stars becomes an increasingly unlikely dream.

So what is an SF heroine to do if she wants to have both family and career? Postwar women writers offered different answers to this question, but they seem to have been in agreement on one central point: if a woman wants to practice science on her own terms, she must leave the patriarchal workplace and strike out for new territory—whether that territory is in the kitchen or outer space. They also seem to have agreed that the most effective way to tell such stories was to refashion those cultural myths that depict science and technology as masculine activities. By redefining women's work to include both scientific and domestic labor and putting that work at the center of their stories, such authors refuted the logic of the feminine mystique. And in imagining that women might have it all—or that they might at least pursue it all—they created some of the first versions of what Roberts describes as "the feminist fairy tales that are needed to counteract the misogynistic stories of our culture."

For example, Katherine MacLean's "And Be Merry . . ." (1950) rewrites the relations of science, society, and gender codified in what many scholars and fans consider to be the first SF story: Mary Shelley's *Frankenstein*. Donawerth explains that Shelley's text has inspired and frustrated women writers since its publication because it depicts both science and storytelling about science as masculine activities. Because women nonetheless continue to write SF—and to look for themselves in the stories they tell—they "have returned again and again to the complexities of the questions that Shelley raised: making a science that does not exclude women, creating an identity for woman as alien, and finding a voice in a male world" (*Frankenstein's Daughters* xviii). MacLean does all this in her version of the Frankenstein myth, simply enough, by recasting Victor Frankenstein as a married professional woman.

Much like her literary predecessor, Dr. Helen Berent is a brilliant young scientist who hopes to discover the secrets of life and death, but is convinced she can only do so by rejecting scientific society and its conventions. More specifically, Helen hopes to stop the aging process by identify the endocrines responsible for cellular rejuvenation. As she explains: "That Russian scientist started me on this idea. He gave oldsters a little of their lost elasticity by injections of an antibody that attacked and dissolved some of their old connective tissue and forced a partial replacement. I just wanted to go him one better, and see if I can coax a replacement for every creaking cell in the body. [But] you can see how it would be a drastic process. . . . There is nobody I dare try it on except myself" (83). Fearing censure from her more conservative scientific peers, Helen retreats to the privacy of her home and builds herself a "laboratory kitchen," complete with a sleeping alcove where she can eat, rest, and work all at once. From the very beginning of her story, MacLean invites comparisons between her protagonist and Shelley's while insisting on one key difference: Helen may share Victor Frankenstein's arrogant disregard for the rest of the scientific community, but she is sensible enough to feed and care for herself while she works. (Victor, as readers may remember, gets so caught up in his work that he forgets to do just that and nearly dies from the resulting illness.)

Helen is also like Victor Frankenstein in that her scientific and social transgressions seem to yield monstrous results. Helen's experiments exceed beyond her wildest dreams and she gives herself the body of a healthy eighteen-year-old. In this respect she is a far cry from the misshapen creature that Victor creates. Her mind, however, is a more complex matter. After spending months uncovering the secrets of life, Helen finds that once she does so she cannot stop thinking about death. "There is something wrong," she worries. "I have to be very critical. People are too careless. I never realized that before, but they are" (41).

Eventually Helen's obsession with the many ways that her new body might be damaged or destroyed lands her in Bellevue State Hospital. As the hospital's psychiatric resident puts it, "she's afraid all right. Even afraid of me! Says I have germs. Says I'm incompetent. It's a symptom of some other fear of course. . . . It's not rational" (42). Like Victor's creature, Helen becomes alien to her own society. Once again, however, MacLean departs from her source material. While the humans who fear and loathe Frankenstein's creature do so irrationally, MacLean suggests that Helen has every right to fear those doctors who dismiss the story of her scientific breakthrough as mere imagination and instead try to silence her with a "cure" of psychoanalysis, drugs, and shock therapy.

At this point, MacLean fully departs from the Frankenstein myth. In Shelley's novel Victor is truly alone, rejecting the company of both other scientists and his own family. In fact, Shelley suggests that her protagonist's problems ultimately stem from this lack of family. Victor has no mother to provide moral guidance, and he refuses to share his work with his fiancée, Elizabeth. Helen, however, has a domestic partner who serves as both moral compass and scientific confidante: her husband, archeologist Alec Berent. In the experimental records she leaves for her husband, Helen details the success of her experiment and concludes that

[i]t is hard to be practical, darling. My imagination keeps galloping off in all directions. Did you know that your hair is getting thin in back? Another two years with that crew cut and you would have begun to look like a monk.

I know, I know, you'll tell me it is not fair for you to be a juvenile when everyone else is gray, but what is fair? To be fair at all everyone will have to have the treatment available free, for *nothing*. And I mean *everyone*. We can leave it to an economist to worry out how. . . .

It would be good for the race I think. It may even help evolution. Regeneration would remove environmental handicaps, old scars of bad raising, and give every man a body as good as his genes. . . . And look at cultural evolution! For the first time we humans will be able to use our one talent, learning, the way it should be used, the way it was meant to be used from the very beginning. (39)

In direct contrast to Victor Frankenstein, who believes he can create "a new species that would bless me as its creator and source," Helen dreams of transforming her entire race into gods (Shelley 49). Moreover, it is precisely her love for another person that leads her to those unorthodox practices that will best enable her to achieve this dream.

Helen further differs from Victor in that she has the admiration of at least one other scientist: her husband, Alec. "Besides being your wife," Helen writes to Alec as a way of explaining why she decides to stay home and pursue her own research while he is away on a dig, "I am an endocrinologist, and an expert. If you can cheerfully expose me to cliffs, swamps, man-eating tigers and malarial mosquitoes, all in the name of Archeology, I have an even better right to stick hypodermics in myself in the name of Endocrinology" (32). Although Alec is never fully convinced that Helen should play with needles in such a cavalier fashion, he respects her fiercely independent mind, roundly chastising the Bellevue psychiatrist for failing to acknowledge Helen as a scientific colleague and knocking him unconscious when he continues to treat her like a madwoman. Thus, MacLean uses the trope of marriage as a microcosm through which to imagine a new kind of scientific community that respects both women's voices and their scientific practices.

Finally, MacLean uses the love affair between the Berents to show that the practice of alternative science does not necessarily have to end in monstrosity and madness. Alec believes that Helen has discovered the secret of eternal life for the simple reason that he knows that she is "just too rational" to have made it up (42). Accordingly, he determines that the best way to bring Helen back to her senses is to appeal to her intellect. And sure enough, when Alec points out that her work in cell regeneration might produce cancerous mutations, Helen immediately puts her own fears aside and begins to outline the next step in her research, asking Alec to "work it out on a slide rule for me, Hon" (44). Delighted to realize that "Helen was back," Alec seems more than ready to comply—but not before giving her a wildly romantic kiss (45). Because MacLean ends with this image, rather than explaining how the Berents will get out of Bellevue and convince the scientific community of Helen's discovery, the moral of her story might seem open to debate. And yet this final image of the vindicated female scientist and her devoted husband, replete as it is with connotations of fertility and generation, suggests that Helen will escape the tragic fate of Victor Frankenstein and realize her dream of leading humanity toward godhood.

While MacLean looks to the private sphere of domestic relations as the basis for a new and more egalitarian kind of scientific community, Doris Pitkin Buck suggests that women can practice science successfully only by abandoning their homes and husbands. This is particularly apparent in Buck's short story "Birth of a Gardner" (1961), which rewrites Nathaniel Hawthorne's 1843 classic, "The Birthmark." Brian Attebery explains that SF scholars have long been interested in Hawthorne as a precursor to modern SF because, much like Mary Shelley, he "was usually careful to ground [his] plots in the science of his day" (23). "The Birthmark" is of particular interest to feminist SF scholars because it treats science in a specifically gendered manner. Hawthorne's story revolves around the brilliant scientist Aylmer and his wife, Georgiana. Georgiana possesses a tiny, hand-shaped birthmark on her left cheek that most men find enchanting but that Aylmer perceives as the single imperfection marring his wife's beauty. Dedicated to proving his control over nature, Aylmer vows to eradicate Georgiana's birthmark at any cost. Eventually the scientist attains his goal, but only by sacrificing his wife's self-confidence and her life. Thus, Hawthorne's story crystallizes a set of themes that would become central to much later SF, including "men's reduction of women to physical appearance; their denial of their own bodily existence and projection onto women of the body's imperfections, and the male scientist's resentment of and subversion of a nature perceived as powerfully female" (24).

These themes are central to the first part of Buck's story. "Birth of a Gardner" relates the tale of Payne, a physicist "famous in two hemispheres for his work on anti-matter," who vows to rid his wife, Rosalie (whom he nicknames Lee), of what he perceives as her only flaw: an abiding interest in physics (50). A small-minded man who cannot think past the logic of the feminine mystique, Payne tells himself, "a woman with Lee's hair didn't have to be intellectual. After all, she had a green thumb" (50). Events come to a head when, after months of silently enduring her husband's mockery, Lee marshals the courage to tell Payne that she has developed a theory concerning the existence of mirror worlds based on his ideas about matter and antimatter. Infuriated by what he perceives as sheer idiocy, Payne silences his wife with a curt "Darling, you bore me"—a response that he comes to regret when Lee retreats to their bedroom and dies of a brain aneurysm in the middle of the night (54). Much like Aylmer, who sees Georgiana's birthmark as an affront to his expert control over nature, Payne sees Lee's interest in physics as an affront to his own area of expert knowledge. And in both cases the male scientist ends up sacrificing his wife to prove this expertise.

But this is where the similarities between the two stories end. Much of the tragedy from Hawthorne's tale derives from the fact that Georgiana eventually surpasses her husband in scientific expertise and recognizes that his experiments are bound to kill her. Convinced by Aylmer that death is preferable to imperfect beauty, however, she gives in to Aylmer's tinkering and becomes "the victim not only of her husband's ambitions but also of her own acquiescence" (Attebery 24). In contrast, Lee recognizes her own scientific expertise and uses it to actively challenge her husband. Not only does Lee believe that the existence of matter and antimatter points to the existence of worlds and antiworlds, but also she also believes that once an individual understands the physical principles behind various kinds of matter he or she can change the course of events in one world and even call another into being. Moreover, Lee believes she has already done this, telling an astonished Payne, "I evoked you" (51). She further warns her husband that if he continues to ridicule her she will evoke a world where she is free of him: "I find myself adding detail to detail, the way I used to [when I first evoked you], and sort of beaming it out—somewhere. . . . Aren't we ever going to be married, really married?" (53). Thus, Buck's heroine bravely asserts her own scientific voice and agency in a patriarchal world. As such, she anticipates the kind of bold scientific heroine that Donawerth and Roberts attribute to later feminist SF.

Buck further reclaims Hawthorne for her own purposes by "writing beyond the ending" of his original story, as literary critic Rachel Blau DuPlessis puts it. Given Lee's warning to Payne, it should come as no surprise to readers that Lee is not actually dead—or, more precisely, that she is only dead in Payne's world. Soon after he buries his wife, Payne begins to catch glimpses of Lee furiously reading and writing. Although he tries to dismiss these sightings as hallucinations, he is finally forced to admit that what he sees is the life Lee has created for herself in another (clearly better) world: "The closed volume was on her knee. Its name, Payne noted, was lettered in gold, clear and legible: *On the Validity of Thought Patterns as Determined by Their Elegance*. Payne blinked. Automatically, he checked the author's name and read below the title, Rosalie Payne" (57). Thus, Payne learns that Lee was right all along about both the existence of alternate worlds and her own scientific authority. Buck further underscores this point by subtly shifting her protagonist's name: although she is clearly married and retains her husband's surname in both worlds, in the mirror world where she is a recognized scientific expert, she abandons the patriarchal diminutive "Lee" and reclaims the proper (and decidedly feminine) "Rosalie" for herself. Much like MacLean, Buck insists that there might someday be times and places where women can practice science and earn the admiration of men who support them in this practice.

Whether or not the relations of science, society, and gender might change in our own world, however, seems open for debate in Buck's story. Throughout the first half of the story Payne spends a great deal of time and energy trying to steer Lee away from the traditionally masculine pursuit of scientific knowledge and toward the more traditionally feminine pursuit of gardening, telling her that "if you would be happy for an hour, get drunk . . . and happy for life, plant a garden" (51). When he first sees the mirror-world Rosalie, he tries to capture her attention by taking over her neglected garden, vowing, "if you come back a second time, this place will be in shape for you" (59). When Payne finally acknowledges that Rosalie (like Lee) prefers science to gardening, he decides to show her copies of his own latest work. But this is the mirror world and so, inevitably, Rosalie dismisses Payne with his own favorite putdown: "Darling, you bore me." In retaliation, Payne considers taking his own life but ultimately concludes, "He could, he would be happy in spite of everything. Savagely he resolved that tomorrow he would spend the whole day bedding the garden down for winter" (59). So what are readers to make of this resolution? On the one hand, it seems to be one more instance of Payne's childish egotism: if he cannot best his wife in scientific matters, he will give them up altogether. On the other hand, Buck crafts her tale in such a way that readers might surmise Payne has been displacing his own desire for a more nurturing mode of labor onto Lee all along, and that in the end he is learning to embrace this desire. In this case, readers might conclude that scientific and social change is possible in the here and now.

In contrast, Judith Merril's "Daughters of Earth" (1952) directly asserts that women (and men) *must* leave Earth if they are ever to truly effect scientific and social change. This is clear from the opening lines of Merril's story, which boldly revises the origin story of Judeo-Christian culture:

> Martha begat Joan, and Joan begat Ariadne. Ariadne lived and died at home on Pluto, but her daughter, Emma, took the long trip out to the distant planet of an alien sun.
>
> Emma begat Leah, and Leah begat Carla, who was the first to make her bridal voyage through sub-space, a long journey faster than the speed of light itself.
>
> Six women in direct descent—some brave, some beautiful, some brilliant: smug or simple, willful or compliant, all different, all daughters of Earth, though half of them never set foot on the Old Planet. (97)

By rewriting the patriarchal genealogies of the Old Testament and the Torah, Merril proposes a radical break from history: while earthly civilizations of the past may have been founded by men, both the greater universe and the future as a whole belong to their daughters.

Merril also appropriates one of the classic origin stories of SF for her own purposes: the space story. As Stableford explains, "it is natural that SF should be symbolized by the theme of space flight, in that it is primarily concerned with transcending imaginative boundaries, with breaking free of the gravitational force which holds consciousness to a traditional core of belief and expectancy" ("Space Flight" 1135). In Merril's hands, this theme serves to symbolize freedom from the gravitational force of patriarchy. Joan, for example, leaves Earth for Pluto because "in the normal course of things, [she] would have taken her degree . . . and gone to work as a biophysicist until she found a husband. The prospect appalled her" (103). Similarly, Emma volunteers for the first mission from Pluto to Uller because her stepfather, Joe Prell, is an Earthman who loves her dearly but believes that Emma is "too direct, too determined, too intellectual, [and] too *strong*" to be a proper lady like her mother, Ariadne (112). Thus, Merril literally conflates repressive patriarchal thinking with Earth and the past, insisting that the further women are from "the Old Planet," the freer they will be to shape their lives as they see fit.

Merril further underscores this point by opposing her Earth-born men to their offworld counterparts. For example, readers learn that when Emma's Martian husband first sets foot on Uller, "he wanted to shout; he wanted to run; he wanted to kiss the ground under his feet, embrace the man next to him. He wanted to get Emma and pull her out of the ship" (119). Rather than simply bask in the glory of being the first human to step foot on Uller, Ken longs to share the experience with his wife. Later, when Carla leaves for Nifleheim, it is her Uller-born father, Louis, who "was there first, folding the slender girl in a wide embrace [and] laughing proudly into her eyes" (164). And so the sons of Earth turn out to be just as different from their fathers as the daughters of Earth are from their mothers.

Merril also suggests that new and more egalitarian modes of social relations will result in new and more holistic modes of scientific practice. This is particularly true for those of her protagonists whose personal lives serve as professional inspiration. Joan's initial work on Pluto is largely theoretical, but after her husband is killed in a domed city construction accident she devises a terraforming process that will ensure no other family suffers this tragedy (108). Later, when an Uller native accidentally kills Emma's husband, she rejects the retaliatory attitude of the other colonists and devotes her life to initiating real communication with the silicone-based creatures. Eventually Emma succeeds in this task, and when her granddaughter Carla leaves for Nifleheim, she does so "in profitable comradeship with the Ullerns" (159). The further removed Merril's heroines are from their planet of origin, the more able they are to think of themselves in new ways: not just as rugged individuals who must bend nature to their wills, but as intelligent, sympathetic beings enmeshed in complex webs of life that must be preserved at all costs. As such, they practice a utopian mode of science much like that which MacLean and Buck ascribe to their own protagonists. Indeed, Merril takes this scientific practice a step further than her literary peers by imagining how it might enable women to make new connections not just with their families and societies but with entirely new species as well.

Finally, in "The Ship Who Sang" (1966), Anne McCaffrey appropriates the genre of the *bildungsroman*, or "novel of development," to imagine new futures for scientifically and technologically inclined women. Like other stories in this genre, "The Ship Who Sang" follows the adventures of a gifted child who grows, learns, and changes in the process of finding his or her place in society. The child in this case is

Helva, a "shell person" born with a brilliant mind but severe physical disabilities. Like other children with this condition, she is raised by scientists who enclose her in a mechanical life support system and then provide her with extensive intellectual, social, and aesthetic training before implanting her into the spaceship that she will run in tandem with human pilots or "brawn" for the next several centuries. As McCaffrey explains at the very beginning of the story, brainships are elite members of this future society, and so as a shell person Helva is assured "a rewarding, rich, and unusual life, a far cry from what she would have faced as an ordinary, 'normal' being" (2). Thus, McCaffrey uses the classic Western narrative of human development to explore not just how children become useful adult members of society, but how humans might become useful members of an exciting new posthuman society as well.

However, McCaffrey does not simply reiterate the narrative trajectory of the *bildungsroman*. Like MacLean, Buck, and Merril before her, she strategically revises her chosen story form to create a feminist fairytale. While the classic novel of development generally revolves around boys who become men by engaging in intergenerational conflict and competition, McCaffrey frames the tale of Helva's development with scenes of intergenerational harmony and friendship. At the beginning of "The Ship Who Sang" Helva defuses the potential hostility of unmodified human adult visitors to her school with grace, wit, and a charmingly innocent pity for "you people [who] don't have adjustable vision" (4). In doing so, she transforms her potential enemies into staunch allies for all shell children. And at the end of McCaffrey's tale, Helva recovers from the shock of losing Jennan, her first human pilot (and first adult love) with the help of Silvia, a much older ship who reminds her that she is not alone in her grief: "Central's very worried, and so, daughter, are your sister ships. I asked to be your escort [because I] don't want to lose you" (23). As is appropriate to her status as a posthuman cyborg with intimate connections to both the organic and technological worlds, Helva comes into her own as an adult not by isolating or alienating herself from others but by forging and maintaining connections with them.

But "The Ship Who Sang" is also a strategically revised version of the feminine *bildungsroman*. In *Unbecoming Women: British Women Writers and the Novel of Development*, Susan Fraiman explains that stories about the development of female characters historically have been marked by extreme anxiety about sex: "in fact, the female protagonist's progress is generally contingent on . . . preventing 'things' from happening to her. Her paradoxical task is to see the world while avoiding the world's gaze" (7). While McCaffrey's shell people do not engage in the act of physical sex per se, their lives are highly eroticized ones marked by conventionally gendered milestones. Helva may be "born a thing," but when she is implanted in her own ship as a teenager she enjoys a cybernetic version of the traditional sweet sixteen party in which "unusually fine-looking, intelligent, well-coordinate and adjusted young men" gather "to do each other dirt [and] get possession of her" (1, 9).

Eventually Helva chooses Jennan as her first partner in what both brainships and their brawns describe as "marriage" precisely because he respects both her mind and her physical presence within the core of the ship, and the two are deliriously happy until Jennan's untimely death. At this point Helva takes on the persona of the grieving widow, stoically supervising the funeral of her beloved pilot/husband while taking comfort in the company of older female ships who have undergone similar experiences. By imagining a future where women like Helva might be able to see the world while being seen by it in gendered terms, McCaffrey provides a powerful antidote to the postwar American assumption that women must chose between career and family and, in turn, between professional and gendered identities. Instead, she suggests that new forms of technoculture might enable women to combine adventure and romance in truly innovative ways.

And indeed, it is precisely Helva's dual identity as a both technological and gendered subject that enables her to rise to the top of her profession and resolve dilemmas beyond the ken of unmodified (and often male) humans. When Helva and Jennan are sent to evacuate the planet Chloe before its sun goes nova, the nuns who inhabit this world decline to go with them; in fact, the more Jennan pleads with them, the more stubborn they become in their refusal. Helva quickly realizes that the problem is Jennan himself, as the brawn's flip demeanor and rugged good looks have convinced the nuns that this is just one more trick on the part of men to seduce them back into the material world.

Accordingly, Helva marshals her own unique combination of technological and gendered authority to resolve this crisis, providing the convent's Mother Superior with detailed information about the dangerous climate changes that are already taking place on Chloe and then assuring her that "under my protection you and your sisters-in-faith may enter safely and be unprofaned by association with a male. I will guard you and take you safely to a place prepared for you"

(19). When the nuns continue to resist evacuation, Helva publicly stops Jennan from dragging them into her hold, noting that it is their choice as free women to do as they please—at which point the nuns overcome their fears and agree to board the brainship. While conventionally heroic men like Jennan might still be the objects of desire for New Women like Helva (and by extension, McCaffrey's readers), it is the New Woman herself who becomes the true heroine of the future.

Finally, McCaffrey proposes that women who are encouraged to develop their intellectual expertise might develop new modes of art as well. When Helva receives a compliment on her voice as a child, she decides to cultivate her talent as a singer. Accordingly, she turns her formidable mind to the task of analyzing sound reproduction and altering her shell body to mimic the voice of an unmodified human. But, of course, Helva is a modified human—and a brilliant one to boot—so she succeeds beyond her wildest dreams: "She found herself able to sing any role and any song which struck her fancy. It would not have occurred to her that it was curious for a female to sing bass, baritone, tenor, mezzo, soprano, and coloratura as she pleased. It was, to Helva, only a matter of the correct reproduction and diaphragmic control required by the music attempted" (6–7). As with her intellect, Helva's artistic abilities make her even more attractive to those male pilots who vie to become her partner. For example, when other pilots tease Jennan about Helva's art, the brawn vows, "if I have to black eyes from here to the Horsehead to keep the snicker out of the title, we'll be the ship who sings" (15). Much like MacLean and Merril before her, McCaffrey imagines a future in which New Women are accompanied by New Men who love and support them unconditionally, and that the union between these two figures might come to represent the possibility of a whole new society that respects women for their intellectual and aesthetic practices. As such, the story of Helva is the story of all female characters who live in—and all women who write about—galactic suburbia.

Why Not a Woman? Science and Technology as Women's Work in the Postwar Science Fiction Community

In this chapter I have shown how women in the postwar SF community used both fact and fiction writing to create feminine and even protofeminist modes of scientific and technological authority. Although the decades following World War II marked record growth in almost every aspect of American science and technology, women were generally relegated to the margins of professional technoscientific labor. This marginalization was justified by the rhetoric of the feminine mystique, which suggested that women must choose between family and career—and that left to their own devices they would naturally choose the former over the latter. Indeed, antifeminist commentators actively insisted that women who tried to have it all were doomed to fail at it all, as the incompatible demands of motherhood and science would necessarily impinge upon one another in ways that endangered both the well-being of the individual scientist's family and the well-being of American science as a whole.

Nonetheless, women continued to study and practice science and technology in growing numbers. Moreover, as cold war tensions exploded with the advent of the Space Race, a small but increasingly vocal number of scientists and politicians began to argue that the United States could only maintain its position as a global leader by recruiting both men and women into technoscientific professions. New ideas about science and technology as women's work were reflected in the National Defense Education Act of 1958, which allocated funds to ensure the intellectual development of boys and girls alike, and the short-lived Women in Space Early program, which provided Americans with new images of women who were both intensely feminine and technologically adept. Slowly but surely, it seemed that American thinking about the relations of gender, science, and society were changing, and that truly patriotic women might use their talents in both the living room and the laboratory.

Women associated with the postwar SF community both anticipated and greatly extended new ideas about science, technology, and women's work in two distinct ways. Science journalists including June Lurie, Sylvia Jacobs, and Kathleen Downe drew upon a centuries-old tradition of women's science popularization to establish their scientific expertise. By taking on the traditionally feminine personas of the trained educator and the scientist's wife, these authors made spaces for themselves as critical and creative members of the scientific community without ever directly challenging the widespread notion that scientific research was an inherently masculine activity. This enabled such authors to critically assess the work of male scientists and writers while conveying their own social, political, and even scientific ideas to readers.

Meanwhile, SF authors including Marion Zimmer Bradley, Katherine MacLean, Doris Pitkin Buck, and Judith Merril all wrote stories that looked forward to feminist SF in their radical reassessments of science, technology, and women's work. These authors challenged the feminine mystique by telling tales about the personal and cultural tragedies that would occur if women of the future were forced to choose between family and work. These stories make literal Betty Friedan's claim that such choices were mistaken ones that denied the true range of women's talents. Women SF writers also revised the great scientific and social origin stories of Western culture to imagine future worlds where women engage in both scientific and domestic labor. In direct contrast to the superwomen scientists of the mid-century mass media, however, these protofeminist characters do not have to sacrifice all other elements of their lives to keep their personal and professional worlds distinct from one another. Instead, they combine family and work in ways that profitably transform both.

As I have argued in this chapter and throughout this book, women writers turned to SF in significant numbers after World War II because it gave them an ideal source of narratives with which to assess both America's emergent technoculture and their own place within it. By telling stories about gender, science, and society from distinctly feminine perspectives, these authors developed a brave new mode of critical storytelling that would quickly become known as women's SF. So why did this speculative tradition all but disappear with the revival of feminism in the 1960s and the emergence of feminist SF in the 1970s? As I will conclude, women's SF may have disappeared in name, but the thematic concerns and narrative practices that postwar women brought with them to their chosen genre continue to inform SF storytelling today.

PROGENITORS

I M△C *INE IT.* One world where mothers and activists work together to save their children from the destructive religion of physical perfection called "Afterfat." Another world where young women earn celebrity status for their work as globetrotting professional consumers. And yet another world where one lone scientist takes on the combined political and military force of the United States in a desperate attempt to save the superchild he has come to love as his own. By now readers of this book might assume that such stories are just a few more examples of the new women's SF that flourished in the decades following World War II. After all, with their emphasis on women's work and domestic relations in a high-tech world, they seem very much part of galactic suburbia.

And yet all of these stories were written years and even decades after SF authors supposedly turned their attention away from galactic suburbia to other, more radically estranging science-fictional settings. The first, Kit Reed's *Thinner Than Thou* (2004), is a new novel from an SF veteran which recently received the Alex Award for outstanding adult/young adult fiction. The second, James Tiptree Jr.'s Hugo Award–winning "The Girl Who Was Plugged In" (1974), is a classic example of feminist SF and an important precursor to cyberpunk SF. And finally, Trent Hergenrader's "From the Mouth of Babes" (2006)—

which *Fantasy and Science Fiction* editor Gordon van Gelder recently described as an "affecting little tale of father and son"—reflects an emergent interest in the future of domestic relations as they impact both women *and* men (106). Taken together, such stories demonstrate both the very real staying power of postwar women writers and the equally real extent to which the thematic issues and narrative techniques of galactic suburbia continue to inform SF today.

Throughout this book I have argued that postwar women writers used stories set in galactic suburbia to critically assess the new relations of science, society, and gender as they emerged in the decades following World War II. Although issues of romance, marriage, and parenthood might seem to have little or no necessary relation to images of sleek spaceships, strange new worlds, or exotic alien creatures, tales that combined them were part of the Golden Age effort to put a human face on scientific and technological development. Postwar women writers put this new literary ideal into practice by strategically revising SF story types so wives and mothers were at the center of technoscientific action. By telling tales about women who were equally at ease in laboratories and laundry rooms, such authors created new narrative situations that enabled readers to better recognize the impact of America's emergent technoculture on both interpersonal and social relations.

Women writing for the postwar SF community created these new characters and narrative situations by incorporating effects from other literary traditions into their speculative fiction. Most obviously, they drew upon feminist utopian fiction, mainstream magazine fiction, and postmodernism to create shocking—and sometimes shockingly funny—stories about space-age sex therapists, homicidal housewives, and shopping lists that herald the end of the world as we know it. But women writers did not limit themselves to these three narrative traditions. To better stake out spaces for women in America's future imaginary, they looked backward to older modes of women's science writing and antiwar protest and forward to new narrative forms created by civil rights activists, advertisers, and scientists as well. Thus, postwar stories set in galactic suburbia evince the kind of generic hybridity that Roger Luckhurst has recently claimed is a defining characteristic of SF as a literary tradition in its own right.[1] Little wonder, then, that postwar women writers such as Reed still

---

1. For a detailed exploration of generic hybridity in SF, see Luckhurst's *Science Fiction* (*Cultural History of Literature*).

receive accolades for their work and that subsequent generations of SF authors including both luminaries like Tiptree and newcomers like Hergenrader continue to incorporate the themes and techniques of galactic suburbia into their own critical fictions.

But if traces of galactic suburbia are everywhere in SF, then why has postwar women's speculative fiction all but disappeared from our collective memory? As I explain in the first chapter of this book, the SF community vigorously debated the meaning and value of women's SF throughout the 1940s, '50s, and '60s. But within just a few decades this SF was relegated to the margins of literary history by artists and critics who wished to distinguish older modes of women's speculative fiction from the more overtly feminist SF that developed in the 1970s and that continues to flourish today. As women—and a few pioneering men—turned their attention to the question of how new sciences and technologies might foster new sex and gender relations, stories set in what Joanna Russ described as a future version of "white, middle-class, suburban America" seemed increasingly to be relics of a bygone era ("The Image of Women" 81).

This growing sense that galactic suburbia was a thing of the past was likely reinforced by the steady disappearance of postwar women writers from the pages of SF magazines and publisher booklists. This occurred over the course of several decades for several reasons. Science journalists including June Lurie and Mildred Murdoch left the SF community in the middle of the 1950s when *Fantastic Universe* folded and *Amazing Stories* and *Astounding Science Fiction* were revamped to meet the needs of what editors perceived to be an increasingly adult SF audience.[2] In the 1960s the careers of several popular fiction writers including Rosel George Brown and Shirley Jackson were cut short by their untimely deaths. And by the end of the 1970s, other leading architects of galactic suburbia including Margaret St. Clair, Mildred Clingerman, Zenna Henderson, Doris Pitkin Buck, Katherine MacLean, and Judith Merril had all but stopped publishing original fiction. Stories by these authors were subsequently reprinted in a few SF anthologies and single-author collections, but by and large it

---

2. Editor Howard Browne explains why *Amazing Stories* eliminated science journalism and readers' forums from its pages in an editorial from May 1955: "Fandom, they said—with some justification—was growing up, and what was interesting science fiction ten years ago no longer could hold a reader's attention. The editors listened and believed" ("Editorial" 5). Interestingly, these changes had occurred nearly two years earlier without any editorial comment; at the time Browne published this editorial, *Amazing* had revamped itself once again to include more action-oriented stories and the much-missed letters page. Science journalism, however, did not reappear.

seemed that science, technology, and domesticity had all but disappeared as an object of inquiry from women's speculative fiction.

But postwar women writers did not completely disappear from the literary scene. Some simply took on different positions in the SF community. For example, Judith Merril first earned the nickname "little mother of science fiction" for her key role in the development of women's SF as a discrete mode of storytelling after World War II. But she continued to live up to this moniker in subsequent years as editor of the groundbreaking *Year's Best in SF* anthologies and then, after she left the United States in protest against the Vietnam War, as a foundational figure in the development of Canadian SF. In 1965, Merril's sister, Futurian Virginia Kidd, became the first female literary agent in speculative fiction, and over the course of the next three decades represented some the genre's most important authors, including Ursula K. Le Guin, Anne McCaffrey, Gene Wolfe, Alan Dean Foster, and Kathleen Ann Goonan. Like Merril, she also edited a number of SF anthologies including *The Best of Judith Merril* (1976), *Millennial Women* (1978), and, with Le Guin as coeditor, *Interfaces* (1980) and *Edges* (1980). Although Merril always called herself a feminist and Kidd generally avoided this label, both were, as editors and as mentors, instrumental in paving the way for a new generation of women writers.

Other women who published SF in the decades following World War II went on to literary careers in other fields. When Alice Eleanor Jones burst onto the SF scene in 1955 with five well-received SF stories, Anthony Boucher predicted that she would become another Judith Merril. Although Boucher was correct to forecast literary success for Jones, he was wrong about the genre in which she would find that success. After 1955 Jones never published another SF story, choosing instead to work in the more lucrative (and at that time, still more respectable) field of mainstream women's magazine fiction. In addition to writing for *Good Housekeeping, Redbook,* and *Ladies' Home Journal,* Jones produced a regular column for *The Writer,* in which she provided young authors with advice about how to get ahead in the world of commercial fiction writing. Meanwhile, Cornelia Jessey went on to establish herself as a prolific religious author. In addition to publishing scholarly monographs with her husband, Irving Sussman, Jessey wrote at least half a dozen books of her own, including *The Prayer of Cosa: Praying in the Way of Francis of Assisi* (1985) and *Profiles in Hope* (1978). For such authors, SF writing was not an end in and of itself but the means by which they launched their multifaceted writing careers.

A good number of postwar women writers did stay within their chosen field, establishing themselves as leaders in feminist and other new modes of SF. Like Merril, Kit Reed and Carol Emshwiller were regularly featured in early feminist SF anthologies such as Pamela Sargent's *Women of Wonder* (1974) and Virginia Kidd's *Millennial Women* (1978). In contrast to Merril, however, both Reed and Emshwiller continue to produce new SF. Since the turn of the millennia alone Reed has published one collection of short stories and five novels, including the aforementioned award-winning *Thinner Than Thou* and, most recently, *The Baby Merchant* (2006). As the titles of these books suggest, Reed continues to write satirically about those domestic issues that are most central to the American imagination at any given moment in time. In the same time frame Emshwiller has produced over a dozen new short SF stories (many for *The Magazine of Fantasy and Science Fiction,* where she began her career), two anthologies, and two new novels including *The Mount,* winner of the 2002 Philip K. Dick Award. One of her best-known novels, *Carmen Dog* (1988), recently was republished by Small Beers Press. Like Reed, Emshwiller continues to explore many of the same themes that first interested her—including the relation of humans to alien others and the status of women under patriarchy—as they have evolved over time.

Two other women writers who began publishing SF in the 1950s, Marion Zimmer Bradley and Anne McCaffrey, also enjoy immense popularity as feminist SF and fantasy authors. Bradley, who passed away in 1999, is best remembered for *The Planet Savers* (1962), which initiated the Amazonian *Darkover* series, and *The Mists of Avalon* (1979), a retelling of the Camelot legend from the perspectives of Morgaine and Guinevere, which initiated the *Avalonian* series. As editor of the *Sword and Sorcery* series she mentored a generation of new authors including Diana L. Paxson and Mercedes Lackey who write about strong, nontraditional heroines. In a similar vein Anne McCaffrey established a huge fan base with novels such as *Dragonflight* (1968) and *The Ship Who Sang* (1969), which became the bases for her long-running *Dragonriders of Pern* and *Brainship* series. Like Bradley, McCaffrey is well known for mentoring new writers such as Margaret Ball, Elizabeth Scarborough, S. M. Stirling, and Jody Lynn Nye who have coauthored novels with her in various book series. Much like Merril and Kidd, these authors have been instrumental in creating and sustaining a vibrant, mutigenerational community of critically engaged and aesthetically innovative women writers.

Furthermore, although stories that combine the distinctive thematic interests and narrative techniques of postwar women's SF have all but disappeared, the themes and techniques themselves still flourish in the contemporary SF community.[3] This is particularly apparent in feminist SF, where authors grapple with many of the same issues as their literary predecessors. As Joanna Russ explains in "The Image of Women in Science Fiction," postwar women's SF differs from feminist SF in that the former examines the impact of science and technology on what women already are while the latter explores the impact of science and technology on what women might someday be (88). As such, the differences between these two modes of speculative fiction are less a matter of kind than degree.[4]

As I discuss in the second chapter of this book, postwar women writers revised one of SF's oldest tropes, that of the female alien other, to demonstrate the debilitating limits of the feminine mystique for women as homemakers and to celebrate communal modes of mothering as a way to mitigate the isolation of the nuclear family. These same themes were central to the first-generation of feminist SF authors as well. For example, in *The Female Man* (1975) Joanna Russ uses the meeting between four women of the same genotype raised in different timelines to demonstrate the social construction of gender. In contrast to earlier stories like April Smith and Charles Dye's "Settle to One," Russ's protagonists are not divided by their interest in men but put aside their differences to engage in battle together against those who are most truly alien to them: men themselves. Meanwhile, Marge Piercy's *Woman on the Edge of Time* (1976) and Suzy McKee Charnas's *Holdfast* series (1974–99) both revolve around women much like ourselves whose encounters with female alien others (or more precisely, as in Russ's novel, women from different times and places) lead them to embrace the values of cooperative motherhood. But in contrast to the relatively safe suburbs of Rosel George Brown and Zenna Henderson's worlds, these seemingly alien women inhabit

3. Interestingly, *The Magazine of Fantasy and Science Fiction* continues to publish a handful of stories set in galactic suburbia. Two recent examples include Delia Sherman's "Walpurgis Afternoon" (December 2005) and James L. Cambias's "Parsifal (Prix Fixe)" (February 2006). As this latter story indicates, men are now just as likely as women to write from the perspective of wives and mothers.

4. My thanks to the women and men who have compiled comprehensive lists of SF authors and themes on *The Feminist Science Fiction, Fantasy, and Utopia* Web site, http://feministsf.org/bibs/, and *The Ultimate Science Fiction Web Guide,* http://www.magicdragon.com/UltimateSF/SF-Index.html. I have used their work to supplement my own ideas about the thematic and technical development of women's SF throughout this concluding chapter.

wildly estranging postholocaust futures where men either modify themselves to participate in communal motherhood as well or are replaced altogether by bioengineered animals who provide both fresh genetic material and simple physical comfort to their lover/owners. In essence, then, feminist SF authors do not reject but extend the ideas of their postwar counterparts, imagining radical solutions to the problems first identified by women writers in the wake of World War II.

More recently, lesbian and gay SF authors have engaged similar issues in their own fiction. Both Rachel Pollack's *Godmother Night* (1996) and Melissa Kwasny's *Modern Daughters and the Outlaw West* (1990) address the promises and perils of lesbian motherhood in alternate futures much like our own. As such, it seems galactic suburbia (much like real-world suburbia) has expanded at least nominally to include women who refuse both the heterosexual norms of the feminine mystique and the heterosexual togetherness of the nuclear family. In a more fantastic vein, Storm Constantine's *Wraeththu* trilogy (1987–89) asks how androgynes that were once male might deal with the experience of birth and parenting. In Constantine's stories, the narrative drama emerges not so much from the radical differences between humanity and posthumanity but from the ways in which the two remain bound together through the desire for love, family, and children. Like Brown and Henderson before them, Pollack, Kwasny, and Constantine are profoundly interested in the different modes of parenting and family already available in our own society. The primary difference is that they expand their explorations to consider the complex and sometimes contradictory relations of science, society, gender, *and* sexual orientation.

Feminist SF authors also continue to use variations of the media landscape story to investigate women's roles as consumers. While the most obvious example of this is certainly James Tiptree Jr.'s short story "The Girl Who Was Plugged In," other classic feminist SF novels including Russ's *The Female Man* and Octavia Butler's *Kindred* (1979) incorporate aspects of the media landscape narrative into their critiques of patriarchal scientific, social, and sexual relations.[5] Like Garen Drussaï before them, all three of these authors insist that consumption is a job much like any other one. However, while postwar authors such as Ann Warren Griffith and Drussaï locate that

5. For further discussion of Tiptree's story as a feminist critique of advertising, see chapter 2 of Jane L. Donawerth's *Frankenstein's Daughters;* for discussion of Russ and Butler's novels as critiques of the same, see chapter 3 of my book, *The Self Wired: Technology and Subjectivity in Contemporary American Narrative.*

work in the home, Tiptree, Russ, and to a lesser extent Butler show how women's work as consumers merges seamlessly with the work of production itself, as women leave the home to become professional spokespersons extolling the virtues of domestic goods to other women.[6]

Over the past two decades feminist SF authors increasingly have turned their attention to women's work as consumers and producers in what I call the "new media landscape" of cyberpunk. Pat Cadigan's *Synners* (1991), Wilhelmina Baird's *Crashcourse* trilogy (1993–95), and Melissa Scott's *Trouble and Her Friends* (1994) extend the interest of their postwar and feminist predecessors to explore the promises and perils of women's work as consumers and producers of information rather than material goods. While the protagonists of these novels are rarely wives or mothers, they are passionately committed to the other women, men, and children who comprise their communities. And much like the heroines of media landscape stories by Margaret St. Clair and Kit Reed, they use their skills to strategically rewire the world around them in accordance with their own critical and creative needs.

Feminist SF authors also extend the activist tradition of their postwar counterparts. In chapter 3 of this book I examine how women writing SF at mid-century used the nuclear holocaust narrative to protest the new social and moral orders of the atomic age, especially as they threatened to destroy those very families they were meant to preserve. Not surprisingly, women continued to write antinuclear stories throughout the cold war, such as those by Mary Gentle, Pamela Zoline, and Lisa Tuttle that feature prominently in Jen Green and Sarah Lefanu's *Despatches from the Frontiers of the Female Mind* (1985). Feminists also extend the project of their postwar predecessors through more general expressions of antiwar sentiment. For example, Kit Reed's *Little Sisters of the Apocalypse* (1994) imagines that women might take up arms to fend off the men who abandon them for war and then expect a welcoming return, while the seventeen women writers included in Lois McMaster Bujold and Roland J. Green's *Women at War* (1988) explore the diverse roles that women take on during times of conflict as mothers and soldiers, heroes and villains,

6. Butler is actually more interested in how black women—and all African Americans—are duped into consuming false images of their own past, but the point remains much the same: women both consume these images and, by embodying them in their own lives, reproduce them in dangerous ways. For further discussion, see my essay "'A grim fantasy': Remaking American History in Octavia Butler's *Kindred*."

and artists and warriors. Much like Judith Merril, Alice Eleanor Jones, Virginia Cross, Mary Armock, and Carol Emshwiller before them, contemporary women writers assume that the personal is always political and that war impacts individuals on the home front every bit as much as those on the battlefield. But they also extend the ideas first put forth by their postwar counterparts to show how women might move from the home to the front lines of war itself.

Feminist authors also continue to explore the notion that politically engaged women might work together with like-minded scientists to prevent war or build new kinds of community after war has occurred. Much like Merril's *Shadow on the Hearth,* novels including Charnas's *Holdfast* series, Pamela Sargent's *The Shore of Women* (1986), and Joan Slonczewski's *The Wall Around Eden* (1989) illustrate the devastation wrought by nuclear war while treating such war as a potentially fortunate event that might herald the end of patriarchy and the rise of alternate social and political structures. However, while Merril only provides readers with a glimpse of one possible new world order via the quasi-utopian community that her characters create within the confines of a single suburban home, later writers imagine that women might seize control of science and technology to actively create new and distinctly nonsuburban, nonpatriarchal societies. As such, they grant their protagonists a kind of critical and creative agency that postwar authors could only gesture toward.[7]

But perhaps the most significant evolution of themes in SF written by women over the past half century occurs in the treatment of race. In direct contrast to authors like Margaret St. Clair, Kay Rogers, Cornelia Jessey, and Mildred Clingerman, who told science-fictional versions of the mid-century racial conversion narrative centered on white people and their perceptions of race relations, feminist authors writing in the wake of the civil rights movement write about protagonists of color who live in worlds extrapolated from stories and histories of the protagonists themselves. For example, African American author Octavia Butler's *Patternist* (1976–84), *Lilith's Brood* (1987–89), and *Parable* (1993–98) series feature heroes and villains of color who must learn how to negotiate potentially disastrous encounters with alien others of different races and species. Meanwhile, Caribbean-

---

7. Other SF authors write ecofeminist variants of the "nuclear holocaust as fortunate fall" narrative in which manmade plagues and other ecological disasters engender the demise of patriarchy and rise of new cultures based on alternate sex and gender relations. For excellent examples of this, see Joanna Russ's *The Female Man* (1975), Emma Bull's *Bone Dance* (1991), and Starhawk's *The Fifth Sacred Thing* (1993).

Canadian author Nalo Hopkinson builds strange new worlds extrapolated from Afrodiasporic religions, mythologies, and histories in short stories such as "Ganger (Ball Lightning)" (2000) and "Greedy Choke Puppy" (2000) and in novels such as *Midnight Robber* (2000) and *The Salt Roads* (2003). But other feminist authors also tell stories about protagonists of color. Both Marge Piercy's *Woman on the Edge of Time* (1976) and Starhawk's *The Fifth Sacred Thing* (1993) feature Latina heroines, while novels such as Chitra Bannerjee Divakaruni's *The Mistress of Spices* (1998) and Cynthia Kadohata's *In the Heart of the Valley of Love* (1997) demonstrate the compatibility of Western speculative storytelling traditions with Indian mythology and Japanese history, respectively.

But post–civil rights SF stories are much like their mid-century predecessors in that authors continue to use romantic encounters with the alien other and interspecies family dramas as focusing lenses through which to explore larger race relations. Both Butler's Hugo and Nebula Award–winning short story "Bloodchild" (1985) and her *Lilith's Brood* trilogy revolve around humans and aliens who must relinquish their prejudices against one another and interbreed to ensure the survival of their races, while the Indian goddess Tilo of Divakaruni's *The Mistress of Spices* embarks on a love affair with an American man named Raven in part to better understand how she can help her people adjust to the new world of the West. As in Kay Roger's "Experiment" and St. Clair's "Brightness Falls from the Air," the protagonists of recent SF stories about race relations quickly learn that attempts to build bridges across race and species lines are often thwarted by the ignorance, indifference, and even outright hostility on both sides. However, while this situation usually leads to death in early SF stories about race relations, later ones often end with scenes of marriage and birth—reflecting, perhaps, the very real hope that while love does not conquer all, hatred and fear do not always do so either.

Postwar and feminist SF authors also share a common interest in women's work in science and technology. As I discuss in chapter 4 of this book, the decades immediately following World War II marked a difficult time for scientifically and technologically inclined women. On the one hand, the rhetoric of cold war domestic security suggested that women could best serve their country at home. Nonetheless, women continued to leave their homes to pursue science, math, and engineering careers in record numbers. SF authors including Judith

Merril, Marion Zimmer Bradley, Katherine MacLean, Doris Pitkin Buck, and Anne McCaffrey responded to this situation with their own inspirational stories about women scientists, engineers, and explorers. Similar characters featured in feminist SF include Mary, the biologist and alien communications specialist of Naomi Mitchison's *Memoirs of a Spacewoman* (1962); Margaret, the computer scientist of James Tiptree Jr.'s *Up the Walls of the World* (1978); and more recently, Anna Senoz, the geneticist of Gwyneth Jones's *Life* (2004). But feminist authors also imagine that women might practice alternative forms of science in the guise of magic or witchcraft, as in Andre Norton's *Witch World* series (1963–1998), Joan Vinge's *Snow Queen* series (1980–2000), and Melissa Kwasny's *Modern Daughters and the Outlaw West* (1990). Meanwhile, in novels such as Melissa Scott's *Trouble and Her Friends* (1994) and Pat Cadigan's *Synners, Tea from an Empty Cup* (1998), and *Dervish Is Digital* (2000), women play key roles in both the physical world and cyberspace as hackers, video artists, and cybercops. Like their counterparts from postwar women's SF, these feminist protagonists do not make tidy distinctions between work and home but instead draw upon their domestic lives as inspiration for scientific and technological discovery.

Feminist authors also continue to grapple with many of the same questions about the necessary relations of family and career for women that first emerged after World War II. While postwar authors such as Bradley and Merril warned about the individual and cultural tragedies that come from forcing women to choose between work and family, others including Buck and MacLean (and Merril once again) wrote about future women who avoid this mistaken choice by seeking out nonpatriarchal spaces (ranging from the kitchen to deep space) where they combine work and family as they see fit. Feminist utopian writers of the 1970s offered additional solutions to the dilemma of the mistaken choice. Women might use science and technology to bioengineer men so they could participate equally in childcare (thus freeing women to continue their work outside the family, as in Piercy's *Woman on the Edge of Time*); they might abandon men altogether and use science and technology to transform animals into repositories for human genetic materials (as in Charnas's *Motherlines* trilogy); or they might use science and technology to kill off all the men and develop new reproductive technologies suited to a world of women (as in Russ's *The Female Man*). And so, feminist SF authors extend the ideas of their literary predecessors by imagining that women might not need to leave their homes to escape patriarchal culture, but instead might use science and technology to eliminate the problem of patriarchy itself.

Feminist SF authors also extend the ideas of their literary predecessors with stories about the benefits that accrue to women—and all people—when female scientists combine family and career in new ways. Like the heroine of MacLean's "And Be Merry . . . ," the women who comprise the community of Sharers in Joan Slonczewski's *A Door into Ocean* (1986) combine their laboratories and kitchens under the roofs of their individual homes. The new biological sciences that result from this arrangement enable the Sharers to reproduce parthenogenically and adapt themselves to life on their waterworld. In addition, this arrangement enables them to successfully thwart the plans of the invading male army that hopes to control this planet of women by destroying their scientific bases precisely because it never occurs to the invaders that anyone might practice science at home.

In a related vein, the protagonists of novels including Scott's *Trouble and Her Friends* and *The Roads of Heaven* series (1985–87) and Jones's *Life* survive the heterosexist, patriarchal cultures they live in and make astonishing discoveries about information security, star travel, and genetics in large part because they have the full support of their lovers and spouses. Much like MacLean, Buck, and McCaffrey, Scott and Jones use the trope of the nontraditional marriage to represent the dream of new communities that fully support women's work in science and technology. However, while postwar women writers depict such marriages in modest terms as those in which working husbands support their wives' careers, contemporary authors like Scott and Jones expand the concept of alternative matrimony to include lesbian relationships, group marriages, and role-reversed unions in which husbands serve as homemakers to better support the careers of their wives.

Finally, while feminist authors continue to explore many of those issues first raised by women writing for the SF community after World War II, today it is primarily men who incorporate the settings and characters of galactic suburbia into their SF. While a handful of mid-century SF stories written by men—such as Philip Jose Farmer's *The Lovers* (1961) and Theodore Sturgeon's *Venus Plus X* (1960) use tropes of love, marriage, and motherhood and even in Sturgeon's case the setting of galactic suburbia itself to raise questions about the necessary relations of sex and gender in technologically and socially advanced societies, such stories generally retreat from the radical implications of their own premises, thereby ultimately reinforcing heterosexist and patriarchal ideals.[8] In the 1970s and 1980s, however, male authors began to experiment with these tropes and settings in different ways. For example, John Crowley's *Little, Big* (1981) and many of John Varley's *Eight World* stories, including the *Picnic on Nearside* collection (1984), as well as the novels *The Opiuchi Hotline* (1977) and *Steel Beach* (1992), use family dramas as focusing lenses through which to explore the passing of humanity as we know it and the subsequent emergence of posthumans and other hybrid beings. In direct contrast to authors like Farmer and Sturgeon, both Crowley and Varley refuse to make traditional men the center of their stories, instead relating their tales from the perspective of socially progressive New Men and technologically enhanced mothers whose sex of origin may be either male or female. Much like their female counterparts in both the postwar and feminist SF communities, then, Crowley and Varley exhibit little or no nostalgia for the passing of patriarchy as they stake claims for new kinds of people and societies in the future imaginary.

And just as postwar women used SF stories about families to critically assess the new technocultural arrangements of the atomic age, contemporary men use SF stories about families to critically assess the new technocultural arrangements of the information age. This is particularly apparent in the work of Bruce Sterling, whose novels *Islands in the Net* (1988), *Heavy Weather* (1991), and *Holy Fire* (1996) all revolve around the efforts of women as wives, sisters, and lovers to maintain their families (and in the case of *Holy Fire,* to forge new kinds of posthuman families) in the face of widespread economic, environmental, and technological change. Sterling's work is particularly unusual in that all three novels are either examples of or heavily indebted to cyberpunk, a mode of SF that generally revolves around young, unmarried protagonists who explicitly define themselves in opposition to romance and marriage.[9]

8. Russ first described this tendency on the part of male authors who write about galactic suburbia to simply reiterate patriarchal notions of sex and gender in "The Image of Women in Science Fiction." For further discussion of Farmer's *The Lovers* as a prime example of this tendency, see Robin Roberts's *A New Species: Gender and Science in Science Fiction.* For further discussion of Sturgeon's *Venus Plus X* as another such example, see Brian Attebery's *Decoding Gender in Science Fiction.*

9. This is particularly evident in William Gibson's *Neuromancer* (1984), when Molly leaves Case because past experience teaches her that business partners who become lovers tend to get killed, and in the sequel, *Count Zero* (1986), when another character offhandedly notes that Case has dropped out of the data piracy business to get married and raise children in the suburbs of the Sprawl.

Significantly, many of the authors who write about men's loves and lives in galactic suburbia today publish their work in precisely the same venue as did their postwar predecessors: *The Magazine of Fantasy and Science Fiction,* which maintains its original mission to publish offbeat, off-trail stories. Like earlier stories set in galactic suburbia, current ones tackle a variety of subjects in a variety of ways. For example, Trent Hergenrader's "From the Mouth of Babes" (March 2006) uses the story of a father and son on the run from the law to explore how male scientists might resist the limits of masculinist scientific practices that reduce people to objects of manipulation—and how they might therefore embrace new and more holistic scientific practices, even if the penalty is death. In "Parsifal (Prix Fixe)" (February 2006), James L. Cambias playfully undermines masculinist myths of the Holy Grail with his tale of a young American couple that discovers the real grail is actually a stewpot in which a modest French family has simmered the world's most perfect soup for two millennia. While Cambias deploys a far more lighthearted tone than Hergenrader, both ask readers to think about the gendered implications of our culture's foundational practices and myths. Meanwhile, in stories such as "Animal Magnetism" (June 2006), Albert E. Cowdrey stakes out spaces for gay families in the future imaginary with a tale of two men (and a female dog) who make a new kind of home for themselves in galactic suburbia by embracing their inner werewolves. Like Cambias's tale, "Animal Magnetism" is a piece of serious fun that demonstrates how men also adapt the characters and settings first developed by women writing for the postwar SF community in their quest to creatively revise dominant understandings of science, society, and gender as they structure our thinking at the beginning of the new millennia.

More than mere historical curiosity, postwar women's writing about galactic suburbia has powerfully informed the development of contemporary SF. While some of the original architects of galactic suburbia have passed on or changed career paths, many others continue to participate in the SF community as authors, editors, and mentors to new writers. And over the course of the past three decades, new writers themselves have invoked, revised, and extended the thematic issues and stylistic techniques of early women's SF in their own fiction. This is most apparent in the work of feminist SF authors, who generally liberate their female characters from the confines of the patriarchal home but who continue to explore many of the same issues regarding women's work in a high-tech world. It is also evident in the work of male authors who use the characters and settings of galactic suburbia in their own critical fictions about science, society, and gender. Taken together, these trends demonstrate how postwar women's stories about galactic suburbia comprise one of the key foundations upon which SF authors of all nationalities and genders continue to build today.

WORKS CITED

Ackmann, Martha. *The Mercury 13: The Untold Story of Thirteen American Women and the Dream of Space Flight.* New York: Random House, 2003.

Adams, Annmarie. "The Eichler Home: Intention and Experience in Postwar Suburbia." *Gender, Class, and Shelter: Perspectives in Vernacular Culture, V.* Knoxville: University of Tennessee Press, 1995. 164–78.

Aldiss, Brian. *Billion Year Spree: The True History of Science Fiction.* New York: Schocken Books, 1973.

Alonso, Harriet Hyman. "Mayhem and Moderation: Women Peace Activists During the McCarthy Era." *Not June Cleaver: Women and Gender in Postwar America, 1945–1960.* Ed. Joanne Meyerowitz. Philadelphia: Temple University Press, 1994. 128–50.

Armock, Mary. "First Born." *Fantastic* (Feb. 1960): 85–89.

Attebery, Brian. *Decoding Gender in Science Fiction.* New York and London: Routledge, 2002.

Baird, Wilhemina. *Clipjoint.* New York: Ace, 1994.

——. *Crashcourse.* New York: Ace, 1993.

——. *Psykosis.* New York: Ace, 1995.

Barr, Marleen S. *Alien to Femininity: Speculative Fiction and Feminist Theory.* Westport, CT: Greenwood Press, 1987.

——. *Future Females: A Critical Anthology.* Bowling Green, OH: Bowling Green State University Press, 1981.

——. *Lost in Space: Probing Feminist Science Fiction and Beyond.* Chapel Hill: University of North Carolina Press, 1993.

Basinger, Jeanine. *A Woman's View: How Hollywood Spoke to Women, 1930–1960.* Middletown, CT: Wesleyan University Press, 1995.

Belenky, Mary Field, Blythe McVicker Clinchy, Nancy Rule Goldberger, and Jill Mattuck Tarule. *Women's Ways of Knowing: The Development of Self, Voice, and Mind.* New York: Basic Books, 1986.

Berger, Albert I. "The Triumph of Prophecy: Science Fiction and Nuclear Power in the Post-Hiroshima Period." *Science Fiction Studies* 3 (1976): 143–50.

Best American Short Stories of the Century. Ed. John Updike and Katrina Kenison. Boston and New York: Houghton Mifflin, 1999.

Boucher, Anthony, ed. *The Best of* Fantasy and Science Fiction: *Eighth Series*. New York: Doubleday, 1959.

——. *The Best of* Fantasy and Science Fiction: *Fifth Series*. New York: Doubleday, 1956.

——. "Introduction to Alice Eleanor Jones' 'Created He Them.'" *The Best from* Fantasy and Science Fiction: *Fifth Series*. New York: Doubleday, 1956. 125.

Bradbury, Ray. "The Big Black and White Game." 1946. Rpt. in *Fahrenheit 451/The Illustrated Man/Dandelion Wine/The Golden Apples of the Sun/The Martian Chronicles*. New York: Octopus/Heinemann, 1987. 550–59.

——. "The Day It Rained Forever." 1958. Rpt. in *Ray Bradbury: Classic Stories 2*. New York: Bantam Spectra, 1990. 131–44.

——. "I See You Never." Rpt. in *Fahrenheit 451/The Illustrated Man/Dandelion Wine/The Golden Apples of the Sun/The Martian Chronicles*. New York: Octopus/Heinemann, 1987. 544–46.

——. "The Other Foot." Rpt. in *Fahrenheit 451/The Illustrated Man/Dandelion Wine/The Golden Apples of the Sun/The Martian Chronicles*. New York: Octopus/Heinemann, 1987. 147–58.

Bradley, Marion Zimmer. *The Mists of Avalon*. 1979. New York: Ballantine, 1984.

——. *The Planet Savers*. 1963. New York: Ace, 1998.

——. "The Wind People." *If* (Feb. 1959): 14–27.

Brown, Charles N., and William G. Contento. *The Locus Index to Science Fiction and Index to Science Fiction Anthologies and Collections*. Oakland, CA: Locus Press, 2002.

Brown, Rosel George. "Car Pool." *If* (July 1959): 80–94.

Browne, Harold. "Editorial." *Amazing Stories* 29.3 (1955): 5.

——. "Response to Cathleen M. M. Harlan." *Amazing Stories* 29.4 (1955): 117–18.

Bryant, Marsha. "Plath, Domesticity, and the Art of Advertising. " *College Literature* 29.3 (Summer 2002): 17–34.

Buck, Doris Pitkin. "Birth of a Gardner." *Magazine of Fantasy and Science Fiction* (June 1961): 50–59.

Bujold, Louise McMaster, and Roland J. Green, eds. 1988. *Women at War*. New York: Tor, 1997.

Bull, Emma. *Bone Dance*. New York: Ace, 1991.

Butler, Octavia E. "Bloodchild." 1985. *Bloodchild and Other Stories*. 2nd ed. New York: Seven Stories Press, 2005. 1–32.

——. *Kindred*. 1979. Boston: Beacon Press, 2004.

——. *Lilith's Brood*. 1987–89. New York: Warner Aspect, 2000.

——. *Parable of the Sower*. 1993. New York: Grand Central Publishing, 2000.

——. *Parable of the Talents*. 1998. New York: Grand Central Publishing, 2000.

——. *Seed to Harvest*. 1976–84. New York: Grand Central Publishing, 2007.

Byers, Jackie. *All That Hollywood Allows: Re-Reading Gender in the 1950s Melodrama*. Chapel Hill: University of North Carolina Press, 1991.

Cardigan, Pat. *Dervish Is Digital*. 2000. New York: Tor, 2002.

——. *Synners*. 1991. New York: Four Walls Eight Windows, 2001.

——. *Tea from an Empty Cup*. 1998. New York: Tor, 1999.

Cambias, James L. "Parsifal (Prix Fixe)." *Magazine of Fantasy and Science Fiction* (Feb. 2006): 128–35.

Carpenter, Lynette. "The Establishment and Preservation of Female Power in Shirley Jackson's *We Have Always Lived in the Castle.*" *Frontiers* 8.1 (1984): 32–38.

Carr, Terry, and Martin H. Greenberg, eds.. *A Treasury of Modern Fantasy.* New York: Avon, 1981.

Chafe, William H. *The Unfinished Journey: America Since World War II.* 3rd ed. New York: Oxford University Press, 1995.

Charnas, Suzy McKee. *The Conqueror's Child.* 1999. New York: Tor, 2000.

——. *The Furies.* 1994. New York: Orb, 2001.

——. *Motherlines.* 1978. New York: Berkley Books, 1981.

——. *Walk to the End of the World.* 1974. New York: Berkley Books, 1979.

Chase, Helen Reid. "Night of Fire." *The Avalonian* 1 (1952): 31–34.

Chodorow, Nancy. *The Reproduction of Mothering: Psychoanalysis and the Sociology of Gender.* Berkeley: University of California Press, 1978.

Clark, Clifford E., Jr. "Ranch House Suburbia: Ideals and Realities." *Recasting America: Culture and Politics in the Age of the Cold War.* Ed. Lary May. Chicago: University of Chicago Press, 1989. 171–91.

Clingerman, Mildred. "Mr. Sakrison's Halt." 1956. Rpt. in *Best from* Fantasy and Science Fiction: *Sixth Series.* Ed. Anthony Boucher. New York: Doubleday, 1957. 36–44.

Cohen, Lizbeth. "From Town Center to Shopping Center: The Reconfiguration of Community Marketplaces in Postwar America." *The American Historical Review* 101.4 (Oct. 1996): 1050–81.

Constantine, Storm. *The Wraeththu Trilogy.* 1987–89. New York: Orb, 1993.

Cowan, Ruth Schwartz. *More Work for Mother: The Ironies of Household Technology from the Open Hearth to the Microwave.* New York: Basic Books, 1983.

Cowdry, Albert E. "Animal Magnetism." *Magazine of Fantasy and Science Fiction* (June 2006): 6–37.

Cranny-Frances, Anne. *Feminist Fiction: Feminist Uses of Generic Fiction.* New York: St. Martin's Press, 1990.

Crawford, Vicki L., Jacqueline Anne Rouse, and Barbara Woods, eds. *Women in the Civil Rights Movement: Trailblazers and Torchbearers, 1941–1965.* Bloomington: Indiana University Press, 1993.

Cross, Virginia. "Adversity." *Other Worlds* (May 1995): 84–91.

Crowley, John. *Little, Big.* 1981. New York: Harper Perennial Modern Classics, 2006.

Cummins, Elizabeth. "American SF, 1940s–1950s: Where's the Book? The New York Nexus." *Extrapolation* 40.4 (1999): 314–19.

——. "Judith Merril: A Link with the New Wave—Then and Now." *Extrapolation* 36.3 (1995): 198–209.

——. "Judith Merril: Scouting SF." *Extrapolation* 35.1 (1994): 5–14.

Divakaruni, Chitra Bannerjee. *The Mistress of Spices.* New York: Anchor, 1998.

Doctorow, Cory. "Anda's Game." *The Best American Short Stories 2005.* Ed. Michael Chabon. New York: Houghton Mifflin, 2004. 223–50.

Donawerth, Jane L. *Frankenstein's Daughters: Women Writing Science Fiction.* Syracuse, NY: Syracuse University Press, 1997.

——. "Science Fiction by Women in the Early Pulps, 1926–1930." *Utopian and Science Fiction by Women: Worlds of Difference.* Ed. Jane L. Donawerth and Carol A. Kolmerton, Syracuse, NY: Syracuse University Press, 1994. 137–52.

Donawerth, Jane L., and Carol A. Kolmerton, eds. *Utopian and Science Fiction by Women: Worlds of Difference.* Syracuse, NY: Syracuse University Press, 1994.

Downe, Kathleen. "Why Not a Woman?" *Authentic Science Fiction Monthly* 57 (May 1955): 101–2.

Drussaï, Garen. "Woman's Work." *The Magazine of Fantasy and Science Fiction* (Aug. 1956): 104–6.

DuPlessis, Rachel Blau. *Writing Beyond the Ending: Narrative Strategies of Twentieth Century Women Writers.* Bloomington: Indiana University Press, 1985.

Egan, James. "Sanctuary: Shirley Jackson's Domestic and Fantastic Parables." *Studies in Weird Fiction* 6 (1989): 5–24.

Ehrenreich, Barbara, and Deirdre English. *For Her Own Good.* Garden City, NY: Anchor, 1978.

Ellis, Sophie Wenzel. "Creatures of the Light." *Astounding Science-Fiction* (Feb. 1930): 197–220.

Ellison, Harlan. "The Man Who Rowed Christopher Columbus Ashore." 1991. *Slippage: Previously Uncollected, Precariously Poised Stories.* New York: Houghton Mifflin, 1997. 1–18.

Emshwiller, Carol. "Adapted." 1961. Rpt. in *Rod Serling's Devils and Demons.* Ed. Rod Serling. New York: Bantam, 1967. 31–39.

———. *Carmen Dog.* 1988. Northampton, MA: Small Beer Press, 2004.

———. "Day at the Beach." 1959. Rpt. in *SF: The Best of the Best.* Ed. Judith Merril. New York: Delacourt, 1967. 274–84.

———. *The Mount.* 2002. London: Puffin Press, 2005.

Fairbanks, Paul W. "Response to Mrs. Lucky Rardin." *Fantastic* 6.5 (June 1957): 125.

Flanagan, Mary, and Austin Booth, eds. *Reload: Rethinking Women + Cyberculture.* Cambridge, MA: MIT Press, 2002.

Farmer, Philip José. *The Lovers.* 1961. New York: Del Rey, 1980.

Foreman, Joel, ed. *The Other Fifties: Interrogating Midcentury American Icons.* Urbana and Chicago: University of Chicago Press, 1997.

Foust, James C. "E. W. Scripps and the Science Service." *Journalism History* 21.2 (Summer 1995): 58–64.

Fox, Bonnie J. "Selling the Mechanized Household: 70 Years of Ads in *Ladies' Home Journal*." *Gender and Society* 4.1 (Mar. 1990): 25–40.

Fraiman, Susan. *Unbecoming Women: British Women Writers and the Novel of Development.* New York: Columbia University Press, 1993.

Frederick, Christine. *Selling Mrs. Consumer.* New York: The Business Bourse, 1929.

Freni, Pamela. *Space for Women: A History of Women with the Right Stuff.* Santa Ana, CA: Seven Locks Press, 2002.

Friedan, Betty. *The Feminine Mystique.* 1963. New York: Dell, 1983.

Gamble, Sarah. "'Shambleau . . . and Others': The Role of the Female in the Fiction of C. L. Moore." *Where No Man Has Gone Before: Women and Science Fiction.* Ed. Lucie Armitt. London: Routledge, 1991. 29–49.

Garrison, Dee. "'Our Skirts Gave Them Courage': The Civil Defense Protest Movement in New York City, 1955–1961." *Not June Cleaver: Women and Gender in Postwar America, 1945–1960.* Ed. Joanne Meyerowitz. Philadelphia: Temple University Press, 1994. 201–26.

Gates, Barbara T., and Ann B. Shteir. "Introduction: Charting the Tradition."

Natural Eloquence: Women Reinscribe Nature. Ed. Barbara T. Gates and Ann B. Shteir. Madison: University of Wisconsin Press, 1997. 3–24.

Gibson, William. *Count Zero.* New York: Ace, 1984.

——. *Neuromancer.* New York: Ace, 1984.

Gilbreth, Lillian M., Orpha Mae Thomas, and Eleanor Clymer. *Management in the Home: Happier Living through Saving Time and Energy.* New York: Dodd, Mean & Company, 1954.

Gilligan, Carol. *In a Different Voice: Psychological Theory and Women's Development.* Cambridge, MA: Harvard University Press, 1981.

Gilmore, Glenda Elizabeth. "Admitting Pauli Murray." *Dialogue* 14.2 (Summer 2002): 62–67.

Glanzman, Rita. "The Bantus with the Brains." *Fantastic Adventures* 13.12 (Dec. 1951): 55.

——. "Machines Make the Money." *Fantastic Adventures* 14.2 (Feb. 1952): 93.

Green, Jen, and Sarah Lefanu. *Despatches from the Frontiers of the Female Mind.* 1985. London: Women's Press, 1987.

Griffith, Ann Warren. "Captive Audience." 1953. Rpt. in *The Best from* Fantasy and Science Fiction: *Third Series.* Ed. Anthony Boucher and J. Francis McComas. New York: Doubleday, 1954. 197–212.

Hafemeister, D. W. "A Chronology of the Nuclear Arms Race." *Nuclear Arms Technologies in the 1990s.* Eds. Dietrich Schroeer and David Hafemeister. New York: American Institute of Physics, 1988. 435–43.

Hansen, Lillian Taylor. "What the Sodium Lines Revealed." *Amazing Stories Quarterly* (Winter 1929):120–38.

Haraway, Donna J. "A Cyborg Manifesto: Science, Technology, and Socialist-Feminism in the Late Twentieth Century." 1985. Rpt. in *Simians, Cyborgs, and Women: The Reinvention of Nature.* New York: Routledge, 1991. 149–81.

Harlan, Cathleen M. M. "Letter to the Editor." *Amazing Stories* 29.4 (1955): 117–18.

Harris, Clare Winger. "A Runaway World." Rpt. in *Away from the Here-and-Now: Stories in Pseudo-Science.* Philadelphia: Dorrance, 1947. 7–36.

Hartmann, Susan M. "Women's Employment and the Domestic Ideal in the Early Cold War Years." *Not June Cleaver: Women and Gender in Postwar America, 1945–1960.* Ed. Joanne Meyerowitz. Philadelphia: Temple University Press, 1994. 84–100.

Haskell, Molly. *From Reverence to Rape: The Treatment of Women in the Movies.* Chicago: University of Chicago Press, 1987.

Hattenhauer, Darryl. *Shirley Jackson's American Gothic.* Albany: State University of New York Press, 2003.

Hayles, N. Katherine. *How We Became Posthuman: Virtual Bodies in Cybernetics, Literature, and Informatics.* Chicago: University of Chicago Press, 1999.

——. "The Life Cycle of Cyborgs: Writing the Posthuman." *The Cyborg Handbook.* Ed. Chris Hables Gray. New York: Routledge, 1995. 321–35.

Henderson, Zenna. *Ingathering: The Complete People Stories.* Cambridge, MA: NESFA Press, 1995.

——. *No Different Flesh.* New York: Avon, 1966.

——. *Pilgrimage: The Book of the People.* New York: Avon, 1961.

——. "Pottage." 1955. Rpt. in *The Best from* Fantasy and Science Fiction: *Fifth Series.* Ed. Anthony Boucher. New York: Doubleday, 1956. 75–112.

Hergenrader, Trent. "From the Mouth of Babes." *Magazine of Fantasy and Science Fiction* (2006): 106–13.

Hobson, Fred. "The Southern Racial Conversion Narrative." *The Virginia Quarterly Review* 75.2 (1999): 205–25.

Holliday, Laura Scott. "Kitchen Technologies: Promises and Alibis: 1944–1966." *Camera Obscura* 16.2 (2001): 79–131.

Hopkinson, Nalo. "Ganger (Ball Lightning)." 2000. *Dark Matter: A Century of Science Fiction from the African Diaspora.* Ed. Sheree R. Thomas. New York: Aspect, 2001. 134–51.

———. "Greedy Choke Puppy." 2000. *Dark Matter: A Century of Science Fiction from the African Diaspora.* Ed. Sheree R. Thomas. New York: Aspect, 2001. 103–12.

———. *Midnight Robber.* New York: Warner Aspect, 2000.

———. *The Salt Roads.* 2003. New York: Grand Central Publishing, 2004.

Hume, Janice. "Changing Characteristics of Heroic Women in Midcentury Mainstream Media." *Journal of Popular Culture* 34.1 (Summer 2000): 9–29.

Hyman, Lawrence Jackson, and Sarah Hyman Stewart. *Just an Ordinary Day: The Uncollected Stories of Shirley Jackson.* New York: Bantam, 1997.

Jackson, Shirley. "Bulletin." *The Magazine of Fantasy and Science Fiction* (Mar. 1954): 46–48.

———. *Life Among the Savages.* New York: Farrar, Straus, and Young, 1953.

———. "The Missing Girl." *The Magazine of Fantasy and Science Fiction* (Dec. 1957): 42–52.

———. "The Omen." *The Magazine of Fantasy and Science Fiction* (Mar. 1958): 118–30.

———. "One Ordinary Day, with Peanuts." 1955. Rpt. in *Just an Ordinary Day.* Ed. Lawrence Jackson Hyman and Sarah Hyman Stewart. New York: Bantam, 1977. 296–304.

———. *Raising Demons.* New York: Farrar, Straus, and Young, 1957.

———. *The Sundial.* New York: Farrar, Straus, and Cudahy, 1958.

Jacobs, Sylvia. "Hold That Helium!" *Astounding Science Fiction* 15.1 (Mar. 1955): 132–49.

Jacoway, Elizabeth. "Vivion Brewer of Arkansas: A Ladylike Assault on the 'Southern Way of Life.'" *Lives Full of Struggle and Triumph: Southern Women, Their Institutions, and Their Communities.* Ed. Bruce L. Clayton and John A. Salmond. Gainesville: University Press of Florida, 2003. 264–82.

James, Edward. *Science Fiction in the Twentieth Century.* Oxford: Oxford University Press, 1994.

Jessey, Cornelia. *The Prayer of Cosa: Praying in the Way of Francis of Assisi.* London and New York: Continuum International Publishing, 1985.

———. *Profiles in Hope.* Prescott, AZ: Veritas Publications, 1978.

———. "Put Out the Light." *Fantastic Worlds* (Fall 1955): 18–24.

Johnson, Karen Ramsay, and Diantha Daniels Kesling. "Stories within Stories: Race and Gender Against the Background." *The Centennial Review* 41.3 (1997): 507–14.

Jones, Alice Eleanor. "Created He Them." *The Magazine of Fantasy and Science Fiction* (June 1955): 29–37.

———. "The Happy Clown." *If* (Dec. 1955): 105–15.

———. "The Honeymoon." *Redbook* (June 1957): 31, 88–91.

——. "How to Sell an Offbeat Story." *The Writer* 75 (Mar. 1962): 18–20.

——. "Jenny Kissed Me." *Ladies' Home Journal* (Nov. 1955): 93, 167–71.

——. "Life, Incorporated." *Fantastic Universe* (Apr. 1955): 59–74.

——. "Miss Quatro." *Fantastic Universe* (June 1955): 55–63.

——. "Morning Watch." *Redbook* (Nov. 1958): 42–43, 111–15.

——. "One Shattering Weekend." *Redbook* (July 1960): 40, 72–76.

——. "Ones That Got Away." *The Writer* 78 (May 1965): 17–18, 46.

——. "The Real Me." *Redbook* (Oct. 1962): 62–63, 137–40.

——. "Recruiting Officer." *Fantastic* (Oct. 1955): 87–101.

Jones, Gwyneth. *Life.* Seattle: Aqueduct Press, 2004.

Jones, Jacqueline. "The Political Implications of Black and White Southern Women's Work in the South, 1890–1965." *Women and Political Change.* Ed. Louise A. Tilley and Patricia Gurin. New York: Russell Sage Foundation, 1992. 108–29.

Joshi, S. T. "Shirley Jackson: Domestic Horror." *Studies in Weird Fiction* 14 (1994): 9–28.

Kadohata, Cynthia. *In the Heart of the Valley of Love.* Berkeley: University of California Press, 1997.

Kaledin, Eugenia. *Mothers and More: American Women in the 1950s.* Boston: Twayne, 1984.

Keller, Evelyn Fox. *A Feeling for the Organism: The Life and Work of Barbara McClintock.* New York and San Francisco: W. H. Freeman, 1983.

Keller, Evelyn Fox, and Helen E. Longino, eds. *Feminism and Science.* New York: Oxford University Press, 1996.

Kessler, Carol Farley. *Daring to Dream: Utopian Fiction by United States Women Before 1950.* Syracuse, NY: Syracuse University Press, 1995.

Kevles, Bettyann Holtzmann. *Almost Heaven: The Story of Women in Space.* New York: Basic Books, 2003.

Kidd, Virginia. *The Best of Judith Merril.* New York: Warner, 1976.

——. *Millennial Women.* New York: Delacorte, 1978.

Kidd, Virginia, and Ursula K. Le Guin. *Edges.* New York: Pocket, 1980.

——. *Interfaces.* New York: Aces, 1980.

Killingsworth, M. Jimmie, and Jacqueline S. Palmer. "*Silent Spring* and Science Fiction: An Essay in the History and Rhetoric of Narrative." *And No Birds Sing: Rhetorical Analyses of Rachel Carson's* Silent Spring. Ed. Craig Waddell. Carbondale: Southern Illinois University Press, 2000. 174–204.

Kohlstedt, Sally Gregory. "Sustaining Gains: Reflections on Women in Science and Technology in the Twentieth-Century United States." *NWSA Journal* 16.1 (Spring 2004): 1–27.

Krentz, Jayne Ann, ed. *Dangerous Men and Adventurous Women: Romance Writers on the Appeal of the Romance.* Philadelphia: University of Pennsylvania Press, 1992.

Kwansy, Melissa. *Modern Daughters and the Outlaw West.* Midway, FL: Spinsters Ink, 1990.

Lafollette, Marcel C. "Eyes on the Stars: Images of Women Scientists in Popular Magazines." *Science, Technology, & Human Values* 13.3–4 (1988): 262–75.

Larbalestier, Justine. *The Battle of the Sexes in Science Fiction.* Middletown, CT: Wesleyan University Press, 2002.

Larbalestier, Justine, and Helen Merrick. "The Revolting Housewife: Women and

Science Fiction in the 1950s." *Paradoxa* 18 (2003): 136–47.

"Lava Soap: Guard Against 'Dirt Danger' Days!" 1953. *The Duke Library Ad Access Project.* 19 May 2006. http://scriptorium.lib.duke.edu/adaccess/BH/BH11/BH1180-150dpi.jpeg.

Lefanu, Sarah. *Feminism and Science Fiction.* Bloomington: Indiana University Press, 1989.

Le Guin, Ursula K. "The Professor's Houses." 1982. Rpt. in *Unlocking the Air and Other Stories.* New York: HarperCollins, 1996. 39–46.

——. "Sur." *The Compass Rose: Short Stories.* New York: Harper and Row, 1982. 343–53.

Leiber, Fritz. "The Girl with the Hungry Eyes." 1949. Rpt. in *Blood Thirst: 100 Years of Vampire Fiction.* Ed. Leonard Wolf. Cambridge: Oxford University Press, 1997. 90–102.

Link, Kelly. "Stone Animals." *The Best American Short Stories 2005.* Ed. Michael Chabon. New York: Houghton Mifflin, 2004. 67–108.

Lloyd, Justine, and Lesley Johnson. "The Three Faces of Eve: The Postwar Housewife, Melodrama, and Home." *Feminist Media Studies* 3.1 (2003): 7–25.

Lorraine, Lilith. "Into the 28th Century." *Science Wonder Quarterly* (Winter 1930): 250–67, 276.

Luckhurst, Roger. *Science Fiction (Cultural History of Literature).* Cambridge, UK: Polity, 2005.

Lurie, June. "Artificial Universe." *Amazing Stories* 24.11 (Nov. 1950): n.p.

——. "Bacteria with Brains!" *Amazing Stories* 25.6 (June 1951): 7.

——. "Icy Cold-War." *Amazing Stories* 24.9 (Sept. 1950): 169.

——. "Mars Is Waiting!" *Amazing Stories* 26.3 (Mar. 1952): 93.

——. "Red Atoms." *Amazing Stories* 24.5 (May 1950): 127.

Lynes, Russell. *The Tastemakers.* 1949. New York: Grosset & Dunlap, 1954.

Lynn, Susan. "Gender and Progressive Politics: A Bridge to the Social Activism of the 1960s." *Not June Cleaver: Women and Gender in Postwar America, 1945–1960.* Ed. Joanne Meyerowitz. Philadelphia: Temple University Press, 1994. 103–27.

——. *Progressive Women in Conservative Times: Racial Justice, Peace, and Feminism, 1945 to the 1960s.* New Brunswick, NJ: Rutgers University Press, 1992.

MacLean, Katherine. "And Be Merry . . ." 1950. Rpt. in *Omnibus of Science Fiction.* Ed. Groff Conklin. New York: Crown, 1952. 29–45.

Mack, Pamela. "What Difference Has Feminism Made to Engineering in the Twentieth Century?" *Feminism in Twentieth Century Science, Technology and Medicine.* Ed. Angela N. H. Creager, Elizabeth Lunbeck, Catharine R. Stimpson, and Londa Schiebinger. Chicago: University of Chicago Press, 2001. 149–68.

Margulies, Leo. "The Female Invasion." *Fantastic Universe* 1.4 (Jan. 1954): 161.

May, Elaine Tyler. "Ambivalent Dreams: Women and the Home After World War II." *Journal of Women's History* 13.3 (Autumn 2001): 151–52.

——. *Homeward Bound: American Families in the Cold War.* New York: Basic Books, 1988.

May, Lary, ed. *Recasting America: Culture and Politics in the Age of Cold War.* Chicago and London: University of Chicago Press, 1989.

McCaffrey, Anne. *Dragonflight.* 1968. New York: Del Rey, 2005.

——. "The Ship Who Sang." 1966. Rpt. in *The Ship Who Sang.* New York: Del Rey,

1969. 1–24.

——. *The Ship Who Sang.* New York: Del Rey, 1969.

McCormack, Alma. "A Chat with the Editor." *If* (Aug. 1954): 2–3.

Mechling, Elizabeth Walker, and Jay Mechling. "The Campaign for Civil Defense and the Struggle to Naturalize the Bomb." *Critical Questions: Invention, Creativity, and the Criticism of Discourse and Media.* Ed. William L. Nothstine, Carole Blair, and Gary A. Copeland. New York: St. Martin's Press, 1994. 125–54.

Melzer, Patricia. *Alien Constructions: Science Fiction and Feminist Thought.* Austin: University of Texas Press, 2006.

Mendlesohn, Farah. "Gender, Power, and Conflict Resolution: 'Subcommittee' by Zenna Henderson." *Extrapolation* 35.2 (1994): 120–29.

Merrick, Helen. "Fantastic Dialogues: Critical Stories about Feminism and Science Fiction." *Speaking Science Fiction: Dialogues and Interpretations.* Ed. Andy Sawyer and David Seed. Liverpool, UK: Liverpool University Press, 2000. 52–68.

——. "The Readers Feminism Doesn't See: Feminist Fans, Critics and Science Fiction." *Trash Aesthetics: Popular Culture and Its Audience.* Ed. Deborah Cartmell et al. London and Chicago: Pluto Press, 1997. 48–65.

Merril, Judith. "Daughters of Earth." 1952. Rpt. in *Daughters of Earth.* New York: Dell, 1968. 97–165.

——. "Dead Center." 1954. Rpt. in *A Treasury of Great Science Fiction.* Ed. Anthony Boucher. New York: Doubleday, 1959. 166–86.

——. "Exile from Space." 1956. *The Fantastic Universe Omnibus.* Ed. Hans Stefan Santesson. New York: Prentice-Hall. 114–56.

——. "Homecalling." 1956. Rpt. in *Daughters of Earth.* New York: Dell, 1968. 167–255.

——. "The Lady Was a Tramp." 1957. Rpt. in *The Best of Judith Merril.* New York: Warner Books, 1976. 197–216.

——. "Project Nursemaid." 1955. Rpt. in *Daughters of Earth.* New York: Dell, 1968. 7–96.

——. *SF: The Best of the Best.* New York: Dell, 1967.

——. *Shadow on the Hearth.* Garden City, NY: Doubleday, 1950.

——. "That Only a Mother." 1948. Rpt. in *Science Fiction Hall of Fame.* Ed. Robert Silverberg. New York: Avon, 1970. 344–54.

——. "What Do You Mean: Science? Fiction?" *SF: The Other Side of Realism.* Ed. Thomas D. Clarenson. Bowling Green, OH: Bowling Green State University Popular Press, 1971. 53–95.

——. "Woman's Work Is Never Done!" *Future* (Mar. 1951): 51, 97–98.

Merril, Judith, and Emily Pohl-Weary. *Better to Have Loved: The Life of Judith Merril.* Toronto: Between the Lines, 2002.

Meyerowitz, Joanne. "Beyond the Feminine Mystique: A Reassessment of Postwar Mass Culture, 1946–1958." *Not June Cleaver: Women and Gender in Postwar America, 1945–1960.* Ed. Joanne Meyerowitz. Philadelphia: Temple University Press, 1994. 229–62.

——, ed. *Not June Cleaver: Women and Gender in Postwar America, 1945–1960.* Philadelphia: Temple University Press, 1994.

Miller, Stephen T., and William G. Contento. *The Locus Science Fiction, Fantasy, and Weird Magazine Index (1890–2001).* Oakland, CA: Locus Press, 2002.

Mitchison, Naomi. *Memoirs of a Spacewoman.* 1962. London: Women's Press, 1985.

Modleski, Tania. *Loving with a Vengeance: Mass-Produced Fantasies for Women.* New York: Routledge, 1996.

"Moscow Kitchen Debate." 24 July 1959. *CNN Interactive: The Cold War Experience.* 19 May 2006. http://www.cnn.com/SPECIALS/cold.war/episodes/14/documents/debate/.

Muncie, Robyn. "Cooperative Motherhood and Democratic Civic Culture in Postwar Suburbia, 1940–1965." *Journal of Social History* 38.2 (2004): 285–310.

Murdoch, Mildred. "Superstitions of the Sea." *Amazing Stories* 21.10 (Oct. 1947): 23.

Myers-Shirk, Susan E. "'To Be Fully Human': U.S. Protestant Psychotherapeutic Culture and the Subversion of the Domestic Ideal, 1945–1965." *Journal of Women's History* 12.1 (2000): 112–36.

Nasstrom, Kathryn L. "Down to Now: Memory, Narrative, and Women's Leadership in the Civil Rights Movement in Atlanta, Georgia." *Gender and History* 11 (Apr. 1999): 113–44.

Neuhaus, Jessamyn. "The Way to a Man's Heart: Gender Roles, Domestic Ideology, and Cookbooks in the 1950s." *The Journal of Social History* (Spring 1999): 529–55.

Newell, Dianne. "Judith Merril and Rachel Carson: Reflections on Their 'Potent Fictions' of Science." *Journal of International Women's Studies* 5.4 (May 2004): 31–43.

Newell, Dianne, and Victoria Lamont. "House Opera: Frontier Mythology and Subversion of Domestic Discourse in Mid-Twentieth-Century Women's Space Opera." *Foundation: The International Review of Science Fiction* 95 (Autumn 2005): 71–88.

——. "Rugged Domesticity: Frontier Mythology in Post-Armageddon Science Fiction by Women." *Science Fiction Studies* 32.3 (Nov. 2005): 423–41.

Nickles, Shelley. "More Is Better: Mass Consumption, Gender, and Class Identity in Postwar America." *American Quarterly* 54.5 (Dec. 2002): 581–622.

Nolen, Stephanie. *Promised the Moon: The Untold History of Women in the Space Race.* New York: Four Walls Eight Windows, 2002.

Norton, Andre. *Witch World.* New York: Ace, 1963.

Oakley, J. Ronald. *God's Country: America in the Fifties.* New York: Dembner, 1990.

Ogden, Annegret. *The Great American Housewife: From Helpmeet to Wage Earner, 1776–1986.* Westport, CT: Greenwood Press, 1986.

Oldenziel, Ruth. *Making Technology Masculine: Women, Men, and the Machine in America, 1880–1945.* Amsterdam: Amsterdam University Press, 1999.

——. "Man the Maker, Woman the Consumer: The Consumption Junction Revisited." *Feminism in Twentieth Century Science, Technology, and Medicine.* Ed. Angela N. H. Creager, Elizabeth Lunbeck, and Londa Schiebinger. Chicago: University of Chicago Press, 2001. 128–48.

Oppenheimer, Judy. *Private Demons: The Life of Shirley Jackson.* New York: G. P. Putnam's Sons, 1988.

Packard, Vance. *The Hidden Persuaders.* 1957. New York: Cardinal, 1963.

Parks, John G. "Waiting for the End: Shirley Jackson's *The Sundial.*" *Critique: Studies in Modern Fiction,* 19.3 (1978): 74–88.

Pascal, Richard. "New World Miniatures: Shirley Jackson's *The Sundial* and Postwar American Society." *Journal of American & Comparative Cultures* 23.3 (Fall 2000): 99–111.

Payne, Charles M. "Men Led, but Women Organized: Movement Participation of Women in the Mississippi Delta." *Women and Social Protest.* Ed. Guida West and Rhoda L. Blumberg. New York: Oxford University Press, 1990. 156–63.

Peterson, Bernice J. "What Man Can Imagine . . . [A] Cure for Infantile Paralysis?" *Amazing Stories* 20.9 (Dec. 1946): 152–53.

Pfaelzer, Jean. *The Utopian Novel in America, 1886–1896.* Pittsburgh: University of Pittsburgh Press, 1989.

Piercy, Marge. *Woman on the Edge of Time.* New York: Knopf, 1976.

Pollock, Rachel. *Godmother Night.* London: Abacus, 1996.

Pratt, Tim. "Hart and Boot." *The Best American Short Stories 2005.* Ed. Michael Chabon. New York: Houghton Mifflin, 2004. 339–55.

"Preview of a War We Do Not Want: Russia's Defeat and Occupation, 1952–1960." Special issue of *Collier's* 27 Oct. 1951.

Pringle, David, and Peter Nicholls. "Media Landscapes." *The Encyclopedia of Science Fiction.* Ed. John Clute and Peter Nicholls. New York: St. Martin's Press, 1993. 792–94.

Putney, Mary Jo. "Welcome to the Dark Side." *Dangerous Men and Adventurous Women: Romance Writers on the Appeal of the Romance.* Ed. Jayne Ann Krentz. Philadelphia: University of Pennsylvania Press, 1992. 99–106.

Radway, Janice A. *Reading the Romance: Women, Patriarchy, and Popular Literature.* 1984. Chapel Hill: University of North Carolina Press, 1991.

Raglon, Rebecca. "Rachel Carson and Her Legacy." *Natural Eloquence: Women Reinscribe Nature.* Ed. Barbara T. Gates and Ann B. Shteir. Madison: University of Wisconsin Press, 1997. 196–211.

Rardin, Lucky. "Letter to the Editor." *Fantastic* 6.5 (June 1957): 125.

Reed, Kit. *The Baby Merchant.* 2006. New York: Tor, 2007.

———. "Cynosure." 1964. Rpt. in *The Killer Mice.* London: Gollancz, 1976. 95–106.

———. *Little Sisters of the Apocalypse.* Tuscaloosa, AL: Fiction Collective 2, 1994.

———. *Thinner Than Thou.* 2004. New York: Tor, 2005.

Rice, Louise, and Tonjoroff-Roberts. "Astounding Enemy." *Amazing Stories Quarterly* (Winter 1930): 78–103.

Roberts, Robin. "It's Still Science Fiction: Strategies of Feminist Science Fiction Criticism." *Extrapolation* 36.3 (1995): 184–97.

———. *A New Species: Gender and Science in Science Fiction.* Urbana: University of Illinois Press, 1993.

Rogers, Kay. "Command Performance." *Magazine of Fantasy and Science Fiction* (Aug. 1954): 69–76.

———. "Experiment." 1953. Rpt. in *Best from Fantasy and Science Fiction: Third Series.* Ed. Anthony Boucher and J. Francis McComas. New York: Doubleday, 1954. 96–99.

Rose, Hilary. *Love, Power, and Knowledge: Toward a Feminist Transformation of the Sciences.* Bloomington: Indiana University Press, 1994.

Rosen, Marjorie. *Popcorn Venus.* New York: Avon, 1985.

Rossiter, Margaret W. *Women Scientists in America before Affirmative Action, 1940–1972.* Baltimore: Johns Hopkins University Press, 1995.

Rothman, Sheila R. *Woman's Proper Place: A History of Changing Ideals and Prac-

tices, 1870 to the Present. New York: Basic Books, 1978.

Ruddick, Sara. *Maternal Thinking: Toward a Politics of Peace.* 1989. Boston: Beacon Press, 1995.

Rupp, Leila J., and Verta Taylor. *Survival in the Doldrums: The American Women's Rights Movement, 1945 to the 1960s.* New York: Oxford University Press, 1987.

Russ, Joanna. *The Female Man.* 1975. London: Women's Press, 2002.

——. "The Image of Women in Science Fiction." 1971. Rpt. in *Images of Women in Fiction: Feminist Perspectives.* Ed. Susan Koppleman Cornillion. Bowling Green, OH: Bowling Green University Popular Press, 1972. 79–94.

Sargent, Pamela. *The Shore of Women.* 1986. Dallas: Benbella Books, 2004.

——, ed. *Women of Wonder: Science Fiction Stories by Women about Women.* 1974. New York: Vintage, 1975.

Sawaya, Francesca. *Modern Women, Modern Work.* Philadelphia: University of Pennsylvania Press, 2004.

Scott, Melissa. *Trouble and Her Friends.* 1994. New York: Tor, 1995.

——. *The Roads of Heaven.* New York: Doubleday, 1987.

Scholes, Robert. *The Fabulators.* New York: Oxford University Press, 1967.

——. *Structural Fabulation.* South Bend, IN: University of Notre Dame Press, 1975.

Shelley, Mary Wollstonecraft. *Frankenstein, Or, the Modern Prometheus.* 1818. Chicago: University of Chicago Press, 1982.

Sherman, Delia. "Walpurgis Afternoon." *Magazine of Fantasy and Science Fiction* (Dec. 2005): 8–33.

Slonczewski, Joan. *A Door into Ocean.* 1986. New York: Orb, 2000.

——. *The Wall Around Eden.* 1989. New York: Avon, 1990.

Smith, April, and Charles Dye. "Settle to One." *Astounding Science Fiction* 11.2 (Apr. 1953): 63–82.

Spigel, Lynn. *Make Room for TV: Television and the Family Ideal in Postwar America.* Chicago: University of Chicago Press, 1992.

——. *Welcome to the Dreamhouse: Popular Media and Postwar Suburbs.* Durham, NC: Duke University Press, 2001.

Squier, Susan Merrill. *Babies in Bottles: Twentieth-Century Visions of Reproductive Technology.* New Brunswick, NJ: Rutgers University Press, 1994.

——. "Conflicting Scientific Feminisms: Charlotte Haldane and Naomi Mitchison." *Natural Eloquence: Women Reinscribe Nature.* Ed. Barbara T. Gates and Ann B. Shteir. Madison: University of Wisconsin Press, 1997. 179–95.

——. *Liminal Lives: Imagining the Human at the Frontiers of Biomedicine.* Durham, NC: Duke University Press, 2005.

Stableford, Brian. "Aliens." *The Encyclopedia of Science Fiction.* Ed. John Clute and Peter Nicholls. New York: St. Martin's Press, 1993. 15–19.

——. "Scientists." *The Encyclopedia of Science Fiction.* Ed. John Clute and Peter Nicholls. New York: St. Martin's Press, 1993. 1076–77.

——. "Space Flight." *The Encyclopedia of Science Fiction.* Ed. John Clute and Peter Nicholls. New York: St. Martin's Press, 1993. 1135–36.

Starhawk. *The Fifth Sacred Thing.* 1993. New York: Bantam, 1994.

St. Clair, Margaret. "Brightness Falls from the Air." 1951. Rpt. in *The Science Fiction Century.* Ed. David G. Hartwell. New York: Tor, 1997. 161–65.

——. "New Ritual." 1953. Rpt. in *The Best from Fantasy and Science Fiction: Third*

Series. Ed. Anthony Boucher and J. Francis McComas. New York: Doubleday, 1954. 172–81.

Steidl, Rose E., and Esther Crew Bratton. *Work in the Home.* New York: John Wiley & Sons, 1968.

Sterling, Bruce. *Heavy Weather.* 1991. New York: Bantam, 1995.

——. *Holy Fire.* 1996. New York: Spectra, 1997.

——. *Islands in the Net.* 1988. New York: Ace, 1989.

Stone, Albert E. *Literary Aftershocks: American Writers, Readers, and the Bomb.* New York: Twayne Publishers, 1994.

Stone, Leslie F. "Day of the Pulps." *Fantasy Commentator* 9.2 (1997): 100–103, 152.

——. "Out of the Void." *Amazing Stories* (Aug.–Sept. 1929): 440–55.

——. "Women with Wings." *Air Wonder Stories* (May 1930): 984–1003.

Strasser, Susan. *Never Done: A History of American Housework.* New York: Pantheon, 1982.

Sturgeon, Theodore. *Venus Plus X.* 1960. New York: Vintage, 1999.

Swerdlow, Amy. *Women Strike for Peace: Traditional Motherhood and Radical Politics in the 1960s.* Chicago and London: University of Chicago Press, 1993.

Synnott, Marcia G. "Alice Norwood Spearman Wright: Civil Rights Apostle to South Carolinians." *Beyond Images and Convention: Explorations in Southern Women's History.* Ed. Janet L. Coryell et al. Columbia: University of Missouri Press, 1998. 184–207.

Taylor, Ella. *Prime-Time Families: Television Culture in Postwar America.* Berkeley: University of California Press, 1991.

Thomas, Sheree R. "Introduction: Looking for the Invisible." *Dark Matter: A Century of Science Fiction from the African Diaspora.* New York: Warner Books, 2000. ix–xiv.

Tiptree, James Jr. "The Girl Who Was Plugged In." 1974. *Screwtop/The Girl Who Was Plugged In.* New York: Tor, 1989.

——. *Up the Walls of the World.* 1978. New York: Ace, 1984.

Tolley, Kim. *The Science Education of American Girls: A Historical Perspective.* New York: RoutledgeFalmer, 2003.

Trachtenberg, Mark. "American Thinking on Nuclear War." *Strategic Power: USA/ USSR.* Ed. Carl G. Jacobsen. New York: St. Martin's, 1990. 355–69.

Tressider, Mary. "Women and Science at Science Service." Summer 2005. *The Smithsonian Institution Archives* 30 Dec. 2005. http://siarchives.si.edu/ research/sciservwomen.html.

Tuttle, Lisa. "Women SF Writers." *The Encyclopedia of Science Fiction.* Ed. John Clute and Peter Nicholls. New York: St. Martin's Press, 1995. 1344–45.

Van Gelder, Gordon. "Introduction to Trent Hergenrader's 'From the Mouth of Babes.'" *The Magazine of Fantasy and Science Fiction* (Mar. 2006): 106.

Varley, John. *The Ophiuchi Hotline.* New York: Dial Press, 1977.

——. *Picnic on Nearside.* New York: Berkley Books, 1984.

——. *Steel Beach.* 1992. New York: Ace, 1993.

Vinge, Joan. *The Snow Queen.* 1980. New York: Aspect, 2001.

——. *The Summer Queen.* 1991. New York: Tor, 2003.

——. *Tangled Up in Blue.* 1999. New York: Tor, 2001.

——. *World's End.* 1984. New York: Tor, 1993.

Waddell, Craig, ed. *And No Birds Sing: Rhetorical Analyses of Rachel Carson's*

Silent Spring. Carbondale: Southern Illinois University Press, 2000.

Wajcman, Judy. "Domestic Technology: Labour-Saving or Enslaving?" *Inventing Women: Science, Technology, and Gender.* Ed. Gill Kirkup and Laurie Smith Keller. Cambridge, UK: Polity, 1992. 238–54.

Walker, Nancy. "Humor and Gender Roles: The 'Funny' Feminism of the Post–World War II Suburbs." *American Quarterly* 37.1 (Spring 1985): 98–113.

Weinbaum, Batya. "Sex Role Reversal in the Thirties: Leslie F. Stone's 'The Conquest of Gola.'" *Science Fiction Studies* 24.3 (1997): 471–82.

Westfahl, Gary. *The Mechanics of Wonder: The Creation of the Idea of Science Fiction.* Liverpool, UK: Liverpool University Press, 1999.

Wiley, Catherine, and Fiona R. Barnes. "Introduction." *Homemaking: Women Writers and the Politics and Poetics of Home.* New York: Garland Publishing, 1996. xv–xxvi.

Williams, Kathleen Broome. *Improbable Warriors: Women Scientists and the U.S. Navy in World War II.* Annapolis, MD: Naval Institute Press, 2001.

Winner, Lauren F. "Cooking, Tending the Garden, and Being a Good Hostess: A Domestic History of White Women's Opposition to the Freedom Movement in Mississippi." *Mississippi Folklife* 31.1 (1998): 28–35.

Wolmark, Jenny. *Aliens and Others: Science Fiction, Feminism, and Postmodernism.* Iowa City: University of Iowa Press, 1994.

———. *Cybersexualities.* Edinburgh: Edinburgh University Press, 2000.

Wolf, Virginia L. "Andre Norton: Feminist Pied Piper in SF." *Children's Literature Association Quarterly* 10.2 (Summer 1985): 66–70.

Wosk, Jenny. *Women and the Machine: Representations from the Spinning Wheel to the Electronic Age.* Baltimore: Johns Hopkins University Press, 2001.

Wright, Roscoe E. "Letter to the Editor." *Astounding Science Fiction* 42.2 (Oct. 1948): 158.

Yaszek, Lisa. "Domestic Satire as Social Commentary in Midcentury Women's Media Landscape SF." *Foundation: The International Review of Science Fiction* 95 (Fall 2005): 29–39.

———. "'A grim fantasy': Remaking American History in Octavia Butler's *Kindred.*" *Signs: Journal of Women in Culture and Society* 28.4 (2003): 1053–1067.

———. "A History of One's Own: Joanna Russ and the Creation of a Feminist Science Fiction Tradition." *On Joanna Russ.* Ed. Farah Mendlesohn. Middletown, CT: Wesleyan Press, forthcoming 2008.

———. *The Self Wired: Technology and Subjectivity in Contemporary American Narrative.* New York: Routledge, 2002.

———. "Stories 'That Only a Mother' Could Write: Midcentury Peace Activism, Maternalist Politics, and Judith Merril's Early Fiction." *NWSA Journal* 16.2 (Summer 2004): 70–97.

———. "Unhappy Housewife Heroines, Galactic Suburbia, and Nuclear War: A New History of Midcentury Women's Science Fiction." *Extrapolation* 44.1 (Spring 2003): 97–111.

Zatkin-Dresner, Zita. "The Housewife as Humorist." *Regionalism and the Female Imagination* 3.2–3 (1997–98): 29–38.

I N D E X

"Miss Quatro" (Jones), 48–49
mistaken choice, 18, 155, 177, 178, 205
The Mistress of Spices (Divakaruni), 204
The Mists of Avalon (Bradley), 199
Mitchison, Naomi, 163, 205
Modern Daughters and the Outlaw West (Kwansy), 201
Modleski, Tania, 42n19, 44n20
Moore, C. L., 16, 16n11, 21
Moscow Kitchen Debate, 89
motherhood: in postwar America, 3, 12, 42, 69–74, 109–13, 154–55, 157–58, 200; in science fiction, 4, 29–31, 49–52, 77–78, 82–85, 114–32, 142–43, 176–81, 200–201, 207. *See also* family; home
Motherlines (Charnas), 200, 203, 205
The Mount (Emshwiller), 199
"Mr. Sakrison's Halt" (Clingerman), 146–48
Muncie, Robyn, 74
municipal housekeeping, 108n3, 111
Murdoch, Mildred, 165, 167, 197
Myers-Shirk, Susan E., 73n6

Nasstrom, Kathryn L., 134
National Aeronautics and Space Administration (NASA), 13–15, 150, 160–61, 172
National Defense Education Act (NDEA), 13–15, 159, 159n8
National Manpower Council (NMC), 13, 159
Neuhaus, Jessamyn, 73n6
"New Ritual" (St. Clair), 99–101
Newell, Diane, 5, 5n3, 16n11, 114n8, 174n22
A New Species: Gender and Science in Science Fiction (Roberts), 6n4, 16n11, 36n15, 48n23, 75, 108n3, 175, 207n8
Nicholls, Peter, 47, 93
Nickles, Shelley, 92
"Night of Fire" (Chase), 1
No Different Flesh (Henderson), 83n7
Nolen, Stephanie, 14, 14n9, 161

Norton, Andre, 16, 16n11, 21, 205
nuclear holocaust narrative, 15, 17, 50n24, 114–32, 114n8, 149, 176n23, 202–3, 203n7. *See also* activism; nuclear war
nuclear war: in postwar American discourse, 109, 110, 113, 115, 117, 121; protest against, 17, 109, 111–13, 121, 149; in science fiction. *See also* activism; nuclear holocaust narrative

Oakley, J. Ronald, 72
offbeat romance, 40, 44–45, 64
Ogden, Annegret, 7, 7n6, 9, 10, 12, 110n4
Oldenziel, Ruth, 156n4, 192
"The Omen" (Jackson), 60–61
"One Ordinary Day, with Peanuts" (Jackson), 59–60
"Ones That Got Away" (Jones), 43
The Ophiuchi Hotline (Varley), 207
Oppenheimer, Judy, 22, 54, 63

Packard, Vance, 91, 91n9, 93, 97
Palmer, Jacqueline S., 164
Parable of the Sower (Butler), 203
Parable of the Talents (Butler), 203
Parks, John, 55, 55n26
"Parsifal (Prix Fixe)" (Cambias), 208
Pascal, Richard, 56n27
Payne, Charles M., 134
peace movement, 17, 107, 107n1, 108, 109–13, 111n6, 112n7, 114, 115, 117, 118, 124, 132, 134, 149, 165n15, 176n23
Peterson, Bernice J., 165, 168, 169
Pfaelzer, Jean, 25
Picnic on Nearside (Varley), 207
Piercy, Marge, 200, 204, 205
Pilgrimage: The Book of the People (Henderson), 83n7
The Planet Savers (Bradley), 199
Pohl, Fred, 28, 31n13, 47, 93, 105
Pohl-Weary, Emily, 25, 28, 31n13, 35, 124, 127n10, 132n13
Pollack, Rachel, 201
postmodern literature, 17, 20, 25, 52,